Business Intelligence: A Managerial Perspective

Business Intelligence: A Managerial Perspective

Drew Bentley

CLANRYE INTERNATIONAL
www.clanryeinternational.com

Clanrye International,
750 Third Avenue, 9th Floor,
New York, NY 10017, USA

ISBN: 978-1-64726-075-0

Cataloging-in-Publication Data

Business intelligence : a managerial perspective / Drew Bentley.
p. cm.
Includes bibliographical references and index.
ISBN 978-1-64726-075-0
1. Business intelligence. 2. Industrial management. 3. Confidential business information.
4. Business ethics. I. Bentley, Drew.

HD38.7 .B87 2022
658.472--dc23

For information on all Clanrye International publications
visit our website at www.clanryeinternational.com

Clanrye International

Contents

Preface

Business intelligence refers to the technologies and strategies that are used by enterprises for the data analysis of business information. It provides historical, predictive and current views of business operations. Some of the common functions of business intelligence are online analytical processing, reporting, data mining, complex event processing and business performance management. It is also used for text mining, predictive analytics and prescriptive analysis. Technologies used in business intelligence have the capacity for handling large amounts of structured and unstructured data. This data is used for the identification, development and creation of new strategic business opportunities. This book elucidates the concepts and innovative models around prospective developments with respect to business intelligence. It picks up individual branches and explains their need and contribution in the context of a growing economy. This textbook is appropriate for those seeking detailed information in this area.

To facilitate a deeper understanding of the contents of this book a short introduction of every chapter is written below:

Chapter 1- The practices, skills and technologies which are utilized for continuous iterative exploration and investigation of past business performance is termed as business analytics. Its purpose is to gain insight and drive business planning. This chapter has been carefully written to provide an easy introduction to the varied facets of business analytics.

Chapter 2- The set of strategies and technologies which are utilized by enterprises for the analysis of data related to business information is termed as business intelligence. It can be used for value creation in numerous environments. The topics elaborated in this chapter will help in gaining a better perspective about the varied facets of business intelligence as well as the processes associated with it.

Chapter 3- Business analytics is involved in developing new insights related to business performance by using data and statistical methods. This chapter closely examines the key concepts related to the role of data in business analytics such as data requirements analysis and data integration to provide an extensive understanding of the subject.

Chapter 4- The usage of business data involves the extraction of business intelligence from unstructured data, drawing insights from the collection of data and reusing data. These diverse uses of business data as well as the use of data mining for the purpose of predictive analysis have been thoroughly discussed in this chapter.

Chapter 5- The ethical principles related to the code of conduct which govern the decisions related to the data of consumers, businesses or employees such as data accuracy and involuntary release of personal information are known as professional ethics. This chapter has been carefully written to provide an easy understanding of the varied facets of ethics in business intelligence as well as the diverse principles which fall under it.

Finally, I would like to thank the entire team involved in the inception of this book for their valuable time and contribution. This book would not have been possible without their efforts. I would also like to thank my friends and family for their constant support.

Drew Bentley

1

Introduction to Business Analytics

The practices, skills and technologies which are utilized for continuous iterative exploration and investigation of past business performance is termed as business analytics. Its purpose is to gain insight and drive business planning. This chapter has been carefully written to provide an easy introduction to the varied facets of business analytics.

BI(Business Intelligence) is a set of processes, architectures, and technologies that convert raw data into meaningful information that drives profitable business actions. It is a suite of software and services to transform data into actionable intelligence and knowledge.

BI has a direct impact on organization's strategic, tactical and operational business decisions. BI supports fact-based decision making using historical data rather than assumptions and gut feeling.

BI tools perform data analysis and create reports, summaries, dashboards, maps, graphs, and charts to provide users with detailed intelligence about the nature of the business.

Importance of Business Intelligence

- Measurement: creating KPI (Key Performance Indicators) based on historic data.
- Identify and set benchmarks for varied processes.
- With BI systems organizations can identify market trends and spot business problems that need to be addressed.
- BI helps on data visualization that enhances the data quality and thereby the quality of decision making.
- BI systems can be used not just by enterprises but SME (Small and Medium Enterprises).

Implementation of Business Intelligence Systems

Here are the steps:

- Step 1: Raw Data from corporate databases is extracted. The data could be spread across multiple systems heterogeneous systems.
- Step 2: The data is cleaned and transformed into the data warehouse. The table can be linked, and data cubes are formed.
- Step 3: Using BI system the user can ask quires, request ad-hoc reports or conduct any other analysis.

Examples of Business Intelligence System used in Practice:

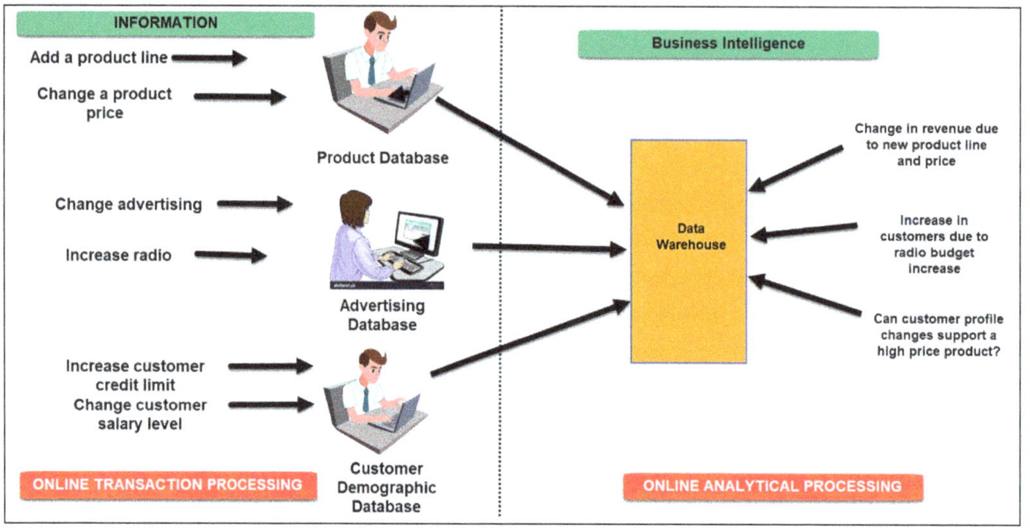

In an Online Transaction Processing (OLTP) system information that could be fed into product database could be:

- Add a product line.
- Change a product price.

Correspondingly, in a Business Intelligence system query that would be executed for the product subject area could be did the addition of new product line or change in product price increase revenues.

In an advertising database of OLTP system query that could be executed:

- Changed in advertisement options.
- Increase radio budget.

Correspondingly, in BI system query that could be executed would be how many new clients added due to change in radio budget.

In OLTP system dealing with customer demographic data bases data that could be fed would be:

- Increase customer credit limit.
- Change in customer salary level.

Correspondingly in the OLAP system query that could be executed would be can customer profile changes support support higher product price.

Example: A hotel owner uses BI analytical applications to gather statistical information regarding average occupancy and room rate. It helps to find aggregate revenue generated per room. It also collects statistics on market share and data from customer surveys from each hotel to decide its competitive position in various markets. By analyzing these trends year by year, month by month and day by day helps management to offer discounts on room rentals.

Example: A bank gives branch managers access to BI applications. It helps branch manager to determine who are the most profitable customer and which customers they should work on. The use of BI tools frees information technology staff from the task of generating analytical reports for the departments. It also gives department personnel access to a richer data source.

Types of BI Users

Following given are the four key players who are used Business Intelligence System:

1. The Professional Data Analyst: The data analyst is a statistician who always needs to drill deep down into data. BI system helps them to get fresh insights to develop unique business strategies.
2. The IT users: The IT user also plays a dominant role in maintaining the BI infrastructure.
3. The head of the company: CEO or CXO can increase the profit of their business by improving operational efficiency in their business.
4. The Business Users: Business intelligence users can be found from across the organization. There are mainly two types of business users:
    - Casual business intelligence user.
    - The power user.

The difference between both of them is that a power user has the capability of working with complex data sets, while the casual user need will make him use dashboards to evaluate predefined sets of data.

Advantages of Business Intelligence

Here are some of the advantages of using Business Intelligence System:

1. Boost productivity: With a BI program, It is possible for businesses to create reports with a single click thus saves lots of time and resources. It also allows employees to be more productive on their tasks.
2. To improve visibility: BI also helps to improve the visibility of these processes and make it possible to identify any areas which need attention.
3. Fix Accountability: BI system assigns accountability in the organization as there must be someone who should own accountability and ownership for the organization's performance against its set goals.
4. It gives a bird's eye view: BI system also helps organizations as decision makers get an overall bird's eye view through typical BI features like dashboards and scorecards.
5. It streamlines business processes: BI takes out all complexity associated with business processes. It also automates analytics by offering predictive analysis, computer modeling, benchmarking and other methodologies.

6. It allows for easy analytics: BI software has democratized its usage, allowing even nontechnical or non-analysts users to collect and process data quickly. This also allows putting the power of analytics from the hand's many people.

BI System Disadvantages

1. Cost: Business intelligence can prove costly for small as well as for medium-sized enterprises. The use of such type of system may be expensive for routine business transactions.
2. Complexity: Another drawback of BI is its complexity in implementation of data warehouse. It can be so complex that it can make business techniques rigid to deal with.
3. Limited use: Like all improved technologies, BI was first established keeping in consideration the buying competence of rich firms. Therefore, BI system is yet not affordable for many small and medium size companies.
4. Time Consuming Implementation: It takes almost one and half year for data warehousing system to be completely implemented. Therefore, it is a time-consuming process.

Trends in Business Intelligence

The following are some business intelligence and analytics trends that you should be aware of:

1. Artificial Intelligence: Gartner' report indicates that AI and machine learning now take on complex tasks done by human intelligence. This capability is being leveraged to come up with real-time data analysis and dashboard reporting.
2. Collaborative BI: BI software combined with collaboration tools, including social media, and other latest technologies enhance the working and sharing by teams for collaborative decision making.
3. Embedded BI: Embedded BI allows the integration of BI software or some of its features into another business application for enhancing and extending its reporting functionality.
4. Cloud Analytics: BI applications will be soon offered in the cloud, and more businesses will be shifting to this technology. As per their predictions within a couple of years, the spending on cloud-based analytics will grow 4.5 times faster.

Improvement of Decision Making

1. As for the marketing department, it helps them grow the top line. It helps them analyze the results of their campaign and promotional yields. And it helps them fine-tune their spending to get better ROI.
2. In the sales department, business intelligence helps them find the best path and best practices, the cost and length of customer acquisition, process improvement, and year-by-year analysis of turnover and sales.

3. Business intelligence helps the human resource department track and manages things like employee turnover, attrition rate, recruitment process, and so on.

Aside these, every other department within a company will benefit directly or indirectly from business intelligence. Correct usage of this strategy has shown excellent results across all sectors; be it e-commerce, media, non-profit organizations, healthcare, telecommunication, financial services, energy, and so on.

Business intelligence helps in decision making due to the multiple powerful elements it entails. These include interactivity, data visualization, database connection, mobile business intelligence, predictive analytics, application integration, and ad hoc reporting.

Ways Business Intelligence Help in Decision Making

1. Interactivity: There should be a high level of interactivity between the dashboard and the difference report. For example, if a person is seeing and analyzing the total sales report, some interaction should be involved. This will help the person dig further into the report to figure out region wise sales, product wise sales, time period wise sales, and so on. The more the level of interaction the more the volume of vital information that will be retrieved and the better the decisions that will be made.
2. Data visualization: Having data visualized in a correct format is very important, as this facilitates better understanding of the data. For example, month-on-month sales could be represented in the form of a line graph rather than just words or verbal communication. Similarly, a component wise contribution could be best represented with a pie chart. Only when data is represented in the correct format can any useful insight be extracted from it.
3. Connection to databases: During a business intelligence procedure, the analysts in charge should be able to fetch information by connecting to different databases and web services, so that they will get access to the right information irrespective of its source. With the right information, helpful recommendations can be made that will help a company grow.
4. Predictive analytics: With the aid of historical data and high-end algorithms, certain predictions can be made, such as the likelihood of customers coming back for repeat business, expected revenue, expected region wise sales, machine failure, and so on. This can help a company to be proactive.
5. Application integration: A business intelligence tool should be easily integrated with your existing application or software regardless of whether it is developed in Java, C, Ruby, PHP, or any other platform.
6. Mobile business intelligence: With more and more workforce going mobile and handling tasks on the move, they need to have the right information on their mobile devices, such as smartphones and tablets. So, all reports dashboards and graphs should be compatible with mobile devices.

According to a survey, a decision made based on data analysis has 79% chances of success more than one made based on pure intuition. Business intelligence helps businesses take a more structured look at data while providing deep interpretations. It aids decision making via real-time, interactive access to and analysis of important corporate information. And it bridges the gaps between information silos in an organization.

Importance of Business Intelligence

There are many important reasons that even small and midsize businesses will want to invest in BI to gain a competitive advantage. Let's take a look at six of the most important:

- BI turns data into usable information. Raw data doesn't tell us what to do in business all on its own. BI systems allow for comprehensive analysis of data to identify important trends that can be used to modify or implement strategic plans and to understand the interconnections between different functions and facets of your business.
- BI improves the visibility of core business components. BI makes it easier to see each component part of your business, including those that are often overlooked. Consequently, you can more easily identify components that need improvement and to make changes.
- BI improves your ROI and ability to achieve goals. BI analysis allows you to understand how best to allocate resources to meet your stated goals. This allows you to increase your ROI by ensuring that resources are deployed strategically to achieve fixed goals and it helps to prevent "mission drift" or "mission creep" where outcomes no longer align to goals.
- BI improves your understanding of consumer behavior. BI analysis allows you to track global, regional, and local consumption patterns to better understand current trends. This, in turn, allows you to develop and deliver products and services that anticipate market needs.
- BI improves your marketing and sales intelligence. By keeping track of data about your clients and customers, BI allows you to understand how they interact with your organization at a deeper level so you can identify solutions to consumer issues and better reach your customers with targeted messages to increase sales.
- BI improves productivity. BI makes the process of analyzing and interpreting data faster and more efficient, giving you the power to understand business data as quickly as it comes in, and it allows you to generate reports with the simple click of a mouse. This gives you and your employees more time to devote to running your business rather than analyzing it.

Information Asset

The idea of an information asset is a powerful new concept that is designed to bridge the gap between how business views information and how computers manage files. The information asset is an entirely new perspective of data and is necessitated by the fact that business users intuitively include much more than just an individual file when referring to their information. Simple things like, what is actually in the file, who it is for, etc., is often confusingly and inconsistently encoded in the file name or implied by its directory location. Other information such as prior revisions, the template that was used to create the file, associated files such as pictures, scanned copies, or other working documents, not to mention the relevant emails, are simply scattered if recorded at all. As one customer put it, "We have more controls, tracking, documentation rules, checks, and management oversight of our petty cash than we do over our information assets". The result of this is that computers are simply not designed to know what an information asset is, and therefore, are completely unable to manage it in any way.

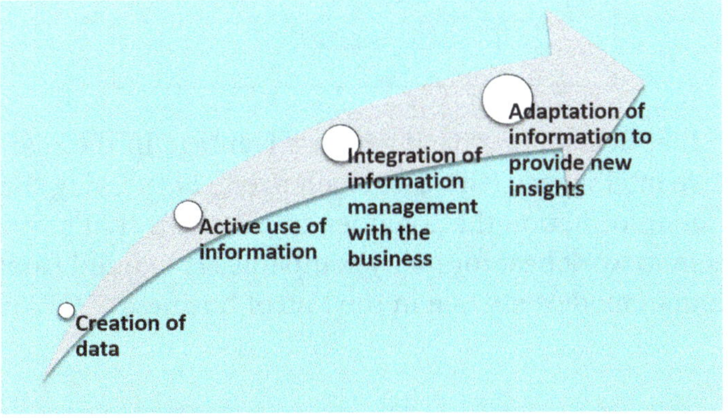

To be clear, information assets are not simply the collection of files on a file server. The formal definition of an information asset is the set of all data, rules, and procedures that, collectively, represents a concept meaningful to the business. This set of data can include not only a collection of files but other important items such as tracking and descriptive information (e.g. the name of the customer), audit logs, emails, supporting documentation, images, etc., that collectively, have meaning to the business. These can range from a few items to very complex asset that might include thousands of files.

Actionable Intelligence

Actionable intelligence is information that can be followed up on, with the further implication that a strategic plan should be undertaken to make positive use of the information gathered. This meaning is distinct from the use of actionable intelligence in a legal context, which means that information meets the legal requirements for a justifiable (actionable) lawsuit.

In information technology (IT), actionable intelligence, also called actionable insight, is often spoken of in the context of big data and predictive modeling. In marketing, artificial intelligence (AI) can help companies shrink the gap between customer intent data and actionable insight by feeding intelligence into customer relationship management (CRM), marketing automation and other operational tools. This type of holistic approach to gaining insights from customer data can help a company meet the challenges associated with working with big data and exploit information that can help make the company more profitable.

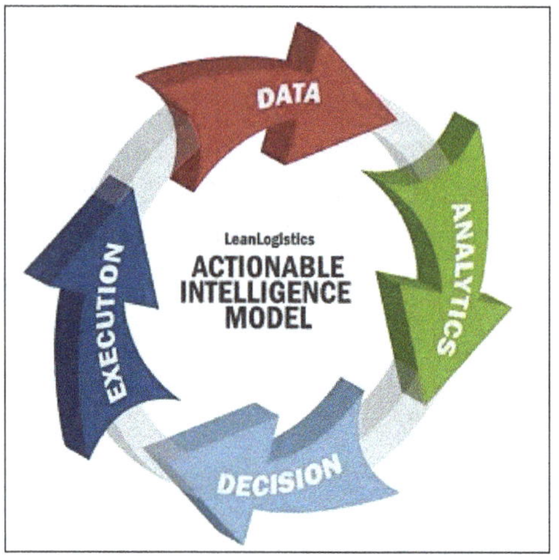

Actionable intelligence that helps a company get an advantage in the marketplace is sometimes referred to as competitive intelligence (CI). The challenge to harnessing the power of competitive intelligence is how to find information that's hidden in a data set that's variable and volatile. One of the solutions that seem to work best for many companies is to build front-end visualization interfaces that present data in models anyone in the line of business (LOB) can easily comprehend and follow up on.

Difference between Big Data, Business Intelligence and Data Mining

Lately, there have been tremendous shifts in the business technology landscape. Advances in cloud technology and mobile applications have enabled businesses and IT users to interact in entirely new ways. One of the most rapidly growing technologies in this sphere is business intelligence, and associated concepts such as big data and data mining.

To help you understand the various business data processes towards leveraging business intelligence tools, it is important to know the differences between big data vs. data mining vs. business intelligence. We've outlined the definitions of each, and detailed how they relate and compare to each other.

Business Intelligence

Business intelligence encompasses data analysis with the intent of uncovering trends, patterns and insights. Findings based on data provide accurate, astute views of one company's processes and the results those processes are yielding. Beyond standard metrics such as financial measures, in-depth business intelligence reveals the impact of current practices on employee performance, overall company satisfaction, conversions, media reach and a number of other factors.

In addition to presenting information on the present state of an organization, the utilization of business intelligence can forecast future performance. Through the analysis of past and current data, robust BI systems track trends and illustrate how those trends will continue as time goes on.

Business intelligence encompasses more than observation. BI moves beyond analysis when action is taken based on the findings. Having the ability to see the real, quantifiable results of policy and the impact on the future of a business a powerful decision-making tool.

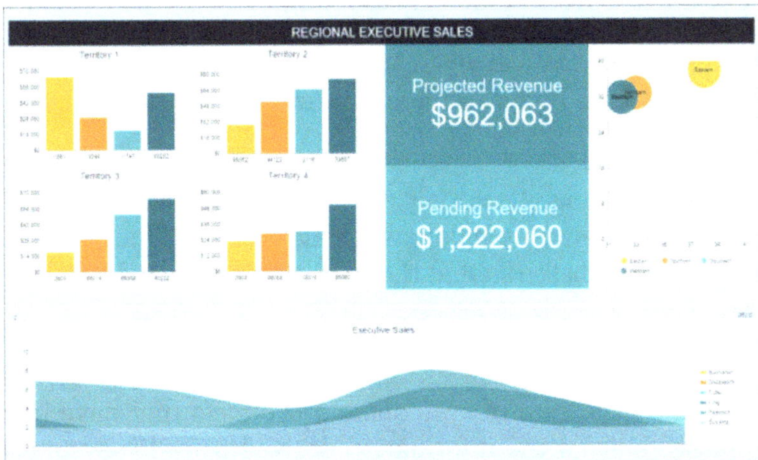

Big Data

The term big data can be defined simply as large data sets that outgrow simple databases and data handling architectures. For example, data that cannot be easily handled in Excel spread sheets may be referred to as big data.

Big data involves the process of storing, processing and visualizing data. It is essential to find the right tools for creating the best environment to successfully obtain valuable insights from your data.

Setting up an effective big data environment involves utilizing infrastructural technologies that process, store and facilitate data analysis. Data warehouses, modeling language programs and OLAP cubes are just some examples. Today, businesses often use more than one infrastructural deployment to manage various aspects of their data.

Big data often provides companies with answers to the questions they did not know they wanted to ask: How has the new HR software impacted employee performance? How do recent customer reviews relate to sales? Analyzing big data sources illuminates the relationships between all facets of your business.

Therefore, there is inherent usefulness to the information being collected in big data. Businesses must set relevant objectives and parameters in place to glean valuable insights from big data.

Data Mining

Data mining relates to the process of going through large sets of data to identify relevant or pertinent information. However, decision-makers need access to smaller, more specific pieces of data as well. Businesses use data mining for business intelligence and to identify specific data that may help their companies make better leadership and management decisions.

Data mining is the process of finding answers to issues you did not know you were looking for beforehand. For example, exploring new data sources may lead to the discovery of causes for financial shortcomings, underperforming employees and more. Quantifiable data illuminates information that may not be obvious from standard observation.

Information overload leads many data analysts to believe they may be overlooking key points that can help their companies perform better. Data mining experts sift through large data sets to identify trends and patterns.

Various software packages and analytical tools can be used for data mining. The process can be automated or done manually. Data mining allows individual workers to send specific queries for information to archives and databases so that they can obtain targeted results.

Business Intelligence vs. Big Data

Business intelligence is the collection of systems and products that have been implemented in various business practices, but not the information derived from the systems and products. On the other hand, big data has come to mean various things to different people. When comparing big data vs business intelligence, some people use the term big data when referring to the size of data, while others use the term in reference to specific approaches to analytics.

So, how do business intelligence and big data relate and compare? Big data can provide information outside of a company's own data sources, serving as an expansive resource. Therefore, it is a component of business intelligence, offering a comprehensive view into your processes. Big data often constitutes the information which will lead to business intelligence insights.

Again, big data exists within business intelligence. This means the two differ in the amount and type of data they include. As business intelligence is an umbrella term, the data that is considered a part of BI is much more all-inclusive than what falls under big data. Business intelligence covers all data, from sales reports hosted in Excel spread sheets to large online databases. Big data, on the other hand, consists of only those large data sets.

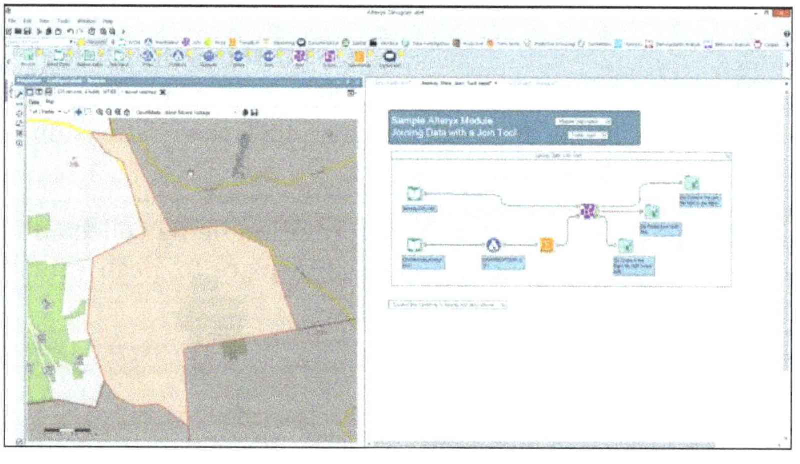

The tools involved in the processes of big data and business intelligence differ as well. Base-level business intelligence software has the ability to process standard data sources, but may not be equipped to manage big data. Other more advanced systems are specifically designed for big data processing.

Of course, in the big data vs BI discussion, there is some overlap involved in the use of comprehensive business intelligence systems that are made to handle large sets of data. Most business intelligence software vendors offer tiered cost models which increase functionality depending on the price. Big data capabilities may also be offered as an add-on to a BI software system. And that's BI vs big data.

BI vs. Data Mining

As previously stated, business intelligence is defined as the methods and tools used by organizations to glean analytical findings from data. It also consists of how companies can gain information from big data and data mining. This means business intelligence is not confined to technology – it includes the business processes and data analysis procedures that facilitate the collection of big data.

Data mining falls under the umbrella term of "business intelligence," and can be considered a form of BI. Data mining can be considered a function of BI, used to collect relevant information and gain insights. Moreover, business intelligence could also be thought of as the result of data mining. As stated, business intelligence involves using data to acquire insights. Data mining business intelligence is the collection of necessary data, which will eventually lead to answers through in-depth analysis.

The link between data mining and business intelligence can be thought of as a cause-and-effect relationship. Data mining searches for the "what" (relevant data sets) and business intelligence processes uncover the "how" and "why" (insights). Analysts utilize data mining to find the information they need and use business intelligence to determine why it is important.

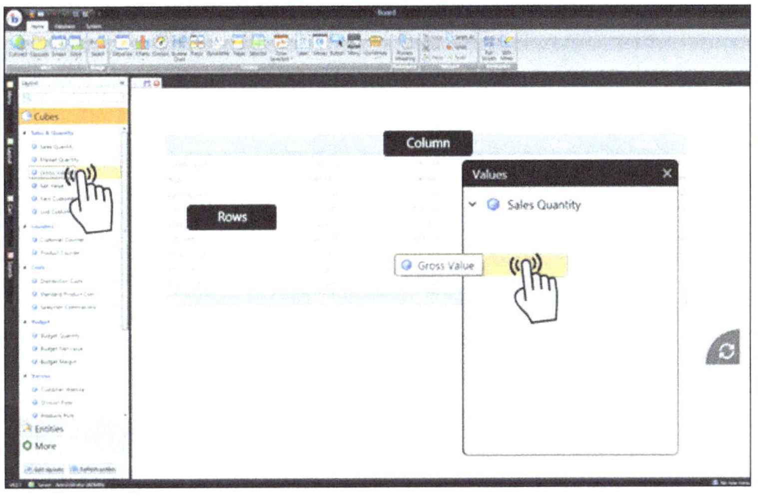

Big Data vs. Data Mining

Big data and data mining differ as two separate concepts that describe interactions with expansive data sources. Of course, big data and data mining are still related and fall under the realm of business intelligence. While the definition of big data does vary, it generally is referred to as an item or concept, while data mining is considered more of an action. For example, data mining may, in some cases, involve sifting through big data sources.

Big data does, by some definitions, include the action of processing large data sets. Conversely, data mining is more about collecting and identifying data. Data mining will usually be the step before accessing big data, or the action needed to access a big data source. These two components of business intelligence work in tandem to determine the best data sets to provide answers to your organization's questions. Following the processes involved in data mining vs big data, analysts can begin evaluating data and eventually offer suggestions for business procedure improvements based on their findings.

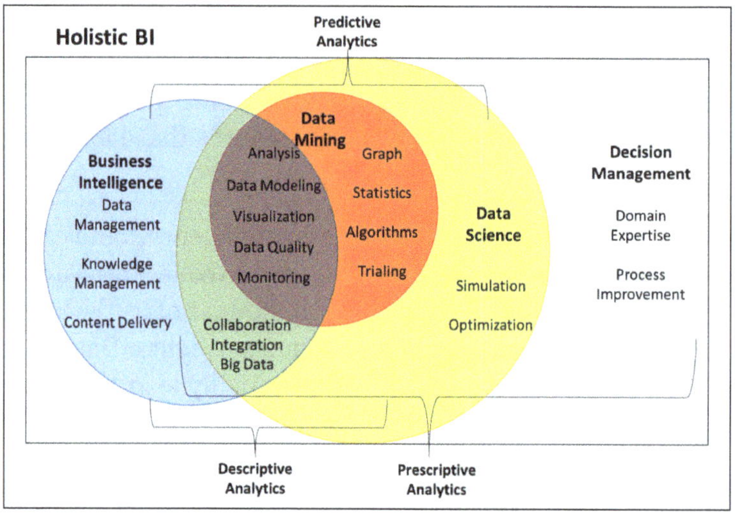

The practices of business intelligence are not a step-by-step operation. It's not as simple as mine for data, complete the big data function of processing the information and perform business intelligence analysis. Analyzing data with the intent of using that data to influence business decisions is an ongoing, interconnected process. During analysis, a company finds out whether they need new data or that their current approach is not successful. Necessary adjustments made to your business intelligence plans along the way will ensure accurate, truly insightful analysis.

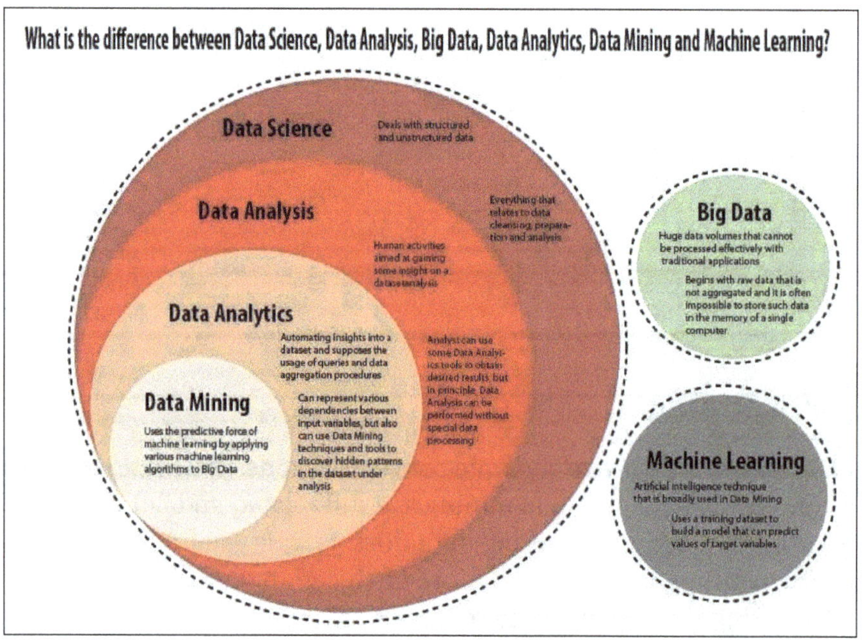

Additionally, as one purpose of business intelligence is to deliver real-time insight, this will be a continuing project. Your company will need to be constantly collecting and investigating data to achieve the most up-to-date information portraits possible.

Business intelligence, big data and data mining are three different concepts that exist in the same sphere. Business intelligence can be considered the overarching category in which these concepts exist, as it can be simply defined as data-based analysis of business practices. Big data is mined and analyzed, resulting in the gain of business intelligence. While these three concepts differ, BI, big data and data mining all work together to serve the purpose of providing data-driven insights. They are tools which can lead to a greater understanding of your business, and ultimately more streamlined processes which increase productivity and financial yield.

References

- Business-intelligence-definition-example: guru99.com, Retrieved 14 July, 2019
- Intelligence-decision-making: profitableventure.com, Retrieved 31 March, 2019
- Importance-business-intelligence-organizations: smartdatacollective.com, Retrieved 17 May, 2019
- Assetmanagementpart, assets: expeditefile.com, Retrieved 19 April, 2019
- Actionable-intelligence, definition: techtarget.com, Retrieved 5 February, 2019
- Bi-vs-big-data-vs-data-mining, business-intelligence: selecthub.com, Retrieved 26 July, 2019

Business Intelligence: Value, Environment and Processes

The set of strategies and technologies which are utilized by enterprises for the analysis of data related to business information is termed as business intelligence. It can be used for value creation in numerous environments. The topics elaborated in this chapter will help in gaining a better perspective about the varied facets of business intelligence as well as the processes associated with it.

Value Drivers

Corporate management has an ongoing mandate to maximize shareholder returns. But while maximizing shareholder value is an important corporate objective, it is not specific and accountable enough for operating management, who must also know which factors most influence value and which factors can be most easily affected. We call these factors "value drivers," and they are the primary focus of companies that succeed in maximizing shareholder value.

Prioritizing Value-creating Activities

Identifying and managing value driver helps management focus their attention on activities that will have the greatest impact on value. This focus enables management to translate the broad goal of value creation into the specific actions most likely to deliver that value.

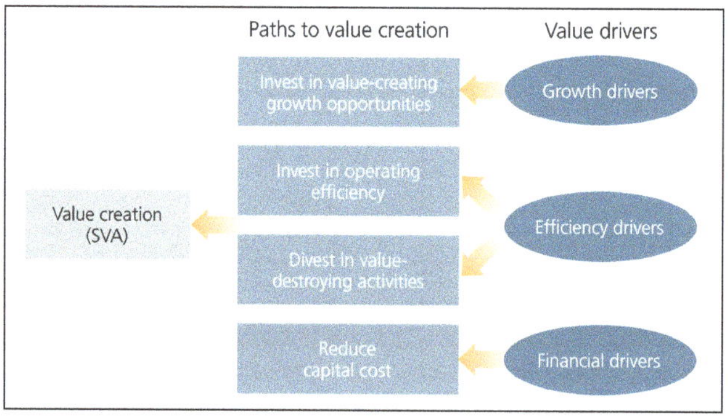

How value drivers link to value creation.

There are three categories of value drivers: Growth drivers, efficiency drivers, and financial drivers. companies tend to manage these value drivers in four ways. By focusing on value drivers, management can prioritize the specific activities that will affect performance in each area.

Examining and defining paths to value creation enables companies to identify and understand responsibilities by function and level within the organization. This in turn helps managers to focus their attention on factors that really matter.

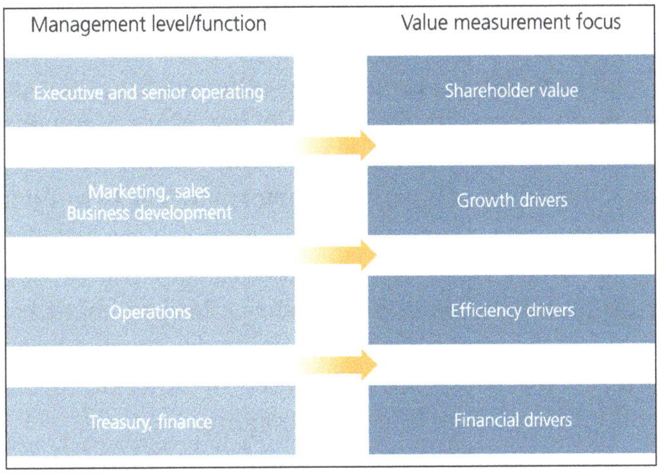

Aligning management responsibility for value drivers.

We find that most companies manage their business as if every operating factor were equally important. Most operating managers have a solid knowledge of the variables that impact business performance and they manage that list aggressively. The problem is that the list of variables is often too long and may be prioritized against goals other than value creation. Valuable resources are marshaled to increase market share, maintain pricing, increase distribution, introduce new products, increase operating efficiency, etc., without a clear sense of what "true" value drivers are.

There are two easy ways to identify value drivers:

- Value drivers have a significant value impact.
- They are controllable. (For example, commodity inputs maybe important to your business, but since they are not easily controlled, they may not deserve significant management attention).

The Value Driver Matrix illustrates a framework for prioritizing value drivers. The task is to identify variables that reside in quadrant IV and manage the resources directed at influencing variables in quadrants I through III.

Value Driver Analysis

Value driver analysis is an important foundation for strategic planning, helping management sort through their operations to define critical strategic levers. If, for example, growth drivers are important to a particular firm, management can direct strategic planning to focus on growth strategies. In short, value drivers ensure that strategy is grounded in the reality of operating performance.

Identifying value drivers is a three-step process:

- Develop a value driver "map" of your business.
- Test for value driver sensitivities.
- Test for controllability.

Manage Value Driver Performance

Once management has built a consensus around key value drivers, they can focus on the logistics of increasing value driver performance. If, for example, inventory management is a key value driver, management can focus on the system and process improvements that will result in increased inventory turns. One way to highlight value driver performance is to build measures of this performance into the regular performance measurement systems and reward structures of the business. Management must agree on which value driver measures they want to track and then develop a regular reporting structure that includes these measures. Management incentives can also be an effective way to highlight value driver performance. Value drivers can be substituted for other objectives in annual incentive plans. These can be tailored by function to ensure that managers are tied to value drivers that they are responsible for managing.

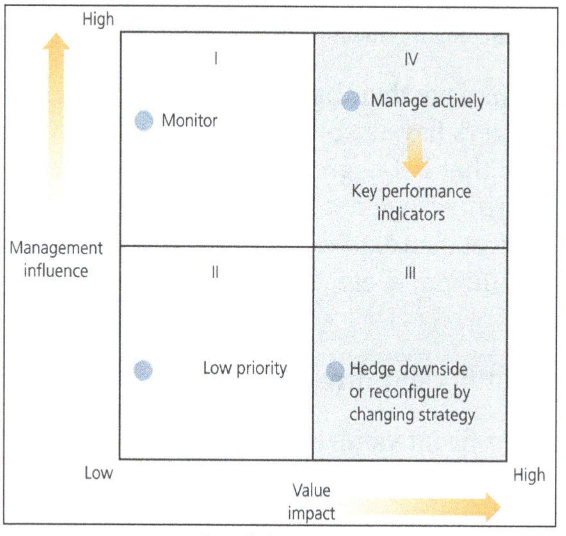

Value driver matrix

Performance Metrics and KPI

A Key Performance Indicator (KPI) is a quantifiable metric that reflects how well an organization is achieving its stated goals and objectives. For example, if one of your goals is to provide superior customer service, you could use a KPI to target the number of customer support requests that remain unsatisfied at the end of each week. This will measure your progress toward your objective.

KPIs link organizational vision to individual action. An ideal situation is where KPIs cascade from level to level in an organization. The pyramid has strategic vision at the top, feeding down to specific actions at the bottom. In the middle you'll find the KPIs that have been derived from the strategy, objectives, and Critical Success Factors (CSFs) of your organization.

CSFs are the areas of activity in which your organization must perform well in order to be successful. KPIs are the means by which these CSFs can be measured. The actions below the KPIs are the tasks and projects that you carry out in order to achieve the KPIs.

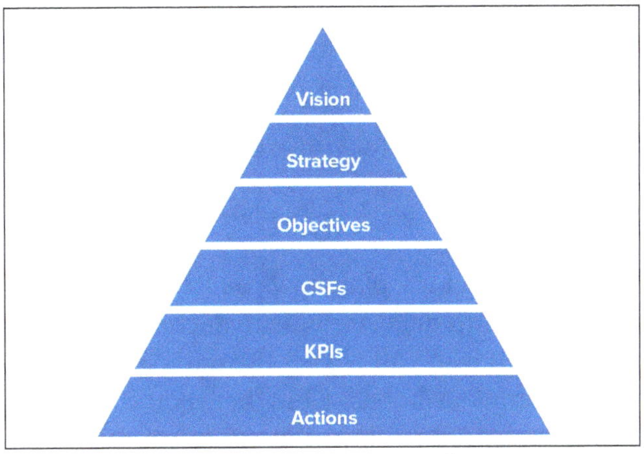

How KPIs fit into an organizational structure.

Used well, KPIs support your organization's goals and strategy. They allow you to focus on what matters most, and to monitor your progress.

How to Set Organizational KPIs

First, your organization needs to choose KPIs that measure the appropriate activity for each area of the business. For example, net profit is a standard KPI for an organization's financial performance. It's easy enough to calculate (total revenue minus total expenses), and you know that the higher it is, the better the company is performing.

Others may be harder to calculate. A customer satisfaction KPI, for example, may require regular, carefully constructed customer surveys to build the right amount of data. You'd then have to decide what sort of customer satisfaction score represents the benchmark you want to achieve.

Setting SMART KPIs

Whatever the nature of your KPIs, you need to make sure that they're SMART. This stands for:

- Specific: Be clear about what each KPI will measure, and why it's important.
- Measurable: The KPI must be measurable to a defined standard.
- Achievable: You must be able to deliver on the KPI.
- Relevant: Your KPI must measure something that matters and improves performance.
- Time-Bound: It's achievable within an agreed time frame.

When you finalize a KPI, it should fulfill all of these SMART criteria. For example, "Increase new paid sign-ups to the website by 25 percent by the end of the second quarter of the financial year." Ask yourself the following questions to help you to understand the context and define effective KPIs:

- What is your organization's vision? What's the strategy for achieving that vision?
- Which metrics will indicate that you are successfully pursuing your vision and strategy?

- How many metrics should you have?
- What should you use as a benchmark?
- How could the metrics be cheated, and how will you guard against this?

Managing your KPIs

When you're deciding which KPIs to set up, plan how you'll capture the information you need. Net profit requires a different set of data than customer satisfaction, for example, and requires access to different systems. Also, establish who will collect the data, and how frequently. Sales data can usually be collected daily, for example, whereas KPIs that require data to be collated from a number of sources might be better measured weekly or monthly.

You'll need to verify the data, too, to make sure it's accurate, and that it covers all the requirements of your KPI.

Communicate KPIs clearly to everyone concerned. If you're responsible for a team or organizational KPI, make sure that your reports know how each KPI impacts their work, and that they know which activities to focus on. You may be able to set up a performance dashboard, or use a balanced scorecard to measure progress efficiently.

How to Set Individual KPIs

"What gets measured gets done" is a common management saying. If you set a goal around a desired outcome, the chances of that outcome occurring are much higher, simply because you have committed to managing and measuring your progress toward it.

When you set goals and KPIs with individual team members, make sure that they align with your team's overall strategy – which, in turn, aligns with the overall strategy of your organization.

Defining an employee's goal with an organizational KPI ensures that their daily activities are well aligned with the goals of the organization. This is the critical link between employee performance and organizational success.

Here's an example of how organizational strategy cascades down to an individual team member's goals and KPIs:

- Organizational Vision: To be known for high customer satisfaction and superior service.
- Organizational Objective: To reduce the number of dissatisfied customers by 25 percent.
- Organizational KPI: The number of customer complaints that remain unresolved at the end of a week.
- Team Member's Goal: To increase the number of satisfactory complaint resolutions by 15 percent in this period.
- Team Member KPI: The weekly percentage difference in complaints handled that result in satisfied customers, as against unsatisfied customers.

Using KPIs for Recognition and Development

When you are satisfied that you have meaningful KPIs to measure the performance of your team, and of your organization as a whole, make sure that the appropriate training, support and incentives are in place to enable your people to perform well.

When you establish your rewards and recognition practices, make sure that they relate directly to the KPIs you've set, and that you're not rewarding potentially counterproductive behaviors.

For example, if you want to measure people on how well they deal with customer complaints, then rewarding them for reducing the number of complaints confuses the message you're trying to send.

Intuitively, you may feel that the fewer complaints you receive, the better your customer service must be. But this is not necessarily true: you may be getting fewer complaints because you have fewer customers, or because your customers can't access your support services.

Conversely, if your organization wants to attract new customers, then you might have a KPI that measures how many new customers you gain each week. Depending on the situation, a well-aligned performance system may reward employees based on the number of new customers they personally help to attract.

Value Adding Business Intelligence

We can confidently say that knowledge derived from a company's data can be used as if it were an asset, as long as senior managers understand that an investment in turning data into actionable knowledge can have a significant payoff. It is important to recognize that this problem cannot be solved solely by the application of technology. In truth, the technology must augment a more serious senior-level management commitment to exploiting discovered knowledge and having a way to measure the value of those activities.

	Analytic Application Areas						
	Sales Analysis	Inventory Analysis	Marketing Analysis	Supplier Analysis	Customer Analysis	Manufacturing Analysis	Financial Analysis
BI Value Proposition							
Manage Enterprise Performance	●	●	●	●	●	●	●
Provide Customer-Centric Analysis	●		●		●		
Provide Supply Chain-Centric Analysis	●	●		●		●	
Identify New Sales Opportunities	●		●		●		
Improve Sales Effectiveness	●		●				
Better Match Supply & Demand	●	●					
Improve Inventory / Service Levels		●					
Drive Manufacturing Efficiencies						●	
Improve Sourcing Abilities				●			
Align Strategy w/Operational Performance							●

There are a number of BI analytics that provide business value. Selecting and integrating these analytic functions depends on the ability to effectively build the underlying information infrastructure to support the applications as well as the ability to configure reporting and visualization of the discovered knowledge.

While Business Intelligence (BI) continues to be closely aligned with sales analysis and reporting, more companies are evolving in their use of it to not only understand, predict and influence the behavior of their customers, but to plan, evaluate and monitor their supply chains.

BI and Enterprise Performance Management

All manufacturing and distribution businesses today are driving for better performance: higher returns on invested capital, lower product and overhead costs, better asset utilization, faster delivery, greater customer retention, higher perfect order rates, reduced working capital needs, faster product innovation, greater sales and marketing productivity, the list goes on. But it's difficult to achieve these goals without having Enterprise Performance Management (EPM) processes and applications in place. More manufacturers and distributors are adopting EPM to help them tie execution to strategy by controlling and managing the full lifecycle of business decision-making.

EPM crosses departmental boundaries to embrace supply chain, customer management, and production-based performance management. It drives operational changes and performance improvements through continuous business planning, real-time performance analysis against objectives (presenting performance indicators to managers in scorecards or dashboards) guidance on what should be done when performance variances occur, and continuous response to changing business conditions.

At a high level, Business Intelligence fosters Enterprise Performance Management through technology and applications that are designed to help companies:

- Better understand, predict and influence the behavior of their customers.
- Better plan, evaluate and monitor their supply chains (or operational areas).

Customer Side of BI

- Understand Customer Behavior and Profitability: BI can offer numerous analytical capabilities for measuring customer profitability and for ranking and score carding customers across a number of areas. This can help companies ensure that their most profitable clients remain satisfied and their sales and marketing efforts are aimed at retaining and optimizing the right customers and attracting the right prospects.
- Predict Customer Demand: Business Intelligence can help business planners improve forecast accuracy and the overall sales and operations planning process. This is accomplished through collaborative forecasting and demand planning applications, open order analysis, and sales performance measurements.

- Influence Customer Behavior: Customer-focused business intelligence can also help Organizations' segment their customer bases for cross-selling and up-selling opportunities. And when integrated with marketing-focused analytics, they can help users better allocate and manage their trade funds and promotions in order to influence customer (retail partner) participation and ultimate end-consumer purchases.

Supply Chain (or Operational) Side of BI

- Plan What the Supply Chain Should Do: Today's more advanced predictive analytic applications additionally offer statistical forecasting down to the product SKU level. This enables companies to determine safety stock and re-order points more accurately by optimizing customer service levels and measuring supplier variability with inventory optimization as the bottom-line result.
- Evaluate Supply Chain Performance: By leveraging operational analytics once a forecast has been generated, supply chain performance can be evaluated in a number of areas such as Inventory, Purchasing and Manufacturing. Operational analytics also allow organizations to drive cost reductions on the sourcing side, reduce sourcing cycle time and decrease assets on the balance sheet by helping them cross-functionally manage spending and their supplier networks. Plus, the analytics can be used to assess and optimize assets in the areas of cash, inventory and both warehousing and manufacturing capacity.
- Monitor Supply Chain Variances: Because of the increased velocity of the supply chain, companies are recognizing that planning and analysis must be tightly integrated. As a result, there's a growing use of event management (or exception management) to monitor operational performance against planned performance in real-time with the goal of proactively identifying and addressing any variances that may arise.

6 Levels of Business Intelligence Value

The following 6 Levels of Business Intelligence Value depict types of analytical capabilities and their related value. The potential is huge.

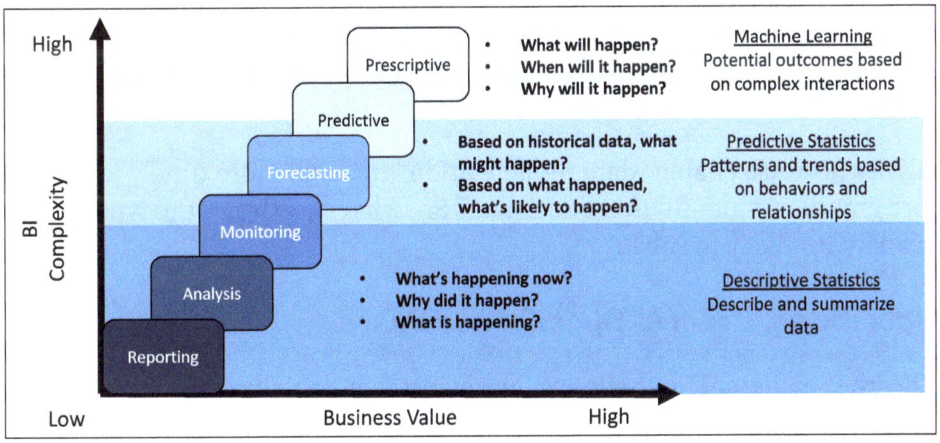

Use Cases for Business Intelligence

Everyone is searching for new ways to turn data into monetized data assets. Everyone is looking for new levers to extract value from data. But data ingesting and modeling is simply a means to an end. The end is not just more reports, dashboards, heatmaps, knowledge, or wisdom. The target is fact based decisions, guided machine learning and actions. Another target is arming users to do data discovery and insight generation without involving IT teams so called User-Driven Business Intelligence.

In other words, what is the use case that shapes the context for "Raw Data -> Aggregated Data -> Intelligence -> Insights -> Decisions -> Operational Impact -> Financial Outcomes -> Value creation." What are the right use cases for the emerging hybrid data ecosystem (with structured and unstructured data)?

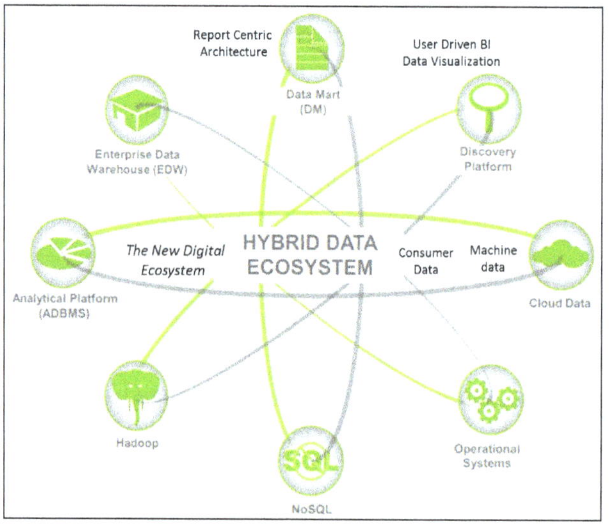

Use Cases by Industry or Function

Many organizations flounder in their Analytics, Data Science and Big Data efforts not because they lack smart talented people or analytics capability but because they lack clear objectives, leadership, experimental mind set or multi-year roadmaps in converting noisy hybrid data into useful signals. Starting with a clear objective is essential in order to pick the right tool to solve the right problem. Some clarity is necessary to drive proof of concepts or even select a technology stack to experiment with.

Big Data Analytics promise enable "data monetization" through more timely more accurate, more complete, more granular, more frequent decisions. So, what exactly are the types of business problems big data analytics likely to solve.

Industry Specific vs. Process Specific use Cases

- Healthcare Providers: The challenge for hospitals, especially as cost pressures tighten, is to treat patients more efficiently, while improving quality and risk KPIs. In care coordination and home-care services, machine and instrument data is being increasingly leveraged to track and optimize treatment, patient flow, and equipment use in hospitals. It is estimated that a 1 percent efficiency gain could yield more than $63 billion in global health care savings.

- Insurance: Individualize auto-insurance policies based on vehicle telemetry data. Insurer gains insight into customer's driving habits delivering: More accurate assessments of risks; Individualized pricing based on actual individual customer driving habits; Influence and motivate individual customers to improve their driving habits.
- Travel: Optimize buying experience through web/mobile log and social media data analysis. Travel site gains insight into customer preferences and desires; Up-selling products by correlating current sales with subsequent browsing behavior Increase browse-to-buy conversions via customized offers and packages; Deliver personalized travel recommendations based on social media data.
- Gaming: Collect gaming data to optimize spend within and across games: Games company gains insight into likes, dislikes and relationships of its users; Enhance games to drive customer spend within games; Recommend other content based on analysis of player connections and similar "likes" Create special offers or packages based on browsing and (non-) buying behavior.
- Predictive Maintenance using sensors (or motes): For instance, high-end cars use telemetry to know that an engine part is likely to break down before it actually does, based on the vibration or temperature patterns, a technique known as predictive maintenance. The idea is that a part does not fail all at once. Instead, it deteriorates over time until it eventually breaks. By monitoring the part real-time, you can spot problems before they become obvious.
- Energy Management: Many firms are using big data for energy management, including energy optimization, smart-grid management, building automation and energy distribution in utility companies. The use case is centers around monitoring and controlling network devices, manage service outages, and dispatch crews. It gives utilities the ability to integrate millions of data points on network performance and let engineers use analytics to monitor the network.

The Organizational Business Intelligence Framework

A major part of the success of a business intelligence program is the approach or methodology used to implement the framework and the related components. For example, if the approach used is one that simply constructs a data mart to support a specific set of business functions with no consideration for the organization strategic direction, scalability or maintainability, this business intelligence solution will certainly become a prime candidate for an expensive re-engineering project once those same business functions outgrow the application.

Incorporating key activities in the Software Development Life Cycle and the use of an architectural framework can implement business intelligence programs that are scalable maintainable and is aligned with the enterprise strategic direction-and of course, with documentation playing an integral part of the approach. Each phase should produce documentation that is used as a method to obtain signed approval to end one phase and begin the next.

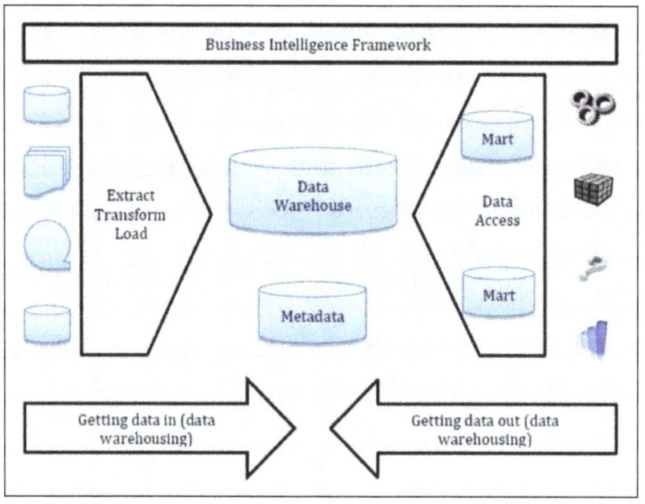

Initial Assessment

One of the most important activities is conducting an initial assessment. This assessment has two components to it; business and IT. The purpose of the assessment is to identify the business needs and the impact that a business intelligence solution would have on the organization. It is an effective way to identify the amount of time, cost and risk to the organization. It also provides the justification for business intelligence. This is a huge plus as it enables continued executive sponsorship.

The IT assessment is a complete evaluation of the current infrastructure. This answers the question "Does our organization have the tools and infrastructure to facilitate a BI solution?" The answer is in the results of a readiness assessment of the organization's ability to support a business intelligence framework and the related applications and solutions. The readiness assessment should include a detailed review of the hardware, BI and database software and operating system.

With this information, the team has everything it needs to produce a high level conceptual design of the BI architectural framework and an executive summary of the assessment. These artifacts are the important business and IT drivers for the remaining activities in the SDLC.

Planning

Planning is the next set of activities that puts the BI framework in place that really and truly, puts everything in motion. It is within this phase that the scope is clearly defined into sufficient detail that sets the expectations of senior management and in essence gets all members of the team to a common understanding of the goals of the project.

Once the scope has been defined and accepted by all members of the team complete with signed approvals, the next step is to define roles and responsibilities needed to complete the BI project. These roles and responsibilities should include both business and IT. It is very important that these roles are defined such that all is taken into account from a budget and time perspective. This task also facilitates the communication protocols for everything from project status reporting to incident management. These roles should include but are not limited to business stakeholders and sponsors, business SMEs, business analysts, architects, DBAs, infrastructure engineers, ETL developers, BI developers (should be specific to the software solution such as COGNOS, SQL Server SSAS, Business Objects, etc) and project managers.

Also in the planning stage, depending on the level of BI maturity in the organization, a training assessment should be conducted to gain an understanding of whether training is required for the BI suite of tools being deployed into the organization. This assessment has direct impact on cost and time lines as well.

The end results of the planning phase should be a fully fleshed out project plan with assigned responsibilities and time lines with alignments to the detailed budget for the project.

Requirements Gathering

With the project plan and budget approved, the functional and non-functional requirements are defined. The functional requirements are the articulated business needs that must be met with this BI solution. It is within these work sessions that requirements related to various types of reporting (ad-hoc and canned), the need for dashboards, key performance indexes (KPIs) and presentation displays are gathered and documented. Metadata management activities are a part of the requirements gathering process as it relates to the business context definitions of data. Also included in the requirements gathering from a business perspective is identifying the data sources that will be used to populate the data mart that will be the supporting data layer for the BI solution (in most cases). Ideally, the identification of these data sources should mainly be contained in the Data Warehouse. This is an important component. Why? Because if the data for the BI solution is sourced from the Data Warehouse, there is a high level of confidence in the quality of the data and minimal use of an ETL solution. If, however the data sources are disparate then the opposite holds true.

Non-functional requirements includes gathering information related to security, an essential and integral part of the BI solution. It is extremely important that the information being delivered is being consumed by authorized users only. Remember, each and every solution/application within the organization must survive an internal or external audit. Think Sarbanes-Oxley and HIPAA.

Other non-functional requirements include the definition of infrastructure needs as it relates to hardware, software and network components. These requirements should address the needs of a BI solution in terms of server memory configuration, use of SAN/NAS for storage, number of CPUs per server and parallel processing capabilities.

Once all this information and data has been compiled, a business requirements document is produced that frames the context of the business and IT requirements related to the BI solution that are in scope of the project.

Design Guidelines

The purpose of the design phase is to translate the business requirements document into design specifications. These specifications will be used as the blueprint for constructing the solution.

However, in designing a BI solution, there is a further refinement of the requirements as it relates to the type of data models that will be designed to deploy the data mart. This means that based on the business needs for reporting and the BI solution proposed, design decisions are made on whether a star schema or snowflake schema or hypercube be used as the supporting data layer for the application. Factors that weigh heavily in this decision are primarily related to the type of BI reporting. For trending, drill through, slice and dice, and analytics, then use of the hypercube works best. However, caution here, loading of the hypercube is resource intensive and complex and should be factored into the availability SLAs. So each design decision does have its tradeoffs; choose wisely.

Other design components within this phase include major enhancements to the security framework. This is often sensitive data. Only the users meant to view specific sets of information should have the required permission. Also included are infrastructure enhancements related to storage, server and network configurations.

The document created that captures the output and results of this phase are the Technical Design Specification.

Construction and Deployment Guidelines

The construction phase is just that. It is constructing, creating or installing the components that have been presented for the BI solution. However, before the actual construction can begin, the details of the Technical Design Specification should be reviewed with all members of the business and IT teams to ensure that there is a common understanding of all components of the BI solution. All work efforts should be focused on building the components of the BI solution. This includes the creation of the data models, the database or hypercube development of the application and presentation layers, installation and upgrade of the hardware and software.

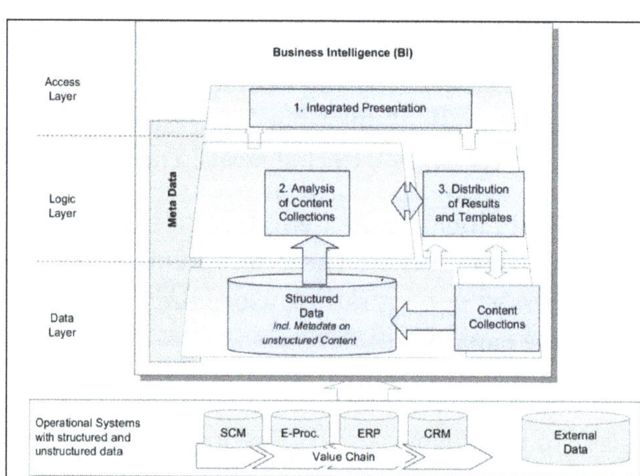

Analytical Information Needs and Information Flows

"Analytics" is a critical component of enterprise architecture capabilities, though most organizations have only recently begun to develop experience using quantitative methods. As Information Technology emerges from a scarcity-based mentality of constrained and costly resources to a commodity consumption model of data, processors and tools, analytics is quickly becoming table stakes for competition.

The emphasis of analytics is changing from one of long-range planning based on historical data, to dynamic and adaptive response based on timely information from multiple contexts, augmented and interpreted through various degrees of quantitative analysis. Analytics now permeates every aspect leading organizations' operations. Competitive, technological and economic factors combine to require more precision and less lag time in discovery and decision-making.

For example, operational processing, the orchestration of business processes and secure capture of transactional data is merging with analytical processing, the gathering and processing of data for reporting and analysis. Analytics in commercial organizations has historically been limited to special groups working more or less off-line. Platforms for transaction processing were separated for performance and security reasons, an effect of "managing from scarcity." But scarcity is not the issue anymore as the relative cost of computing has plummeted. Driven equally by technology and competition, operational systems are either absorbing or at least cooperating with analytical processes. This convergence elevates the visibility of all forms of analytics.

Confusion and mistakes in deploying analytics are common due to imprecise understanding of the various forms and types. Uncertainty about the staff and skills needed for various "types" of analytics are common. Messaging from technology vendors, service providers and analysts is murky and misleading, sometimes deliberately so.

The scope of analytics is vast, ranging from the familiar features of business intelligence to the arcane and mysterious world of applied mathematics. Organizations need to be clear on their objectives and capabilities before funding and staffing an analytic program. Predictive modeling to dramatically improve your results makes for good reading, but the reality is quite different. The four types are meant to help you understand where you can begin or advance.

These categories are not hard and fast. Some activities are clearly a blend of various types. But the point is to add some clarity to the term "analytics" in order to understand its various use cases.

Information Flow

To determine how raw information becomes technical content, you need to understand and map the flow of information. Typically, you work backward from the final information product to determine the original data sources for text and graphics.

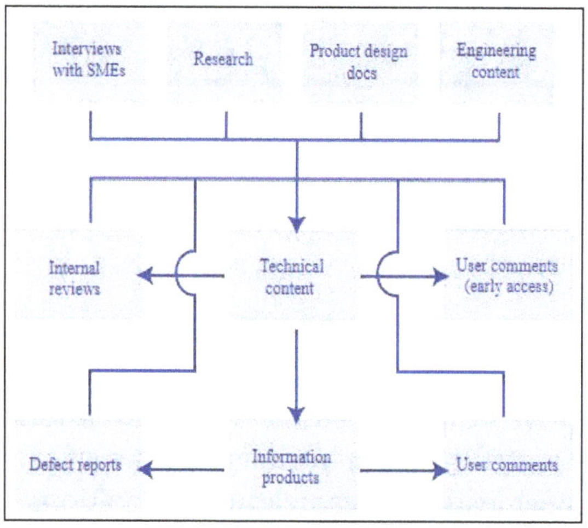

Example of Information Flow (Typical for High-tech)

The information sources are the items at the top of the flowchart. You can further refine this information by specifying who is responsible for each step in the process and when responsibility is handed off from one group to another. For example, in some organizations, engineers write content drafts and give those drafts to the technical publications group so that they can "make it pretty." In other organizations, technical communicators write content independently with minimal input from the engineering team. Some organizations use a hybrid approach: perhaps the technical communicators write user documentation and the engineers write systems documentation. It is important to understand how information flow is currently working and where the problem areas lie.

According to the authors, reviewers are lazy delinquents who give content only a cursory glance but try to prove that they did read the information by nit picking the comma usage, usually incorrectly. According to the reviewers, authors tend to inundate them with 300-page documents, due back in two days, and delivered with no advance notice exactly at the busiest point in the release cycle. Both parties complain about inefficient, annoying processes for marking up documents with comments (reviewers) and integrating comments into the source content (authors).

The distinction between technical content and information products is not always present. In many web-based tools, for example, content is stored in its final form. In most publishing workflows, however, there is a transition between a source content format (maybe XML) and a delivery content format (HTML or PDF).

As you examine the information flow, the goal is to identify bottlenecks and inefficiencies so that a new process can improve upon the current workflow. For example, one common recommendation is to eliminate any content duplication via copy-and-paste and instead carefully manage reusable information. Speeding up the update process so that published information products are current is a priority for many organizations. And often, the integration of a localization workflow into a previously monolingual process is a challenge.

Other considerations may include existing tools, skills, and corporate culture. Staffs who have lots of experience with print production may find a transition to automated document creation annoying—they like having the ability to tweak page breaks. If your corporate culture glorifies last-minute heroics rather than careful planning, you cannot implement a workflow that requires multiple formal signatures on reviews. (By contrast, if you are in a regulated industry, it is unlikely that you can avoid formal review and approval cycles).

The analysis goal is to develop a solution that:

- Streamlines the flow of information throughout the organization.
- Supports efficient content creation and delivery (which reduces costs).
- Maintains or improves the quality of the information delivered to customers.
- Provides an authoring environment that is appropriate for content creators.

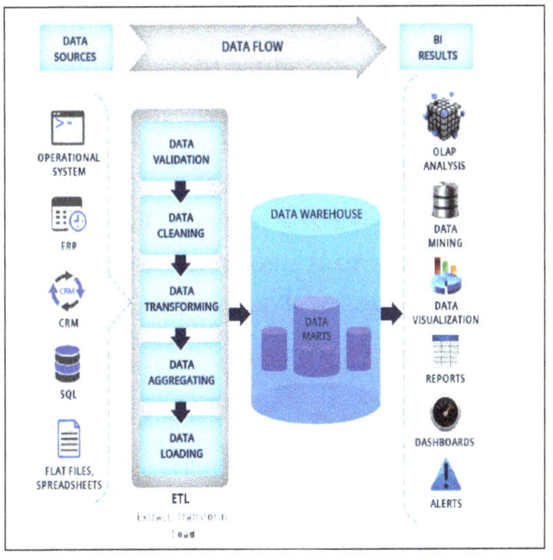

Information Processing and Information Flow

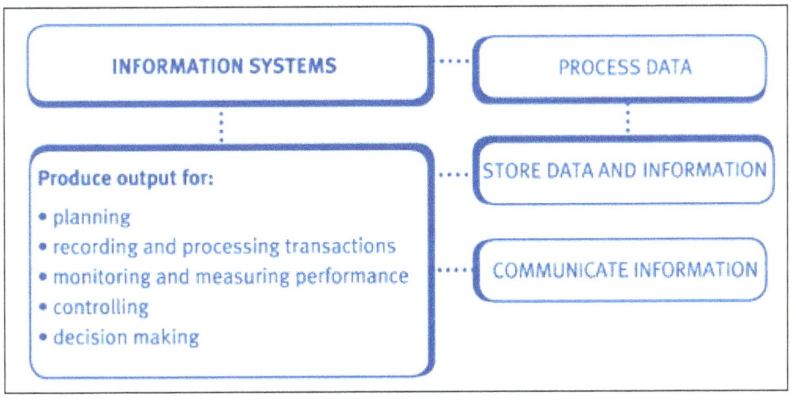

Information processing is the manipulation of data to produce useful information; it involves the capture of information in a format that is retrievable and analyzable. Processing information involves taking raw information and making it more useful by putting it into context. In general, information processing means processing new data, which includes a number of steps: acquiring, inputting, validating, manipulating, storing, outputting, communicating, retrieving, and disposing. The future accessing and updating of files involves one or more of these steps. Information processing provides individuals with basic skills to use the computer to process many types of information effectively and efficiently. The term has often been associated specifically with computer-based operations.

Information Flow Analysis

When timing information is added to the specification of a Multi-Level Secure (MLS) system, it may reveal new information flow: if a classified entity, High, can modify the response time of an unclassified entity, Low, and Low can reliably deduce that the change in its response time is caused by High, High can use this as a mean to transmit illicit information to Low. This timing based information flow leakage is often called a covert-timing channel. As illustrated in figure, a covert (timing) channel has a transmission cycle which consists of a sender–receiver synchronization (S–R) period, a transmission period and a feedback period. During the S–R period, a sender (High) will notify a receiver (Low) that it is ready to transmit new information. However, the S–R period may not be necessary if the sender and the receiver have some prior agreement (e.g. every t units of time, new information is transmitted). In this paper, we assume there exists a prior agreement between the sender and receiver. Therefore, unless stated otherwise, it is assumed that there is no sender– receiver synchronization (S–R) period. If we assume there is an unreliable communication channel between a sender and a receiver, a feedback period must exist to establish reliable communication. Without feedback, the sender is unaware if the receiver has observed the intended information and does not know when to start a new transmission.

Numerous papers have presented covert-timing channel (real-time information flow) analysis for various MLS systems. We are specifically interested in real time systems where time plays a fundamental role and thus timing information must be included in system specifications. Previously, formal frameworks such as timed process algebra or timed automata were used to model timed behaviors of real-time systems and to specify security policies for preventing illicit information leakage through covert timing channels. For the analysis of information flow security in non-real-time systems, a trace-based possibilistic formal framework or model has been quite popular. In the trace-based possibilistic model, the non-timed behavior of a system is modeled by a set of traces, where every trace represents a possible execution sequence of the system and nondeterministic behavior is modeled by the possibility of different execution sequences. In the possibilistic model, system specifications do not require probabilities with which the different possible execution sequence will occur. In this paper, we present a new trace-based possibilistic framework which allows us to:

1. Formally specify traces (histories) of timed actions of real time tasks running under a real-time scheduling algorithm.
2. Define security policies which specify how real-time tasks should behave against covert-timing attacks.

3. Formally show, if a system running under a real-time scheduling algorithm satisfies the proposed security policies, that the system can achieve a high level of real-time information flow security. This satisfactory relation between a system specification and a security policy can reveal that the schedule of tasks generated by a real-time scheduler could leak information through a covert-timing channel.

4. Compare the proposed security policies in terms of their relative strength and specification characteristics.

Approach to a Formal Framework

Designating the level of abstraction to specify timed behaviors of a real-time system is crucial in our approach. A real-time system should function as follows: when multiple tasks arrive at a scheduler for execution, the way in which scheduling priorities are assigned to tasks (if a scheduling algorithm is priority based) and the way in which a task is scheduled to execute on the CPU are determined by the type of a scheduling algorithm in use and the (timing) constraints imposed on task executions. Thus, we model a real-time system as a set of tasks which execute according to a scheduling algorithm to meet their timing constraints. In this paper, we assume that a set of tasks consists of tasks with different security levels, e.g. a high-level (classified) task TH, a low-level (unclassified) task T_L, and a third party1 (trusted) task T_N. The system model we employ throughout this paper is a trace or history-based model, i.e. the timed behavior of a system is modeled by a set of traces where every trace represents a possible timed execution sequence of a real-time task running in the system.

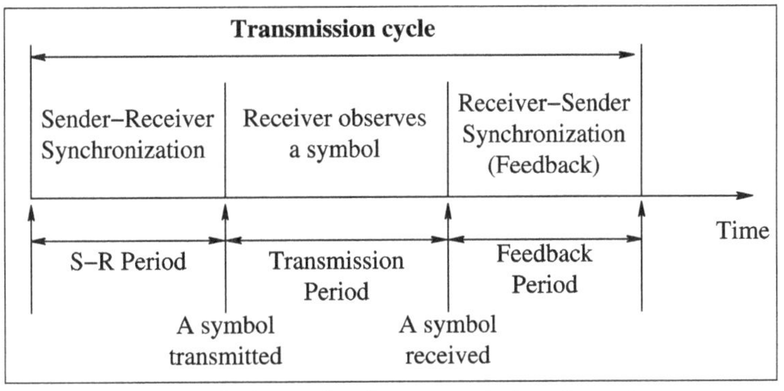

Transmission cycle of a covert-timing channel.

In order to accurately define real-time information flow from High to Low, we first need to specify what Low can observe and what it can reliably deduce from its observation, as well as how High can affect Low's observation. As shown in figure, the model assumes Low is able to assess the response time (the time between the submission of its task to a system and the output event notifying that it is completed) of a low-level task; however, we assume that there is a limit to how accurately Low can record time. Our assumption is that Low cannot measure the time between any two occurrences of context switch. When a high-level task T_H preempts a low level task T_L while T_L is running, or TH locks a resource shared by TL, thereby blocking an execution of T_L, the response time of T_L is affected. The delay or change of the response time of T_L could be used as means of transmitting illicit information. Note that a third party (trusted) task T_N can also affect the response time of T_L in the same way that T_H affects T_L. In our formal framework, the existence of covert-timing channels means that, upon observing the response time of a low-level task, Low can reliably deduce a sequence of timed actions or traces performed by a high-level task.

Real-time Systems

Abstract Model of Real-time Systems

We assume that a real-time system consists of the following components:

- A set of computational real-time tasks that compete for shared resources. These real-time tasks are typically assumed to be software processes or threads.
- A run-time scheduler (or dispatcher) that controls which task is executing at any given moment.
- A set of shared resources used by real-time tasks. These shared resources may include software variables, data bus, CPU, mutual exclusion control, variables, and memory.

Lifecycle of Real-time Task

In a real-time system, which supports the execution of concurrent tasks on a single processor, a task can be defined as being in at least six different unique states:

- Running state – A task with highest priority enters this state as it starts executing on the processor.
- Ready state – A task in the ready state is ready to run but cannot because a higher priority task is executing.
- Blocked state – A task enters the blocked state if it has requested a busy (unavailable) resource or has delayed itself for some duration.
- Null state – A task has not been submitted to a scheduler.
- Activation state – When a task in the null state is submitted to a scheduler for execution, the task becomes activated.
- Termination state - When a task finishes its computation, it terminates; the task state changes from the termination state to the null state.

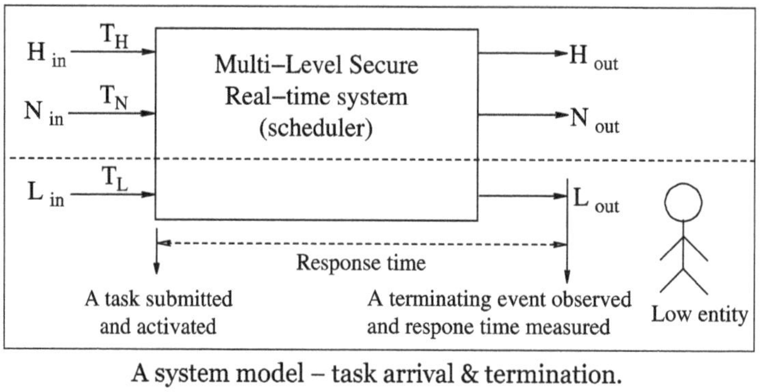

A system model – task arrival & termination.

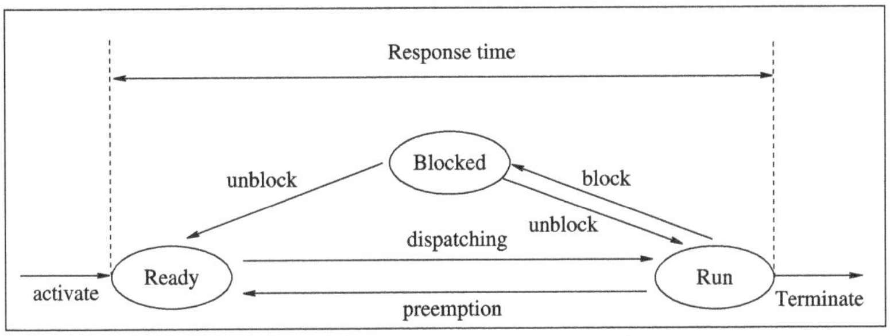

Minimum state transition diagram of a task.

A task moves from one state to another according to the state transition diagram shown in figure. When a real-time task arrives at a run-time scheduler for execution, the task becomes activated. The task is placed in a ready queue and turns to the ready state. The queue is ordered according to the particular run-time scheduling algorithm in force. The task at the ready queue is released for execution and enters the running state. While the task is in the running state, it can be preempted by the arrival of another task with a higher priority. Once preempted, it moves back to the ready state. The running task can also move to the blocked state when blocking on a shared resource occurs or the task delays itself for some duration. A blocked task remains blocked until the blocked resource becomes available or an event (signal) the task is waiting for occurs. When the task is no longer blocked, it moves to the ready state, or it moves directly to the running state by preempting the currently running task if it is the highest priority task. Note that figure shows only the minimum state transition diagram of a real-time task.

We can represent the state of a task using six different atomic propositions (boolean variables). Let $_{Tid}$ be a task with the unique identifier id. Then, the different atomic propositions are $B(T_{id})$, $act(T_{id})$, $ready(T_{id})$, $block(T_{id})$, $run(T_{id})$ and $term(T_{id})$, which describe T_{id} being null (T_{id} has not been submitted to a scheduler), activated, ready, blocked, running, and terminated, respectively.

Timed Kripke Structures (TKS)

We choose to use the Timed Kripke Structure (TKS) to describe timed behaviors of real-time tasks-running under a scheduling algorithm for the following reasons:

- Since TKS is a simple extended version of a state transition system where each transition is labeled by an integer number which denotes the time required to move from one state to another, it is easy to specify a timing constraint between two consecutive actions performed by a task. From TKS, it is also easy to obtain the execution traces (histories) of real-time tasks.
- With TKS, we can easily specify actions performed simultaneously3 by (independent) real-time tasks, e.g. simultaneous arrival of independent tasks at a scheduler.
- Formal verification (model checking) of timed properties of a system over TKS is relatively efficient.

TKS is an extended version of Kripke Structure (KS). Formally it is defined as follows, where N is the set of nonnegative integers.

Timed Kripke Structure of a system is a tuple $M = (AP,\ S\ S_{init}\ R,\ L)$, where:

- AP is a finite set of atomic propositions,
- S is a finite set of states,
- $S_{init} \subseteq S$ is a set of initial states,
- $R_{init} \subseteq S \times N \times S$ is a set of transitions. A transition $(S_i, d_i, S_{i+1}) \in R$ is denoted $S_i \xrightarrow{d_i} S_{i+1}$ by where d_i is the duration of execution in the state s_i.
- $L : S \to 2^{AP}$ is a labeling function; for any states, $L(s) \subseteq AP$ is a set of atomic propositions that hold on s.

The difference of TKS from KS is that in TKS $R \subseteq S \times N \times S$ is a finite set of transitions labeled by a non-negative integer, called the duration of the transition, whereas KS has no duration.

A (computation) path in a TKS is an infinite sequence of states $S_0 \xrightarrow{d_0} S_1 \xrightarrow{d_1} \ldots$ such that $(S_i, d_i, S_{i+1}) \in R$ for all ≥ 0. A finite sequence of transitions $S_0 \xrightarrow{d_0} S_1 \xrightarrow{d_0} | S_2 \ldots\ldots S_n$ in TKS is called a finite computation path.

Timed Computation Tree

In KS, a computation path is formed by designating state sR as initial and then unwinding the KS into an infinite tree with the designated state s_R as the root. Thus, for any KS and state s_R‹ S, there is an infinite computation tree with root labeled sR such that (S_i, S_{i+1}) is an arc in the tree if and only if $(S_i, S_{i+1}) \in R$ in KS.

The same concept is applied to TKS to construct a Timed Computation Tree. The Timed Computation Tree can be constructed by unfolding TKS into an infinite tree. Similarly, for any TKS and state $s_R \in S$, there is an infinite computation tree with root labeled s_R such that (S_i, d_i, S_{i+1}) is an arc in the tree if and only if $(S_i, d_i, S_{i+1}) \in R$ in TKS.

System Model

Labeling States to Model Timed Behaviors of a Task

It is important that a state s_i of TKS should be properly and consistently labeled to model timed behaviors of a task. We assume that a real-time system has a set Γ_A of tasks which constantly change their task states according to a run-time scheduling algorithm A. The task state of each task T_{id} running in a system is described by an atomic proposition $P_{id} \in A_{Pid}$, where,

$$AP_{id} = \{\varnothing(T_{id}),\ act(T_{id}), ready(T_{id}), block(T_{id}),\ run(T_{id}), Term(T_{id})\}$$

For all states $S_i \in S, L(S_i)$ contains the proposition $P_{id} \in AP_{id}$ for each task $T_{id}; L(S_i)$ has the following form if there are n number of tasks running concurrently under scheduling algorithm A, i.e. $\Gamma_A = \{T_{id}\}id \in \{1,.......n\}\}$ and $AP = U_{id \in \{1,.......n\}} AP_{id}$:

$$L(s_i) = P_{id} | id \in \{1,...,n\} \wedge P_{id} \in AP_{id}\}$$

A state s_i of TKS progresses to the next state s_{i+1} if one or more tasks T_{id} in T_A changes their task states, i.e. $P_{id} \in L(s_i) \neq P'_{id} \in L(s_i+1)$; for the remaining tasks with no change in their task states, their atomic propositions at the current state s_{i+1} remain the same as at the previous state s_i.

Let s_d be a state with the duration of d > o units of time and se be a state with zero duration (d = o). We call an atomic proposition P_{id} an action of a task T_{id} if $P_{id} \in L(s_d)$. An atomic proposition P_{id} is called an event of a task T_{id} if $P_{id} \in L(s_e)$. An execution step of a task is represented as an interleaving sequence of actions and events. We denote an action $P_{id} \in L(s_d)$ of T_{id} which requires the task to take d>o units of time by P_{id}^{d}. For example, run $(T_{id})^d$ is used to represent the execution of T_{id} for *d* units of time.

An event of a task is used to describe the following incidents:

1. The event of task activation: a task is activated and placed in a ready queue. There are two cases to consider. The first case is that a task is activated immediately after the system starts (at time zero). The second case is that a task arrives and is activated while other tasks are running. Let $si \in S, i > 0$, and $so \in S_{init}$. The first case is expressed as $s_0 \xrightarrow{0} s_1...$, where act $(T_{id}) \in L(s_0)$, and ready$(T_{id}) \in L(s_1)$. The second case is denoted by $\rightarrow s_i \xrightarrow{d} s_{i+1} \xrightarrow{0} 0\ s_{i+2}...$ where d>o, $\varnothing(Tid) \in L(s\ )$, act $(T_{id}) \in L(s_{i+1})$ and ready$(T_{id}) \in L(s_{i+2})$.
2. The event of task termination: task termination is expressed as $\rightarrow s_i \xrightarrow{d} s_{i+1} \xrightarrow{0} 0\ s_{i+2}...$, where d > o, run$(T_{id}) \in L(s_i)$, term $(T_{id}) \in L(s_{i+1})$ and $\varnothing(Tid) \in L(s_{i+2})$.
3. The event of an immediate release[5] (execution) of a task T_{id} after it is activated: this immediate release of T_{id} is expressed in TKS as follows: $\rightarrow s_i \xrightarrow{0} s_{i+1} \xrightarrow{0} 0\ s_{i+2}...$, where~ $i \geq 0$, act $(T_{id}) \in L(s_i)$, ready$(T_{id}) \in L(s_{i+1})$, and run$(T_{id}) \in L(s_{i+2})$.

In summary, run (T_{id}) and block (T_{id}) are always used to represent an action of a task, and act (T_{id}) and term (T_{id}) always denote an event. The atomic proposition ready (T_{id}) is used as an action to describe a delay before execution or as an event to describe the immediate release (execution) of a task. The atomic proposition $\varnothing(T_{id})$ is used as an action to denote the passage of time during which a task is in the null state or as an event to denote a task being null in a state $s_e \in S$.

Example: Assume Γ_A =]$\{T_N, T_H, T_L\}$.The set Γ_A of tasks is assumed to share no resource between them (no task can be blocked on a busy resource but can delay itself for some duration) and executes according to the timing diagram of figure. There are a few things worth noting in the timing diagram: at time 5, T_H delays itself for three units of time and T_L in the ready queue experiences a delay of one unit of time before execution. At time 6, T_L begins executing. At time 8, T_H preempts T_L and begins executing, and T_L moves back to the ready queue. We construct the corresponding TKS as shown in figure.

Real-time Trace

We define a (real-time) history of a system as:

Definition: For a computation path $\pi \rightarrow s_0 \xrightarrow{d_0} s_1 \xrightarrow{d_1} 0\ s_2 \ldots, s_n$ in TKS, a history $\tau(\pi)$ is an ordered sequence of sets of atomic propositions, $i \geq 0$, where the set $L(s_i)$ holds in state s_i for d_i units of time. Thus, we denote a history τ(π) by $\tau(\pi) = L(s_0)^{d_0}, L(s_1)^{d_1} L(s_i)^{d_i} \ldots L(s_n)^{dn}$.

A history τ(π) describes timing behaviors of a set Γ_A of real time tasks. For convenience when d_i=0, we omit di from the history. To obtain a real-time behavior of an individual task T_{id} from a history, we introduce a restriction operator$|_{id}$:

Definition: Let $\tau(\pi) = L(s_0)^{d_0} \cdot L(s_1)^{d_1} L(s_i)^{d_i} \ldots L(s_n)^{d_n}$. We define $\tau(\pi)|_{id}$ as an ordered sequence of propositions $pi \in AP_{id}$ with a superscript d_i, $i \geq 0$, formed by extracting pi from each $L(s_i)$; thus, $\tau(\pi)|_{id} = \rho_0^{d_0}.\rho_1^{d_1}\ldots.\rho_n^{d_n}$, where $pi \in AP_{id}$ and $pi \in L(s_i)$. We call $\tau(\pi)|_{id}$ a trace of an individual task T_{id}. The same consecutive propositions listed in a trace can be simplified as $\rho_0^{d_0} \cdot \ldots \cdot \rho_{i+k}^{d_k} = \rho_i^{d_0 + \ldots + d_k}$, where $\rho_{i+1} \ldots = \rho_{i+k}$.

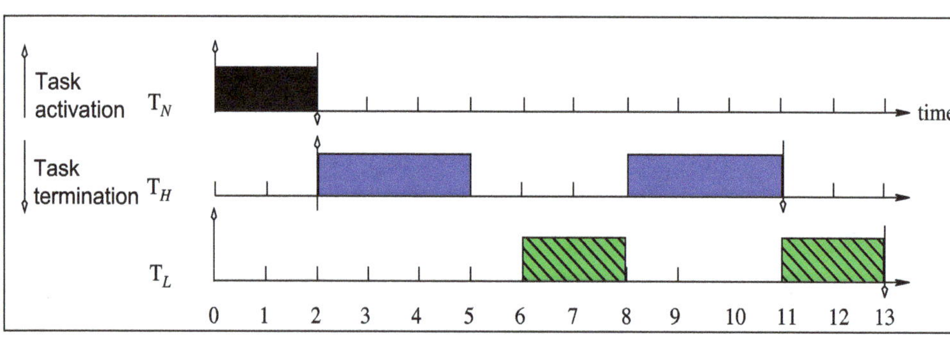

Timing Diagram.

Definition: $D(\tau(\pi)|_{id})$ denotes the cumulative duration of the trace $\tau_\delta|_{id}$ of an individual task T_{id}:

$$D(\tau(\pi)|_{id}) = \sum_{i=o}^{n} d_i, \text{where } \tau(\pi)|_{id} = \rho_0^{d_0} \ldots \rho_n^{d_n}$$

Example: Let π_1 be the computation path shown in figure. Then, the history $\tau(\pi_1)$ is:

$$\tau(\pi_1)=\{act(T_N),\varnothing(T_H),act(T_L)\}...\{ready(T_N),\varnothing(T_H),ready(T_L)\}$$
$$\{run(T_N),\varnothing(T_H),ready(T_L)\}^2...\{term(T_N),act(T_H),ready(T_L)\}.$$
$$\{\varnothing(T_N),ready(T_H),\ ready(T_L)\}...\{ready(T_N),run(T_H),ready(T_L)\}^3.$$
$$\{\varnothing(T_N),block(T_H),\ ready(T_L)\}^1...\{\varnothing(T_N),\varnothing(T_H),term(T_L)\}.$$

The trace of T_L is:

$$\tau(\pi_1)=\mathrm{act}(T_L)\mathrm{ready}(T_L),\mathrm{ready}(T_L)^2...\mathrm{ready}(T_L)\cdot\mathrm{ready}(T_L)$$
$$\cdot\mathrm{ready}(T_L)^3\ \mathrm{ready}(T_L)^1,\mathrm{run}(T_L)^2.\mathrm{ready}(T_L)^3\cdot\mathrm{ready}(T_L)$$
$$\cdot\mathrm{run}(T_L)^2\ \mathrm{term}(T_L),\quad =\mathrm{act}(T_L)\cdot\mathrm{ready}(T_L)^{0+0+2+0+0+3+1}$$
$$\cdot\mathrm{run}(T_L)^2\ \mathrm{ready}\ (T_L)^{3+0}\cdot\mathrm{run}(T_L)^2.\mathrm{term}(T_L)$$
$$=\mathrm{act}(T_L)\cdot\mathrm{ready}(T_L)^6\cdot\mathrm{run}(T_L)^2\cdot\mathrm{ready}(T_L)^3\cdot\mathrm{run}(T_L)^2$$
$$\cdot\mathrm{term}(T_L)$$

Furthermore, $D(\tau(\pi_1)|_L)=0+6+2+3+2+0=13$. In this example, $D(\tau(\pi_1)|_L)$ is the response time of T_L since $\tau(\pi_1)|_L$ represents a sequence of events and actions occurring during the time between act (T_L) and term (T_L).

We introduce a function RUN which takes a trace $\tau(\pi)|_{id}$ of T_{id} as an input and returns an execution trace of T_{id} revealing only act (T_{id}) and run (T_{id}) from $\tau(\pi)|_{id}$. High uses the execution trace RUN $\tau(\pi)|_{id}$ as the means of transmitting illicit information to Low.

Definition: Given a trace $\tau(\pi)|_{id}$, the execution trace RUN- $\tau(\pi)|_{id}$ is obtained by removing all the propositions except act (T_{id}) and run (T_{id}) from $\tau(\pi)|_{id}$ and adding a notation $\downarrow n_i$ right after act (T_{id}) to denote the activation time of T_{id}. Thus, RUN- $\tau(\pi)|_{id}$ has the following form:

$$\mathrm{RUN}(\tau(\pi)|_{id})=\begin{cases} <>_{run},\ \text{if no } run(T_{id}) \text{ is enabled in } \tau(\pi)|_{id}; \\ act(T_{id})\downarrow n_1.\ run(T_{id})^{k_1}\ act(T_{id})\downarrow n_2.\ run(T_{id})^{k_2}; \\ .,.\ .\mathrm{act}(T_{id})\downarrow n_1.\mathrm{run}\ (T_{id})^{k_1}\ ...,\text{otherwise.}\end{cases}$$

$\downarrow n_i$ used in act $(T_{id})\downarrow n_1$ denotes the time n_i of the ith activation of T_{id}. If T_{id} is a periodic task with period p, $n_{i+1} = n_i + p.\ k_i$ used in run $(T_{id})^{k_i}$ ki denotes the total execution (run) time of T_{id} during the ith activation interval. We call RUN $(\tau(\pi)|_{id})$ the run trace of T_{id}.

Example: Let $\tau(\pi_1)|_L$ be the trace of T_L, i.e. $\tau(\pi_1)|_L$ = act(T_L).ready (T_L) ^{6}.run (T_L)^2.ready (T_L)^3.run (T_L)^2.term (T_L). T_L is activated at time 0 and has only one activation interval (not a periodic task). In addition, during the interval, the total execution time of T_{id} is 4 units of time since there are two runs (run(T_L)^2 and run (T_L)^2) in $(\tau(\pi)|_{id})$. Then, the run trace of T_L is:

$$\text{RUN}(\tau(\pi)|_{\text{id}})\text{-act}\left(\text{T}_{\text{id}}\right)\downarrow_0 . \, run\left(\text{T}_{\text{id}}\right) act\left(\text{T}_{\text{id}}\right)^2 . \, run\left(\text{T}_{\text{id}}\right)^2$$
$$= \text{act}\left(\text{T}_{\text{id}}\right)\downarrow \text{n}_0.\text{run}\ \left(\text{T}_{\text{id}}\right)^4.$$

Definition: LET RUN $=(\tau(\pi)|_{\text{id}}) = \text{act}\,(\text{T}_{\text{id}})\downarrow \text{n}_1 \cdot \text{run}\,(\text{T}_{\text{id}})^{k_1} \cdot \text{act}(\text{T}_{\text{id}})\downarrow \text{n}_2 \cdot$ run $(\text{T}_{\text{id}})^{k_2}$... and RUN $(\tau(\pi')|_{\text{id}}) = \text{act}\,(\text{T}_{\text{id}})\downarrow \text{n}_1' \cdot \text{run}\,(\text{T}_{\text{id}})^{k_1'} \cdot \text{act}(\text{T}_{\text{id}})\downarrow \text{n}_2'.$ run $(\text{T}_{\text{id}})^{k_2'}$...Any two run traces RUN$(\tau(\pi)|_{\text{id}})$ and RUN$(\tau(\pi')|_{\text{id}})$ are equivalent if $\forall i \in \{1,2,..\}.n_i = n_i' \wedge k_i = k_i'$.

Real-time Information Flow Security Policies

We provide the general model which can describe the timed behaviors of the set Γ_A of concurrently running tasks. In this section, to specify real-time information flow security policies, we restrict (simplify) our assumption in such a way that the set Γ_A consists only of three tasks with different security levels. Our restricted assumption is that $\Gamma_A = \{T_H, T_L, T_N\}$,, where T_H, T_L, and T_N denote a high-level task, a low-level task, and a third party task, respectively. A tuple *M* of TKS is used to model all possible timed behaviors of the set $\Gamma_A = \{T_H, T_L, T_N\}$, of real-time tasks running under a scheduling algorithm *A, i.e. M* = (*AP, S, S_{init}*, R; L), where, for every state $s \in S$, $L(s) = \{P_N \in AP_N, P_H \in AP_H, P_L \in AP_L\}$ and $AP = \cup_{id \in \{H,L,N\}} AP_{id}$.

Finite Timed Computation Tree (TCT)

For real-time information flow analysis, which is assumed to have a zero sender–receiver (S–R) period, it is important to trace the sequence of state transitions made during a transmission period. In our context, the transmission period means the time between the activation and the termination of T_L. We assume that, during the transmission period, T_L always terminates (in order for Low to observe a response time). Thus, in our model, the timed behavior of a real-time system during the transmission period means a collection of finite computation paths p (each path p consists of an inter leave of actions and events of the set Γ_A of tasks) occurring during the time between T_L's activation and termination. The computation path p is formed by designating state $s_1 \in S$, as initial and then unwinding TKSM into a finite tree ωM with the designated state s_I as the root and a set F of multiple states as leaf nodes, where act $(T_L) \in L'(s_I)$ and $\text{F} = \{s_f \,|\, s_f \in S \wedge term(T_L) \in L(s_f)\}$. We call ωM the finite Timed Computation Tree (TCT) of TKSM. ωM consists of one or more computation paths. The computation path $\pi = s_i \xrightarrow{d_I} \ldots s_f$ of ωM is denoted by $\pi = \left[s_i \ldots s_f\right]$, where act $\left(T_L\right) \in L'\left(s_I\right)$ and $sf \in$ F. Therefore, the finite Timed Computation Tree ωM represents all possible sequences of actions and events of a set Γ_A of tasks occurring during the transmission period. The activation time of T_L is a reference point for the first activation time n_1 of T_H. If T_H is activated before or at the same time as T_L's activation time, we use $n_1 = 0$ (the run trace of T_H starts with act$\left(T_H\right) \downarrow_0$. If TH is activated m units of time after T_L's activation time, $n_1 =$ m (the run trace of TH starts with act$\left(T_H\right) \downarrow_m$).

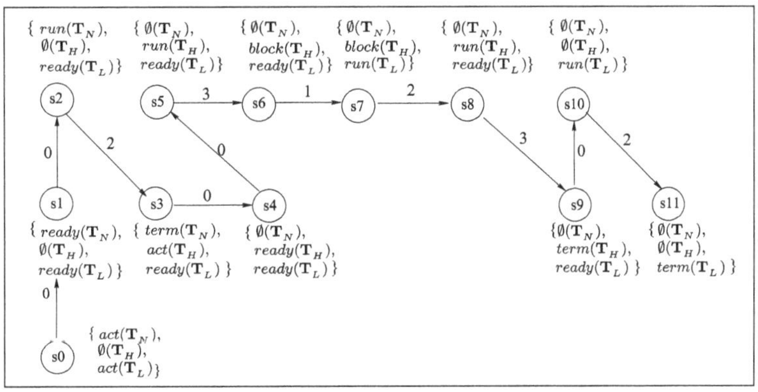

TKS with labels.

Notation

To specify real-time information flow policies, we use the following notations:

1. ρ denotes a finite computation path π from root s_I to a leaf node $s_f \in^2 F$ *of* ωM, *i.e.* $\rho = \pi\left[s_I \ldots s_f\right]$. We call r a complete path in ωM. In addition, $\text{PATHS}_{\omega M}$ denotes a set of all possible complete paths in ωM, i.e. $\text{PATHS}_{\omega M} = \left\{\rho \middle| \rho = \pi\left[S_I \ldots S_f\right]\right.$, $\left. act\left(T_{id}\right) \in L\left(S_I\right), s_f \in F \right\}$.
2. $\left(\tau\right)\rho$ represents the history of a complete path ρ.
3. $R_{\omega M} = \left\{D(\tau\left(\rho\right) | L) \rho \in \text{PATHS}_{\omega M}\right\}$ is a set of all possible response times of T_L which Low can observe.

We need to define all possible execution behaviors (run traces) of T_H. Additionally, we need a way to express which run trace(s) of T_H is/are responsible for a particular response time $t \in R_{\omega M}$.

Definition: The timed behavior set RT^H $RT^H_{\omega M}$ of T_H is defined as a set which contains all possible run traces of complete paths taken by T_H in $_{\omega M}$, i.e. $RT^H_{\omega M} = \left\{\text{RUN}(t\left(\rho\right)|_H)\rho \in \text{PATHS}_{\omega M}\right\}$. $RT^H_{\text{ùM}}$ can be thought of as a set of all possible timed behaviors of T_H which can affect the response time of T_L. The response time specific behavior set $RT^H_{\text{ùM}}$ (t) of T_H, $RT^H_{\text{ùM}}$

$(t) \subseteq \mathrm{RT}^{\mathrm{H}}_{\grave{u}\mathrm{M}}$, is a set of run traces which is responsible for the response time $t \in R_{\omega M}$ of T_L, i.e. $RT^{H}_{\omega M}(t) = \{\mathrm{RUN}(\tau(\rho)|_{\mathrm{H}}) \forall \rho \in \mathrm{PATHS}_{\omega M} \cdot D(\tau(\rho)|_{L}) = t\}$.

Example: Assume a set $\Gamma A = \{T_H, T_L, T_N\}$ of tasks concurrently runs on a single processor and the finite Timed Computation Tree ωM shown in figure represents all possible sequences of actions and events of a set Γ_A of tasks occurring during the transmission period of T_L. For better readability, we omit the states with zero duration except initial state sI and terminal states $s_f \in F$. In addition, the state s_d with the duration d are labeled by only run(T_{id}) to indicate T_{id} executes for d units of time at s_d. The terminal states s_f are labeled by only term(T_L) to indicate that T_L terminates at s_f. The finite Timed Computation Tree w_M has the following characteristics:

– s0 as the initial state sI and a set F of leaf nodes, i.e. F = {s7, s8, s9, s10}.

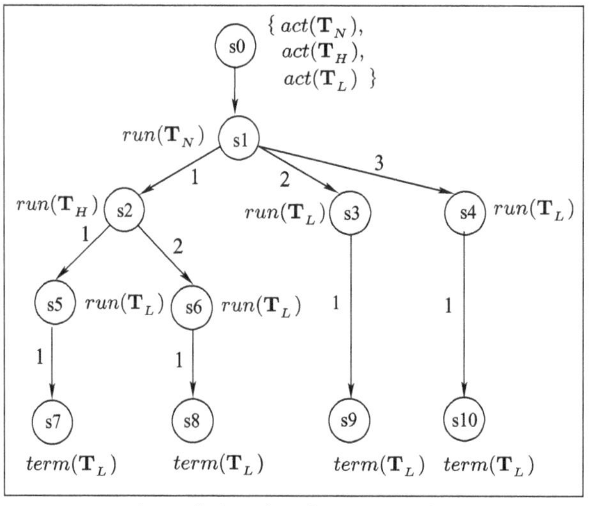

Example - a finite Timed Computation Tree.

$\mathrm{PATHS}_{\omega M} = \rho 1 = \pi[s0...s7], \rho_2 = \pi\ [s0...s8], \rho_3 = \pi[s0...s9],\ \rho_4 = \pi[s0...s10]$.

– Since $D(\tau(\rho_1)|_L)) = D(\tau(\rho_3)|_L)) = 3$ and $D(\tau(\rho_2)|_L)) = D(\tau(\rho_4)|_L)) = 4,\ R_{\omega M} = \{3,\ 4\}$.

–In path ρ_1, T_H is activated at time 0 and executes for 1 unit of time. Thus, $\mathrm{RUN}(\tau(\rho_1)|_H) = \mathrm{act}(T_H)\downarrow_0 \cdot \mathrm{run}(T_H)^1$. Similarly, $\mathrm{RUN}(\tau(\rho_2)|_H) = \mathrm{act}(T_H)\downarrow_0 \mathrm{run}(T_H)^2$ and $\mathrm{RUN}(\tau(\rho_3)|_H) = \mathrm{RUN}(\tau(\rho_4)|_H) = <>$ run

$- \mathrm{RT}^{H}_{\omega M} = \{<>_{run};\ \mathrm{act}(T_H)\downarrow_0 \cdot \mathrm{run}(T_H)^1, \mathrm{act}(T_H)\downarrow_0 \cdot \mathrm{run}(T_H)^2\}$

$-\mathrm{RT}^{H}_{\omega M}(3) = <>_{run},\ \mathrm{act}(T_H)\downarrow_0 \cdot \mathrm{run}(T_H)^1$ and

$\mathrm{RT}^{H}_{\omega M}(4) = <>_{run},\ \mathrm{act}(T_H)\downarrow_0 \cdot \mathrm{run}(T_H)^2$.

Timing Channel Free Policies

We propose four Timing Channel Free (TCF) policies. If a finite Timed Computation Tree ω_M of TKSM has the characteristics which can satisfy the TCF policy, we show that the system is free from covert-timing channels (to a certain degree). Formally, we use $\omega_M \mid\mid= \text{P}$ to denote that the characteristics of ω_M satisfies the TCF policy P. We provide the formal definitions of the TCF policies as follows.

Weak Timing Channel Free Policy

To satisfy the Weak Timing Channel Free (WTCF) policy, for every complete path with a response time $t \in R_{\omega M}$, which has one or more high-level actions run(T) enabled, there must exist a complete path with the same response time t which does not have any high-level action enabled. The formal definition of the WTCF policy is:

Definition: Weak Timing Channel Free (WTCF) policy

$$\forall t \in R_{\omega M}.\text{WTCF}\left(RT^{H}_{\omega M}(t)\right), \text{ where WTCF } (T) \equiv \exists r \in T \cdot r = <>_{run}$$

Lemma: If $\omega_M \mid\mid= \text{WTCF}$, upon observing a response time $t \in R_{\omega M}$, Low cannot reliably deduce occurrences of any run trace $r \in RT^{H}_{\omega M}(t)\ of\ T_H$.

Proof: We assume $\omega_M \mid\mid= \text{WTCF}$, Using above Definition, for every response time t of T_L, the response time specific timed behavior set $RT^{H}_{\omega M}(t)$ has at least one element ($<>_{run}$) which does not have any high-level action run(T_H) enabled. Therefore, Low cannot reliably deduce occurrences of any run trace $RT^{H}_{\omega_M}(t)$ of T_H since the response time t could have been observed without an intervention of timed actions of a high level task.

There still exists real-time information flow in a real-time system which satisfies WTCF policy. Although Low cannot reliably deduce occurrences of a run trace of TH, when Low observes a response time t, it can still deduce which run trace of TH cannot be responsible for the response time t. This type of a covert channel is called a negative channel. To prevent Low from deducing non occurrences of run traces of TH, we need a stronger security policy than WTCF.

Strong Timing Channel Free Policy

We propose the Strong Timing Channel Free (STCF) policy to prevent Low from deducing not only occurrences, but also non occurrences of any run trace of T_H. To prevent Low from deducing non occurrences of run traces of TH, for every response time t, the response specific behavior set $RT^{H}_{\omega_M}(t)$ must include all run traces that a high-level task can possibly execute. The formal definition of STCF policy is:

$$\forall t \in R_{\omega_M}.\text{STCF}\left(RT^{H}_{\omega_M}(t)\right), \text{ where STCF } (T) \equiv WTCF(T) \wedge NON(T),$$

where $NON(T)\ RT^{H}_{\omega_M} = T$

Theorem: If ωM ||=STCF, there is no real-time information flow from High to Low in a real-time system M.

Proof: Assume ωM ||=STCF, From Definition above, ω_M || = WTCF, which prevents Low from reliably deducing occurrences of any run trace r of T_H. By definition, uM also satisfies NON(T), where T = $RT^{H}_{\omega_M}$ =(t). NON(T) requires that the response time specific behavior set $RT^{H}_{\omega_M}$ =(t) must be equal to the set of all run traces which T_H can possibly produce (any measured value of the response time t will not rule out any possible run trace of T_H since $RT^{H}_{\omega_M}$ =(t) $RT^{H}_{\omega_M}$ for every t). These two predicates together (WTCF and NON) prevent Low from reliably deducing anything about the run traces of T_H upon observing a response time.

Example: The finite Timed Computation Tree ω_M satisfies the WTCF policy because the response time specific timed behavior set $RT^{H}_{\omega M} = (t)$ includes $<>_{\text{run}}$ for every response time t. However, the finite computation tree ω_M does not satisfy the STCF policy because $RT^{H}_{\omega_M} = (t) \neq RT^{H}_{\omega_M}$ for every response time t.

Rigid Timing Channel Free Policy

$\left|R_{w_M}\right| = 1 \wedge STCF\left(RT^{H}_{\omega_M}(t)\right)$, where $t \in R_{w_M}$

The difference between STCF and RTCF is that RTCF requires that Low should always observe the same response time $\left(\left|R_{w_M}\right| = 1\right)$, while STCF does not.

The definition of the RTCF policy, which is a special case of STCF, may be useful to convert a system satisfying only WTCF to a system satisfying RTCF; it is easier to design and verify a system satisfying RTCF than STCF. In addition, from Shannon's information theoretic view point the quantity (capacity) of real-time information flow from T_H to T_L over a covert channel for an RTCF system is zero no matter what probability distribution the channel has since Low, as an information receiver, always observes the same value (response time).

Non-Preemptive Timing Channel Free Policy

The Non-preemptive Timing Channel Free (NTCF) policy prevents the existence of covert-timing channels for both real-time and non-real-time systems. It simply says that a low-level task T_L must not be preempted by a high-level task T_H. The formal definition of NTCF is:

$$\forall r \in RT^{H}_{\omega M} \cdot r = <>_{run}$$

We demonstrate a few examples of how our formal framework can be applied to more realistic problems.

Comparing Real-Time Information Flow Policies

Relative Strength of Real-time Information Flow Policies

In this topic, we compare Timing Channel Free (TCF) policies to evaluate the relative strength of each policy. We first define what it means to compare TCF policies. Assume we have two TCF policies P_1 and P_2. To compare two policies, P_1 and P_2, we evaluate $P_1 \Rightarrow P_2$ and $P_2 \Rightarrow P_1$. If the first statement is true, P_1 is at least as strong as P_2, and vice versa. If both are true the policies are of equal strength. If neither is true, they are not comparable.

Theorem: The hierarchical strength of Timing Channel Free requirements follows the partial ordering shown in figure.

Proof: We first prove NTCF $\Rightarrow$ STCF and STCF $\Rightarrow$ NTCF: (NTCF $\Rightarrow$ STCF) Let ω_M be a finite Timed Computation Tree model of $TKSM_1$. If ω_{M_1} ||= NTCF, meaning that no run(T_H) is performed during an execution of T_H, the set $RT^H_{\omega M}$ has a single element $<>_{run}$. Since $RT^H_{\omega M}(t) \subseteq RT^H_{\omega M}, RT^H_{\omega M}(t) = RT^H_{\omega M} = \{<>_{run}\}$ for all response times $RT^H_{\omega M}$ this condition satisfies the predicate NON of STCF. In addition, for every response time t, the response specific behavior set $RT^H_{\omega M}(t)$ contains the element $<>_{run}$, which satisfies the predicate WTCF. Therefore, ω_{M_1} ||= NTCF implies that ω_{M_1} satisfies both predicates WTCF and NON of STCF.

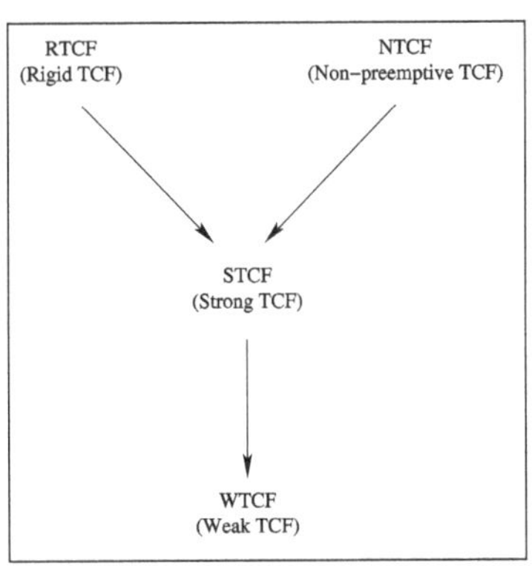

Partial ordering of Timing Channel Free requirements.

(STCF $\Rightarrow$ NTCF) Let ω_{M_2} be a finite Timed Computation Tree model of $TKSM_2$. If ωM_2 ||= STCF, any run trace $r \in RT^H_{\omega M}$ of T_H could have the running action run(T_H) enabled in it (meaning that T_H preempts T_L while T_L is running). This violates the NTCF policy.

Next, we prove NTCF $\not\Leftrightarrow$ RTCF: while NTCF requires that T_L should not be preempted by T_H, a system satisfying RTCF may allow the preemption. Thus, RTCF $\not\Rightarrow$ NTCF. While RTCF requires that Low should only observe a single response time, a system satisfying NTCF may produce multiple response times (due to interference caused by timed action of T_N) observable by Low. Thus, NTCF $\not\Rightarrow$ RTCF.

We do not include the proofs showing the hierarchical strength of Timing Channel Free policies between WTCF, STCF, and RTCF since the careful observation of each definition can easily reveal the relative strength; the definition of RTCF is a more restrictive form of STCF and the definition of STCF includes one of WTCF.

Specifying Security Policies

The Alpern–Schneider's framework has been the dominant model in the specification of programs: a system is identified with the set Π of possible execution sequences π (an execution sequence p can be thought of as a history of a single computation path in TKS) that a system can produce and a property is regarded as the set of execution sequences. A property is often called a property of traces. A system satisfies a property of traces if the system's set of execution sequences is a subset of the property's set. A set of execution sequences is called a property of traces if set membership is solely determined by each element and not by other members of the set. This implies that a security policy or a requirement P is a property if the security policy or the requirement P can be specified by a predicate $\hat{p}$ of the form:

$$P(\Pi) = \forall \pi \in \Pi \cdot \hat{p}(\pi)$$

The above equation reads as: the security policy or the requirement P is a property of traces if every execution sequence π in the set Π satisfies the predicate $\hat{p}$ (form of the security policy) on an individual execution sequence. From the equation (1), it is obvious that, given $P\Pi$, $P\Pi'$ must also hold for any subset Π' of Π.

Lemma: The NTCF policy is a property of traces.

Proof: Let ω_M satisfy NTCF and π be an individual execution sequence (computation path), i.e. $\pi \in \text{PATHS } \omega_M$. To prove NTCF is a property of traces, we must demonstrate that we can construct a predicate $\hat{p}$ defined on a single execution sequence π such that $\forall \pi \in PATHS_{\omega_M} \cdot \hat{P}(\pi)$.

The NTCF policy specifies that a low-level task TL must not be preempted by a high-level task T_H during the transmission period (the time between T_L' activation and termination Thus, the predicate $\hat{P}$ can be constructed to establish if any individual execution path p should not include any high-level action run(T_H) enabled. Therefore, NTCF is a property of traces.

In general, an information flow security policy is not a property of traces unless we restrict its definition. It is generally known that information flow security policies are expressed as a closure condition on a trace set Π of possible execution sequences π. A closure condition is often called a property of a trace set. For example, the simplest form of a closure condition on a trace set can be expressed as: $\pi \in \Pi \Rightarrow f(\pi) \in \Pi$ for some function f which returns an execution sequence for an input π. This implies the following: given an information flow security policy P, two sets of executions Π and Π', and $\Pi' \subset \Pi$, $p(\Pi') \not\Rightarrow P\Pi'$.

WTCF, STCF and RTCF policies have the following characteristics:

Lemma: The WTCF, STCF and RTCF policies are not properties of traces; each policy is a property of a trace set.

Proof: We use a proof by contradiction to show that the WTCF, STCF and RTCF policies are not properties of traces. Let us assume that WTCF is a property P of traces and a TCT model w_M satisfies P. Thus, the following must hold: $P(PATHS\, w_M) \equiv \forall \pi \in PATHS_{\omega M}.\widehat{P}(\pi)$. Further, for any subset Π' of $PATHS_{\omega M}$, $P(\Pi')$ must also hold. Specifically, let Π' be a set with a single execution path in which a high-level action run(T_H) is enabled. This set Π' cannot satisfies WTCF since WTCF requires another execution path with the same response time in which no high-level action is enabled. This clearly shows that WTCF is not a property of traces but a property of a trace set. The same reasoning can be applied to STCF and RTCF.

The big difference between NTCF and other policies is that only NTCF demands that a low-level task TL should not be preempted by a high-level task TH. This difference and the previous two lemmas lead to the following corollary.

Corollary: To define a real-time information flow security policy for a system, where a low-level task must be preempted by a high level task to meet the timing constraints, the policy must be specified by a property of a trace set.

Proof: A preemption of T_L by T_H, while T_L is running, always affects (delays) an execution of T_L. This preemption may cause possible information leakage through a covert-timing channel. For a computation path in which the preemption of T_L by T_H occurs, there must exists at least one (or more) different computation paths which can obfuscate Low's view on timed actions taken by High. Therefore, the policy must be specified by the property of a trace set.

References

- Identifying-and-Managing-Key-Value-Drivers-LEK-Executive-Insights, insights, default: lek.com, Retrieved 21 May, 2019
- Actionable-knowledge, computer-science, topics: sciencedirect.com, Retrieved 8 January, 2019
- 6-levels-of-business-intelligence-value, white-papers, insights: arbelatech.com, Retrieved 13 May, 2019
- Big-data-analytics-use-cases: practicalanalytics.com, Retrieved 25 February, 2019
- The-Business-Intelligence-Framework-Built-to-Last: databasejournal.com, Retrieved 16 January, 2019
- Understanding-analytical-types-and-needs: wordpress.com, Retrieved 29 March, 2019
- Information-flow, assessing-the-situation, developing, contents: contentstrategy101.com, Retrieved 30 April, 2019
- Information-processing, computers-and-computing, computers-and-electrical-engineering, science-and-technology: encyclopedia.com, Retrieved 11 January, 2019

3

Role of Data in Business Analytics

Business analytics is involved in developing new insights related to business performance by using data and statistical methods. This chapter closely examines the key concepts related to the role of data in business analytics such as data requirements analysis and data integration to provide an extensive understanding of the subject.

Data Requirements Analysis

It would be a disservice to discuss organizational data quality management without considering ways of identifying, clarifying, and documenting the collected data requirements from across the application landscape. This need is compounded as there is increased data centralization, governance, and growing organizational data reuse.

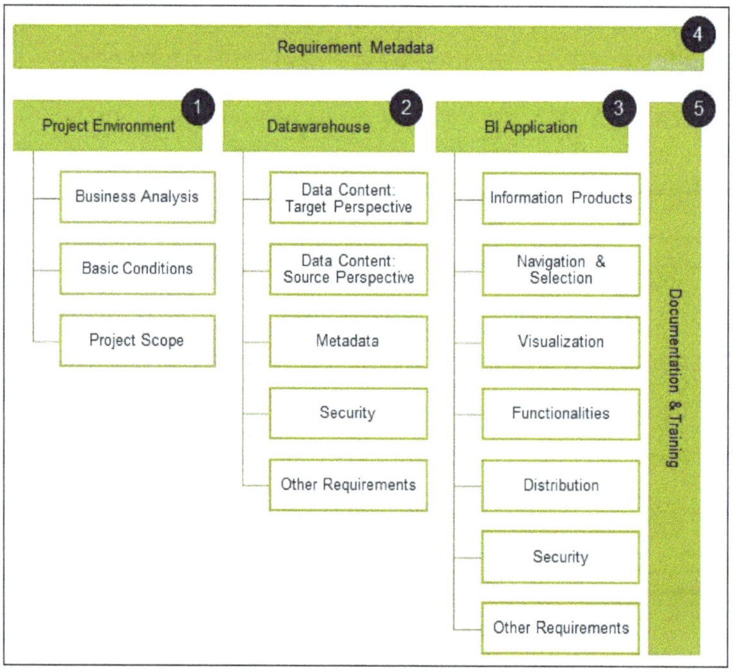

The last item may be the most complex nut to crack. Since the mid 1990s, when decision support processing and data warehousing activities began to collect and restructure data for new purposes, there has been a burning question: Who is responsible and accountable for ensuring that the quality characteristics expected by all data consumers are met? One approach is that the requirements, which often are translated into availability, data validation, or data cleansing rules, are to be applied by the data consumer. However, in this case, once the data is "corrected" or "cleansed," it is changed from the original source and is no longer consistent with that original source. This inconsistency has become the plague of business reporting and analytics, requiring numerous hours spent in reconciling reports from various sources. The alternate approach is to suggest that the business process creating the data must apply all the data quality rules. However, this can become a political hot potato, because it implies that additional work is to be performed by one application team even though the results do not benefit that team's direct customers.

That is where data requirements analysis comes into play. Demonstrating that all applications are accountable for making the best effort for ensuring the quality of data for all downstream purposes, and that the organization benefits as a whole when ensuring that those requirements are met, will encourage better adherence to the types of processes.

Business uses of Information and Business Analytics

Business intelligence and downstream reporting and analytics center on the collection of operational and transactional data and its reorganization and aggregation to support reporting and analyses. Examples are operational reporting, planning and forecasting, score carding and dashboards presenting KPIs, and exploratory analyses seeking new business opportunities. And if the objective of these analyses is to optimize aspects of the business to meet performance targets, the process will need high-quality data and production ready information flows that preserve information semantics even as data is profiled, cleansed, transformed, aggregated, reorganized, and so on. To best benefit from a business intelligence and analysis activity, the analysts must be able to answer these types of questions:

- What business process can be improved?
- What is the existing baseline for performance?
- What are the performance targets?
- How must the business process change?
- How do people need to change?
- How will individuals be incentivized to make those changes?
- How will any improvement be measured and reported?
- What resources are necessary to support those changes?
- What information is needed for these analyses?
- Is that information available?
- Is the information of suitable quality?

In turn, the results of the analyses should be fed back into the operational environments to help improve the business processes, while performance metrics are used to continuously monitor improvement and success.

Business uses of Information

The results of business analyses support various users across the organization. Ultimately, the motivating factors for employing reporting and analytics are to empower users at all levels of decision making across the management hierarchy:

- Strategic use, such as organizational strategic decisions impacting, setting, monitoring, and achieving corporate objectives.
- Tactical use, such as decisions impacting operations including supplier management, logistics, inventory, customer service, marketing, and sales.
- Team-level use, influencing decisions driving collaboration, efficiency, and optimization across the working environment.
- Individual use, including results that feed real-time operational activities such as call center scripts or offer placement.

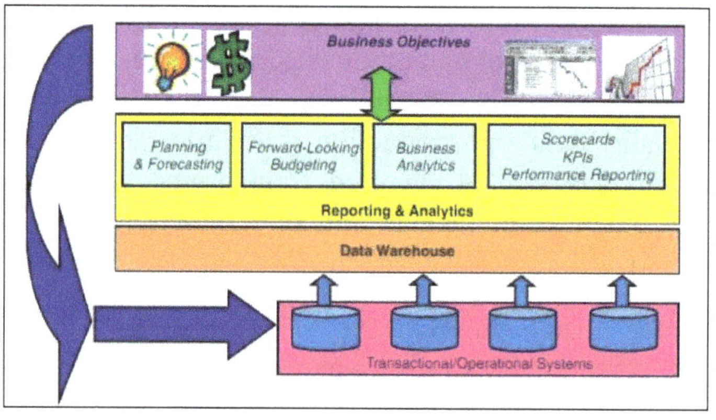

Table: Sample Business Analyses and their Methods of Delivery.

Level of Data Aggregation	Users	Delivery
Detailed operational data	Frontline employees	Alerts, KPIs, queries, drill-down (on demand)
Aggregated management data	Midlevel and seniorv	Summary stats, alerts, queries, and scorecards
Summarized internal and external data	Executive staff	Dashboards
Structured analytic data	Special purpose – marketing, business process analysis	Data mining, Online Analytical Processing (OLAP), analytics, etc.
Aggregate values	Individual contributors	Alerts, messaging

The structure, level of aggregation, and delivery of this information are relevant to the needs of the target users. The following are some examples:

- Queries and reports support operational managers and decision requirements.
- Scorecards support management at various levels and usually support measurement and tracking of local objectives.

- Dashboards normally target senior management and provide a mechanism for tracking performance against key indicators.

Business Drivers and Data Dependencies

Any reporting, analysis, or other type of business intelligence activity should be driven from the perspective of adding value to core areas of business success, and it is worthwhile considering a context for defining dimensions of value to ensure that the activity is engineered to properly support the business needs. We can consider these general areas for optimization:

- Revenues: Identifying new opportunities for growing revenues, new customer acquisition, increased same-customer sales, and generally increasing profitability.
- Cost management: Managing expenses and the ways that individuals within the organization acquire and utilize corporate resources and assets.
- Productivity: Maximizing productivity to best match and meet customer needs and expectations.
- Risk and compliance: Compliance with governmental, industry, or even self-defined standards in a transparent and audit- able manner.

Organizations seek improvement across these dimensions as a way to maximize profitability, value, and respect in the market. Although there are specific industry examples for exploiting data, there are a number of areas of focus that are common across many different types of businesses, and these "horizontal" analysis applications suggest opportunities for improvements that can be applied across the board. For example, all businesses must satisfy the needs of a constituent or customer community, as well as support internal activities associated with staff management and productivity, spend analysis, asset management, project management, and so on. The following are some examples used for analytics:

- Business productivity represents a wide array of applications that focus on resource planning, management, and performance.
- Customer analysis applications focus on customer profiling and segmentation to support targeted marketing efforts.
- Vendor analysis applications support supply chain management.
- Staff productivity applications focus on tracking and monitoring operational performance.
- Behavior analysis applications focus on analyzing and modeling customer activity and behavior to support fraud detection, customer requirements, product design and delivery, and so on.

Data Requirements Analysis

Though traditional requirements analysis centers on functional needs, data requirements analysis complements the functional requirements process and focuses on the information needs, providing a standard set of procedures for identifying, analyzing, and validating data requirements and quality for data-consuming applications. Data requirements analysis is a significant part of an enterprise data management program that is intended to help in:

- Articulating a clear understanding of data needs of all consuming business processes,
- Identifying relevant data quality dimensions associated with those data needs,
- Assessing the quality and suitability of candidate data sources,
- Aligning and standardizing the exchange of data across systems,
- Implementing production procedures for monitoring the conformance to expectations and correcting data as early as possible in the production flow, and Continually reviewing to identify improvement opportunities in relation to downstream data needs.

During this process, the data quality analyst needs to focus on identifying and capturing more than just a list of business questions that need to be answered. Analysis of system goals and objectives, along with the results of stakeholder interviews, should enable the analyst to also capture important business information characteristics that will help drive subsequent analysis and design activities: data and information requirements must be relevant, must add value, and must be subject to availability.

Relevance

Relevance is understood in terms of the degree to which the requirements address one or more business process expectations. For example, data requirements are relevant in support of business processes when they address a need for conducting normal business transactions and also when they refer to reported performance indicators necessary to manage business operations and performance. Alternatively, data requirements are relevant if they answer business questions – data and information that provide managers what they need to make operational, tactical, and strategic decisions. In addition, relevance may be reflected in relation to real-time windows for decision making, leading to real-time requirements for data provisioning.

Added Value

Data requirements reflect added value when they can trace directly to improvements associated with our business drivers. For example, enabling better visibility of transaction processing and workflow processes helps in monitoring performance measures. In turn, ensuring the quality of data that captures transaction volume and duration can be used to evaluate processes and identify opportunities for operational efficiencies, whereas data details that feed analysis and reporting used to identify trends, patterns, and behavior can improve decision making.

Availability

Even with well-defined expectations for data requirements, their utility is limited if the required data is not captured in any available source systems, or if those source systems are not updated and available in time to meet business information and decision-making requirements. Also, in order to meet the avail- ability expectations, one must be assured that the data can be structured to support the business information needs.

Data Requirements Analysis Process

The data requirements analysis process employs a top-down approach that emphasizes business-driven needs, so the analysis is conducted to ensure the identified requirements are relevant and feasible. The process incorporates data discovery and assessment in the context of explicitly qualified business data consumer needs.

The data requirements analysis process consists of these phases:

1. Identifying the business contexts.
2. Conducting stakeholder interviews.
3. Synthesizing expectations and requirements.
4. Developing source-to-target mappings.

Once these steps are completed, the resulting artifacts are reviewed to define data quality rules in relation to the dimensions of data quality.

Identifying the Business Contexts

The business contexts associated with data consumption and reuse provide the scope for the determination of data requirements. Conferring with enterprise architects to under- stand where system boundaries intersect with lines of business will provide a good starting point for determining how (and under what circumstances) data sets are used.

The steps in this phase of the process:

1. Identify relevant stakeholders: Stakeholders may be identified through a review of existing system documentation or may be identified by the data quality team through discussions with business analysts, enterprise analysts, and enterprise architects. The pool of relevant stakeholders may include business program sponsors, business application owners, business process managers, senior management, information consumers, system owners, as well as frontline staff members who are the beneficiaries of shared or reused data.

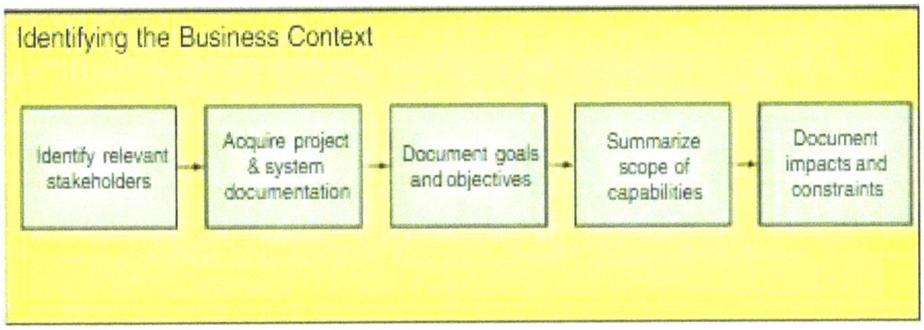

Identifying the business contexts.

2. Acquire documentation: The data quality analyst must become familiar with overall goals and objectives of the target information platforms to provide context for identifying and assessing specific information and data requirements. To do this, it is necessary to review existing artifacts that provide details about the consuming systems, requiring a review of project charters, project scoping documents, requirements, design, and testing documentation. At this stage, the analysts should accumulate any available documentation artifacts that can help in determining collective data use.

3. Document goals and objectives: Determining existing performance measures and success criteria provides a baseline representation of high-level system requirements for summarization and categorization. Conceptual data models may exist that can provide further clarification and guidance regarding the functional and operational expectations of the collection of target systems.

4. Summarize scope of capabilities: Create graphic representations that convey the high-level functions and capabilities of the targeted systems, as well as providing detail of functional requirements and target user profiles. When combined with other context knowledge, one may create a business context diagram or document that summarizes and illustrates the key data flows, functions, and capabilities of the downstream information consumers.

5. Document impacts and constraints: Constraints are conditions that affect or prevent the implementation of system functionality, whereas impacts are potential changes to characteristics of the environment to accommodate the implementation of system functionality. Identifying and understanding all relevant impacts and constraints to the target systems are critical, because the impacts and constraints often define, limit, and frame the data controls and rules that will be managed as part of the data quality environment. Not only that, source-to-target mappings may be impacted by constraints or dependencies associated with the selection of candidate data sources.

The resulting artifacts describe the high-level functions of downstream systems, and how organizational data is expected to meet those systems' needs. Any identified impacts or constraints of the targeted systems, such as legacy system dependencies, global reference tables, existing standards and definitions, and data retention policies, will be documented. In addition, this phase will provide a preliminary view of global reference data requirements that may impact source data element selection and transformation rules. Time stamps and organization standards for time, geography, availability and capacity of potential data sources, frequency and approaches for data extractions, and transformations are additional data points for identifying potential impacts and requirements.

Synthesize Requirements

This next phase synthesizes the results of the documentation scan and the interviews to collect metadata and data expectations as part of the business process flows. The analysts will review the downstream applications' use of business information (as well as questions to be answered) to identify named data concepts and types of aggregates, and associated data element characteristics.

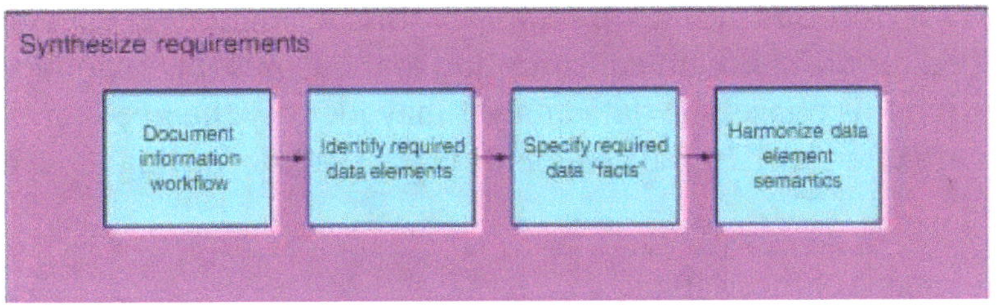

Synthesizing the Results.

Figure shows the sequence of these steps:

1. Document information workflow: Create an information flow model that depicts the sequence, hierarchy, and timing of process activities. The goal is to use this workflow to identify locations within the business processes where data quality controls can be introduced for continuous monitoring and measurement.
2. Identify required data elements: Reviewing the business questions will help segregate the required (or commonly used) data concepts (party, product, agreement, etc.) from the characterizations or aggregation categories (e.g., grouped by geographic region). This drives the determination of required reference data and potential master data items.
3. Specify required facts: These facts represent specific pieces of business information that are tracked, managed, used, shared, or forwarded to a reporting and analytics facility in which they are counted or measured (such as quantity or volume). In addition, the data quality analyst must document any qualifying characteristics of the data that represent conditions or dimensions that are used to filter or organize your facts (such as time or location). The metadata for these data concepts and facts will be captured within a metadata repository for further analysis and resolution.
4. Harmonize data element semantics: A metadata glossary captures all the business terms associated with the business workflows, and classifies the hierarchical composition of any aggregated or analyzed data concepts. Most glossaries may contain a core set of terms across similar projects along with additional project specific terms. When possible, use existing metadata repositories to capture the approved organization definition.

The use of common terms becomes a challenge in data requirements analysis, particularly when common use precludes the existence of agreed-to definitions. These issues become acute when aggregations are applied to counts of objects that may share the same name but don't really share the same meaning. This situation will lead to inconsistencies in reporting, analyses, and operational activities, which in turn will lead to loss of trust in data.

Source-to-target Mapping

The goal of source-to-target mapping is to clearly specify the source data elements that are used in downstream applications. In most situations, the consuming applications may use similar data elements from multiple data sources; the data quality analyst must determine if any consolidation and/or aggregation requirements (i.e., transformations) are required, and determine the level of atomic data needed for drill-down, if necessary. Any transformations specify how upstream data elements are modified for downstream consumption and business rules applied as part of the information flow. During this phase, the data analyst may identify the need for reference data sets. Reference data sets are often used by data elements that have low cardinality and rely on standardized values.

Figure shows the sequence of these steps:

1. Propose target models: Evaluate the catalog of identified data elements and look for those that are frequently created, referenced, or modified. By considering both the conceptual and the logical structures of these data elements and their enclosing data sets, the analyst can identify potential differences and anomalies inherent in the metadata, and then resolve any critical anomalies across data element sizes, types, or formats. These will form the core of a data sharing model, which represents the data elements to be taken from the sources, potentially transformed, validated, and then provided to the consuming applications.

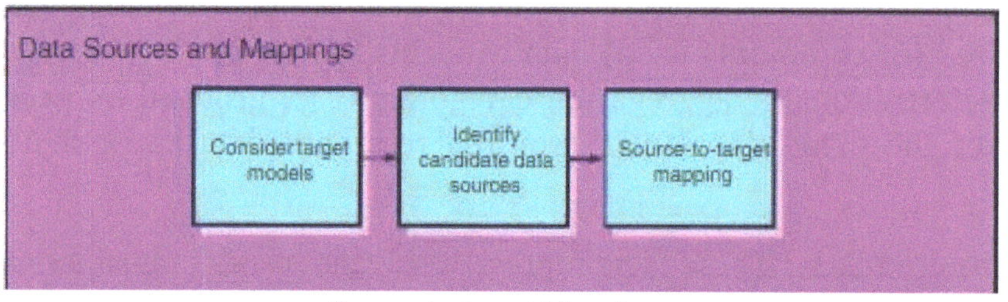

Source-to-target Mapping.

2. Identify candidate data sources: Consult the data management teams to review the candidate data sources containing the identified data elements, and review the collection of data facts needed by the consuming applications. For each fact, determine whether it corresponds to a defined data concept or data element, exists in any data sets in the organization, or is a computed value (and if so, what are the data elements that are used to compute that value), and then document each potential data source.

3. Develop source-to-target mappings: Because this analysis should provide enough input to specify which candidate data sources can be extracted, the next step is to consider how that data is to be transformed into a common representation that is then normalized in preparation for consolidation. The consolidation processes collect the sets of objects and prepare them for populating the consuming applications. During this step, the analysts enumerate which source data elements contribute to target data elements, specify the transformations to be applied, and note where it relies on standardizations and normalizations revealed during earlier stages of the process.

Data Modeling and Analytics

Some data skills are crucial for business analysts while others are better suited to other job functions -such as data analyst, financial analyst, reporting analyst, marketing analyst, and product management.

We take a look at the set of skills required for both data analysis and data modeling, investigate how data modeling can require some data analysis, and detail how skilled business analysts complete this level of analysis without technical data analysis skills.

Data Analysis

Data analysis is a technique to gain insight into an organisation's data. A data analyst might have the following responsibilities:

- To create and analyse important reports (possibly using a third-party reporting, data warehousing, or business intelligence system) to help the business make better decisions.
- To merge data from multiple data sources together, as part of data mining, so it can be analysed and reported on.
- To run queries on existing data sources to evaluate analytics and analyse trends.

Data analysts will have hands-on access to the organisation's data repositories and use their technical skills to query and manipulate the data. They may also be skilled in statistical analysis, having a high-level of mathemetical experience.

Alternative job titles for this type of role include; Report Analyst, Data Warehousing Analyst, Business Intelligence Analyst, or even Product/Marketing Analyst. The common thread among this diverse set of job titles is that each role is responsible for analysing a specific type of data or using a specific type of tool to analyse data.

Data Modelling

Data modeling is a set of tools and techniques used to understand and analyse how an organisation should collect, update, and store data. It is a critical skill for the business analyst who is involved with discovering, analysing, and specifying changes to how software systems create and maintain information.

Data Modeller Functions

- They create an entity relationship diagram to visualise relationships between key business concepts.

- They create a conceptual-level data dictionary to communicate data requirements that are important to business stakeholders.
- They create a data map to resolve potential data issues for a data migration or integration project.

A data modeller would not necessarily query or manipulate data or become involved in designing or implementing databases or data repositories.

Data Modeling Sometimes Needs Data Analysis

Business analyst often need to analyse data as part of making data modeling decisions, and this means that data modeling can include some amount of data analysis. A lot can be accomplished with very basic technical skills, such as the ability to run simple database queries. This is why you may see a technical skill like SQL in a business analyst job description.

Many business analyst succeed without knowing these more technical skills, instead, they rely on their ability to collaborate with technical professionals and other knowledgeable stakeholders to ensure the data is understood well enough to make the right modelling decisions. The non-technical business analyst can also evaluate sample data, interview stakeholders to discover possible data-related issues, review current state database models, and analyse exception reports. While data analysis skills are valuable for the business analyst, they are not essential. However, data modelling falls squarely within the business analyst's domain.

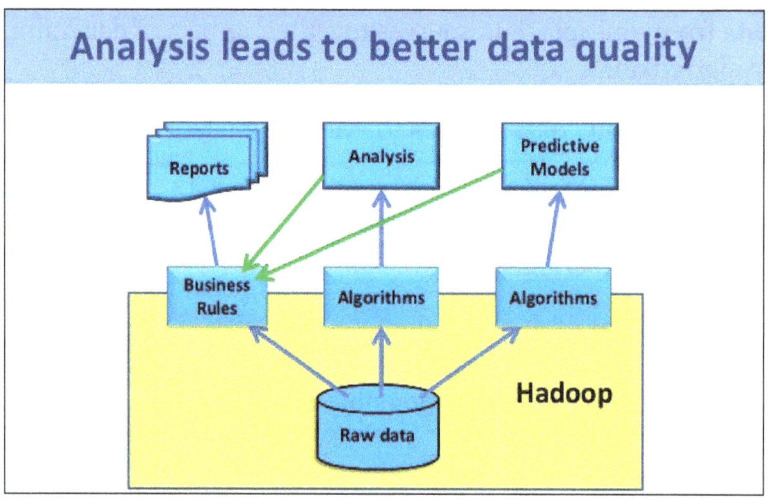

Data Modeling makes Analysis Easier

The fundamental objective of data modeling is to only expose data that holds value for the end user. Clearly delineating what questions a table should answer is essential, and deciding on how different types of data will be modeled creates optimal conditions for data analysis. So, while data modeling itself is highly technical, it nonetheless relies on input from non-technical personnel in order to properly define business objectives.

A good business example to consider is marketing attribution, where comparing and contrasting data from both first touch and last touch attribution perspectives may be very significant. Digging deeper, like building a marketing strategy based exclusively off anything "last touch" in the sales funnel — the final tweet, text alert, email promo, etc., that led to a conversion — requires amassing the raw data and filtering in just the last touch of the journey for analysis. This is hard to do with just a single query, and why it's important to execute before the time of analysis.

With the objectives outlined, database tables can be assembled with each field itself clearly defined. These definitions become part of a data dictionary, an integral part of any successful data model.

Role of the Data Dictionary

Data definition is essential. An effective data dictionary is an inventory that describes the data objects and items in a data model, and will include at least two key ingredients: properly labelled tables and properly defined terms. At its core, these define the rows (elements) and columns (attributes). Clarity is key here, and it's important to remember that tables without definitions are counterintuitive (at best). Whether it's about marketing, web traffic, an email campaign, etc., the goal is exposing clean, raw data. It's imperative to any successful data model that the definitions for the terms used are clear, concise, and uniform, and that any ambiguity when labelling and defining terms has been removed.

The data dictionary should be maintained by all the data's stakeholders but especially those responsible for collection and storage.

Where is the Data Going?

Increased data volumes can produce barriers to accessibility, or provide a wealth of insight. All kinds of business questions arise, requiring data to be structured accordingly. The comprehension level of the end user is a factor, but the guiding principle is modeling data in a way that makes it very easy to query, so that any end user can utilize the data once received. In other words, it's meant to be useful. Flooding the user with extraneous and irrelevant data is as frustrating as it is time-wasting. Because there are always fields for engineers (like an update timestamps or batch IDs) that hold zero benefit for the end user, attention must be paid to the key take away: what fields are exposed to the end users, and how much will those fields denote true business value?

Granularity

All data have different kinds of structure and granularity. Tables are structured to suit end user needs, and granularity defines the level of detail the data provides. Take transactional data as an example. Each row of data could represent an item purchased, and include where it was purchased, how it was purchased, or when it was purchased, even down to the second. (As an example, the latter might be a significant metric for anyone in retail monitoring sales on Black Friday or the day after Christmas).

Another common business reference is the construction of a churn model, and the various parameters inherent in the end user's needs. These needs are loosely defined as a time component, with contractual and non-contractual factors playing a role as well. Customer onboarding and retention behavior can vary substantially, and what the end user needs often exists at a more granular customer level: one day after a promo, one month after a free trial, measuring client satisfaction a year out, and so on.

Since the requirements are clear, a solution is easily modeled: the end user defines the stages or fields they care about, and the data modeler creates the model with tables exposing all relevant data. By exposing churn rate data at specific intervals, interpreting and then "bucketing" the interpreted data — adding an extra column to the table to provide better insight — a data model has been constructed that produces significant business value.

This is part of the best practices approach to data modeling: two deciding (human) factors — someone that understands the right questions to ask, and someone to build the data tables that provide answers and insights.

Data Modeling in Practice

Utilizing a Domain Knowledge Expert

Defining what a table should look like means modeling data in a way that makes it very easy to query — in essence, so any end user or BI tool can use it. The data engineers do the heavy lifting once they understand the business questions to be answered. And just as someone with business domain knowledge is required for providing the right questions to ask, a data domain expert is necessary for interpreting the technical nuances in the data, what it looks like in its raw form, understanding the instrumentation of the data, and translating it into a model that's easy to comprehend. Their knowledge is key to what you can and can't model, and how the tools utilized will be implemented most effectively.

What event the data represents will most likely vary by perspective: for example, a marketing person may see the event as part of a funnel stage — one step has been completed, while another has not — whereas from an engineering standpoint the event might be defined as when a specific POST request was sent. This speaks to another best practice of data modeling: Trust. Both types of expertise require the other to complete the picture and create a model that works for everyone.

As business priorities evolve, the data model must likewise adapt and modify. The entities — and relationships between entities — that make up the schema for queries will change with time and the demands of the enterprise; a data domain expert will ensure that the data model stays up to date and agile enough to continue exposing raw data that is relevant and purposeful.

Runtime vs. Preprocessing: It's about Optimizing Performance

Mapping arcane, technical details within a raw data source and directing it to a user-friendly, easy-to-read outcome can be done with database views and processed at query time. However, if a new table is built on top of that within a data warehouse, modeling the data appropriately as a specific schedule might dictate, that data will be preprocessed.

When weighing the tradeoffs between using runtime for modeling over preprocessed, or pre-calculated, choosing runtime over non-runtime is preferred whenever possible. The more that can be done with the model in runtime, the better (in general), as this translates to less maintenance, while multiple steps with persistent data equate to more management.

Preprocessing is preferred when it's both calculation-intensive and necessary, as in the churn model referenced previously: looping it through logic is inefficient in runtime, since it would require measuring a ton of data — multiple queries — thereby taking too long to deliver timely insights. Documenting past or forecasting future customer churn rates require different models, each using preprocessed output tables to give desired numbers.

Drawing the line between runtime and preprocessing is the job of an experienced data engineer; as a general rule, it's good to start "raw" and trend toward more complex models as enterprise needs become more nuanced. Single query works for some tasks; numerous queries may require preprocessing.

Role of the Analyst

New models are not created overnight. Having to wait hours (or longer) for data processing jobs to arrive, or only receiving once-a-day batched data, will continue to diminish in frequency. End users become more comfortable deploying BI tools for everyday tasks, and the tools themselves continue to become more powerful, reducing the complexity of queries to do analyses, and enabling "self-service" analytics. All arc positive developments, but without the interaction and oversight of a data analyst the potential exists for end users to just as easily draw the wrong conclusions from the accelerated access to data.

An analyst assesses data quality and performs data structure checks, isolating and removing bad values. They may create new tables that track volume of data or row counts of data from a specific raw table. The analyst can also automate a data quality model on top of a model that sets a query for customization, identifying poor quality and outliers.

For example, a query structured to evaluate sales data for the current Monday when compared to the previous six months of Mondays would benefit with build-in exceptions into the quality model — think Cyber Monday or Labor Day Weekend — that furnish more nuanced, useable analytics.

Defining the role of the analyst ties into the essence of defining the data model, helping shape what the tables will look like and what queries those tables will serve. And that analyst is part of a team serving a data warehouse, all operating with the goal of delivering relevant, real-time, 360-degree data for all end users. When a change to the logic of a model occurs, they'll be the ones testing it to make sure it's robust.

The Data Warehouse

A data warehousing is defined as a technique for collecting and managing data from varied sources to provide meaningful business insights. It is a blend of technologies and components which aids the strategic use of data.

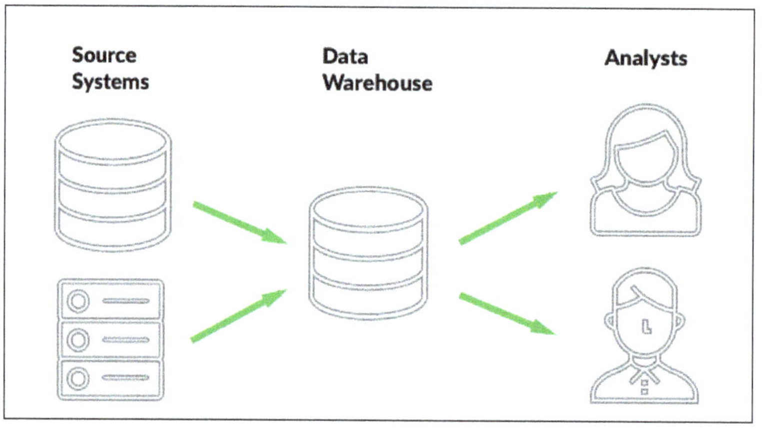

It is electronic storage of a large amount of information by a business which is designed for query and analysis instead of transaction processing. It is a process of transforming data into information and making it available to users in a timely manner to make a difference.

The decision support database (Data Warehouse) is maintained separately from the organization's operational database. However, the data warehouse is not a product but an environment. It is an architectural construct of an information system which provides users with current and historical decision support information which is difficult to access or present in the traditional operational data store. The data warehouse is the core of the BI system which is built for data analysis and reporting.

You many know that a 3NF-designed database for an inventory system many have tables related to each other. For example, a report on current inventory information can include more than 12 joined conditions. This can quickly slow down the response time of the query and report. A data warehouse provides a new design which can help to reduce the response time and helps to enhance the performance of queries for reports and analytics.

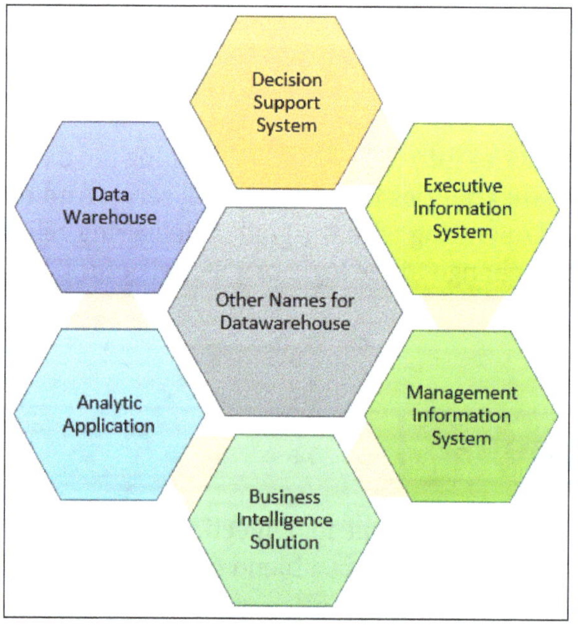

Data warehouse system is also known by the following name:

- Decision Support System (DSS);
- Executive Information System;
- Management Information System;
- Business Intelligence Solution;
- Analytic Application;
- Data Warehouse.

How Datawarehouse Works?

A Data Warehouse works as a central repository where information arrives from one or more data sources. Data flows into a data warehouse from the transactional system and other relational databases.

Data may be:

1. Structured;
2. Semi-structured;
3. Unstructured data.

The data is processed, transformed, and ingested so that users can access the processed data in the Data Warehouse through Business Intelligence tools, SQL clients, and spreadsheets. A data warehouse merges information coming from different sources into one comprehensive database.

By merging all of this information in one place, an organization can analyze its customers more holistically. This helps to ensure that it has considered all the information available. Data warehousing makes data mining possible. Data mining is looking for patterns in the data that may lead to higher sales and profits.

Types of Data Warehouse

1. Enterprise Data Warehouse: Enterprise Data Warehouse is a centralized warehouse. It provides decision support service across the enterprise. It offers a unified approach for organizing and representing data. It also provides the ability to classify data according to the subject and give access according to those divisions.
2. Operational Data Store: Operational Data Store, which is also called ODS, are nothing but data store required when neither Data warehouse nor OLTP systems support organizations reporting needs. In ODS, Data warehouse is refreshed in real time. Hence, it is widely preferred for routine activities like storing records of the Employees.
3. Data Mart: A data mart is a subset of the data warehouse. It specially designed for a particular line of business, such as sales, finance, sales or finance. In an independent data mart, data can collect directly from sources.

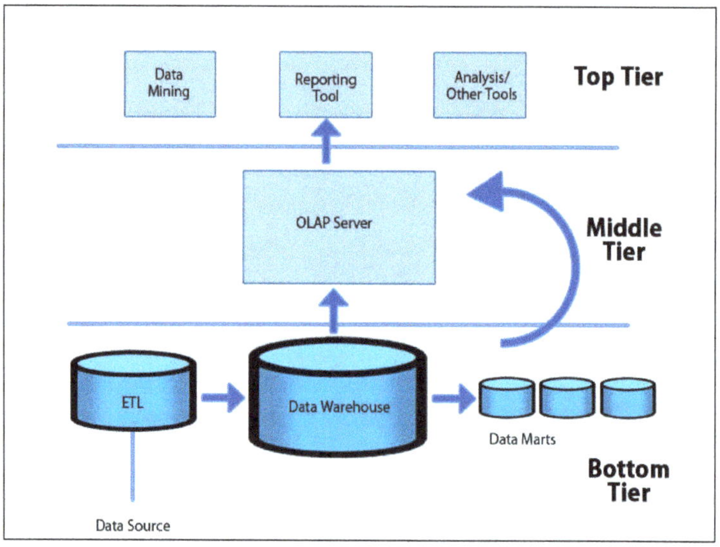

Analytical Platforms

An analytics platform is a unified and proper solution designed to address the demands of users, especially large data-driven companies, on the inadequacy of relational database management systems (RDBMS) in providing contextual analyzed data out of all the stored information. It joins different tools for creating analytics systems together with an engine to execute, a DBMS to store and manage the data, data mining processes, and techniques and mechanisms for obtaining and preparing data that is not stored. This solution can be conveyed as a software-only application or as a cloud-based software as a service (SaaS) provided to organizations in need of contextual information that all their data points to, in other words, analytical information based on current data records.

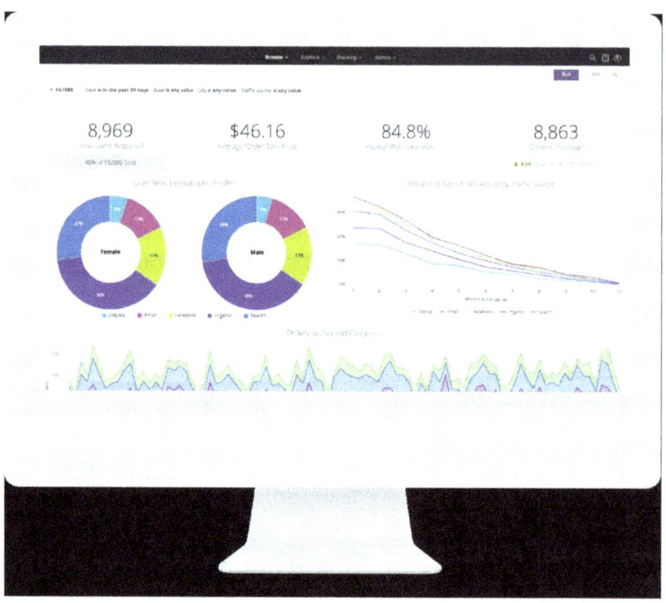

Analytics Platform

The analytics database (ADBMS), the DBMS component of the analytics platform, is designed especially for business administration and analytics applications, usually those concerned with a data warehouse or data mart. This system is read-only, and it stores historical business data, such as sales performance or inventory levels. It features scalability, performance, cost effectiveness and ease of operation advantages over the conventional RDBMS. Users will be able to view different analyzed information like total sales in a given period and be able to compare that to any other desired period, as well as get visual cues like graphs to allow executives to easily view trends and react accordingly to market shift.

Analytics platforms make use of container constructs in memory to secure and synchronize many processes that run in parallel with even more processors. Aside from that, these platforms use inexpensive hardware that are already available. This is because it is a software solution that can be deployed to any organization as a paid service.

As the amount of data, analytic complexity and number of end users increases, analytics platforms offer a variety of options that can help reduce costs and further help in achieving a proper informed decision.

Operational Data Stores

An operational data store (ODS) is a type of database that collects data from multiple sources for processing, after which it sends the data to operational systems and data warehouses.

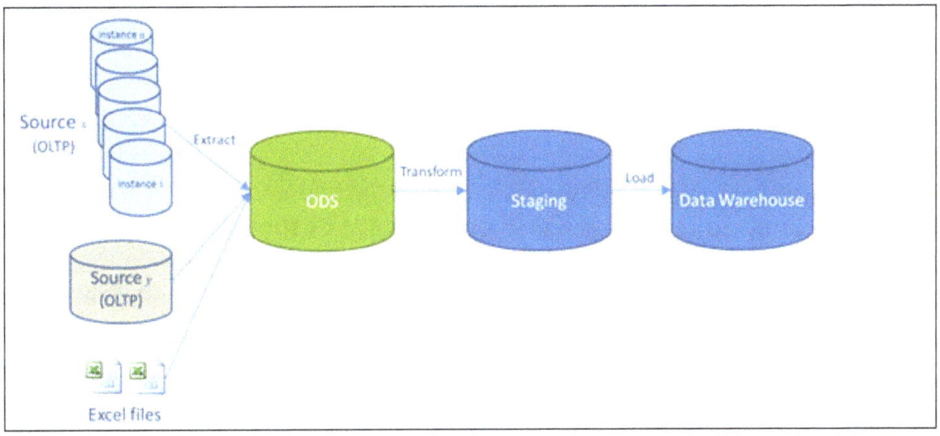

It provides a central interface or platform for all operational data used by enterprise systems and applications.

An ODS is used to store short term data or data currently in use by operational systems or applications, prior to storage in a data warehouse or data repository. Thus, it serves as an intermediate database. An ODS helps clean and organize data and ensure that it meets business and regulatory requirements. It only supports low level data and allows for the application of limited queries.

Metadata

Metadata is data about data. In other words, it's information that's used to describe the data that's contained in something like a web page, document, or file. Another way to think of metadata is as a short explanation or summary of what the data is. A simple example of metadata for a document might include a collection of information like the author, file size, date the document was created, and keywords to describe the document. Metadata for a music file might include the artist's name, the album, and the year it was released.

For computer files, metadata can be stored within the file itself or elsewhere. Metadata represents behind-the-scenes information that's used everywhere, by every industry, in multiple ways. It's ubiquitous in information systems, social media, websites, software, music services, and online retailing. Metadata can be created manually to pick and choose what's included, but it can also be generated automatically based on the data.

Functions and Types of Metadata

Metadata Functions

- Resource discovery:
    - Allowing resources to be found by relevant criteria;
    - Identifying resources;
    - Bringing similar resources together;
    - Distinguishing dissimilar resources;
    - Giving location information.
- Organizing e-resources:
    - Organizing links to resources based on audience or topic.
    - Building these pages dynamically from metadata stored in databases.
- Facilitating interoperability:
    - Using defined metadata schemes, shared transfer protocols, and crosswalks between schemes, resources across the network can be searched more seamlessly.
        - Cross-system search, e.g., using Z39.50 protocol;
        - Metadata harvesting, e.g., OAI protocol.
- Digital identification:
    - Elements for standard numbers, e.g., ISBN.

  - The location of a digital object may also be given using:
    - A file name,
    - A URL,
    - Some persistent identifiers, e.g., PURL (Persistent URL); DOI (Digital Object Identifier).
  - Combined metadata to act as a set of identifying data, differentiating one object from another for validation purposes.
- Archiving and preservation:
  - Challenges:
    - Digital information is fragile and can be corrupted or altered;
    - It may become unusable as storage technologies change.
  - Metadata is key to ensuring that resources will survive and continue to be accessible into the future. Archiving and preservation require special elements:
    - To track the lineage of a digital object,
    - To detail its physical characteristics, and
    - To document its behavior in order to emulate it in future technologies.

Types of Metadata

Type	Definition	Examples
Administrative	Metadata used in managing and administering collections and information resources	• Acquisition information • Rights and reproduction tracking • Documentation of legal access requirements • Location information • Selection criteria for digitization.
Descriptive	Metadata used to identify and describe collections and related information resources	• Cataloging records • Finding aids • Differentiations between versions • Specialized indexes • Curatorial information • Hyperlinked relationships between resources • Annotations by creators and users.

Preservation	Metadata related to the preservation management of collections and information resources	• Documentation of physical condition of resources • Documentation of actions taken to preserve physical and digital versions of resources, e.g., data refreshing and migration • Documentation of any changes occurring during digitization or preservation
Technical	Metadata related to how a system functions or metadata behaves	• Hardware and software documentation • Technical digitization information, e.g., • formats, compression ratios, scaling routines • Tracking of system response times • Authentication and security data, e.g., en cryption keys, passwords.
Use	Metadata related to the level and type of use of collections and information resources	• Circulation records • Physical and digital exhibition records • Use and user tracking • Content reuse and multiversioning information • Search logs • Rights metadata.

Semantic Metadata Processes for Business Analytics

When building a business analytics program, there is no doubt that one requires the standard types of metadata for the physical design and implementation of a data warehouse and corresponding business intelligence delivery methods and tools. For example, it would be impossible to engineer the data integration and transformations needed to migrate data out of the source systems and into an operational data store or a data warehouse without knowledge of the structures of the sources and the target models. Similarly, without understanding the reference metadata (particularly the data types and units of measure), the delivered reports might be difficult to understand, if not altogether undecipherable.

But even presuming the soundness of the management of the technical, structural, and operational metadata, the absence of conceptual data available for shared information will often lead to reinterpretation of the data sets' meanings. The availability of the business metadata, particularly semantic metadata, is somewhat of a panacea, and that means there must be some well-defined processes in place for soliciting, capturing, and managing that semantic information. Some key processes will focus on a particular set of areas of concentration, as we explore here.

Management of Non-Persistent Data Elements

We often will assume that the business terms, data element concepts, and entity concepts that are managed within a metadata framework are associated with persistent data sets, either operational or transactional systems or with data sitting in a data mart or warehouse. It turns out that there are numerous data elements that are used but not stored in a persistent database.

The simplest examples are those associated with the presentation of generated reports and other graphical representations such as column headers or labels on charts. Another example is interim calculations or aggregations that are used in preparing values for presentation. These data elements all have metadata characteristics – size, data type, associated data value domains, mappings to business terms – and there is value in managing that metadata along with metadata for persistent items.

Business Terms

The most opportune place to start is establishing a business term glossary, which is a catalog of the terms and phrases used across the different business processes within (as well as relevant external interfaces to) the enterprise. It would not be a surprise to learn that in most organizations the same or similar words and phrases are used (both in documentation and in conversation) based on corporate lore or personal experience, but many of these terms are never officially defined or documented. When the same terms are used as column headings or data element names in different source systems, there is a tendency to presume that they mean the same things, yet just as often as not there are slight (or sometimes significant) variations in the context and consequently in the definition of the term.

Establishing a business term glossary is a way to identify where the same terms are used with different meanings and facilitating processes for harmonizing the definitions or differentiating them. The metadata process involves reviewing documentation, business applications (their guidelines as well as the program code), and interviewing staff members to identify business terms that are either used by more than one party, or are presumed to have a meaning that is undocumented. Once the terms have been logged, the analysts can review the definitions and determine whether they can be resolved or whether they actually represent more than one concept, each of which requires qualification.

Managing Synonyms

The more unstructured and externally streamed data consumed by the analytical platforms, the greater the potential for synonyms, which are sets of different words or terms that share the same meaning. The synonym challenge is the opposite problem of the one posed by variation in definitions for the same term. For example, the words "car," "auto," and "automobile" in most situations will share the same meaning, and therefore can be considered synonyms.

This process becomes more challenging when the collections of terms are synonyms in one usage scenario but not in another. To continue the example, in some cases the words "truck," "SUV," and "minivan" might be considered synonyms for automobile, but in other cases, each of those terms has its own distinct meaning.

Developing the Business Concept Registry

We can take the idea of a business term glossary one step further by combining it with the management of synonyms to create a business concept registry that captures the ways that the different business terms are integrated into business concepts. For example, we can define the business term "customer," but augment that description with the enumeration of the business terms and concepts that are used to characterize a representation of a customer.

This can be quite complex, especially in siloed organizations with many implementations. Yet the outcome of the process is the identification of the key concepts that are ultimately relevant to both running the business (absorbed as a result of assessing the existing uses) and to improving the business, as the common concepts with agreed-to definitions can form the basis of a canonical data model supporting business reporting and analytics.

Mappings from Concept to use

If one goal of a business intelligence program is to accumulate data from the different areas of the business for reporting and analysis, the designers' and developers' understanding of the distribution of content in the source systems must be comprehensive enough to pinpoint the lineage of information as it flowed into the data warehouse and then out through the reports or analytical presentations. That suggests going beyond the structural inventory of data elements and encompassing the business term glossary, mapping those terms to their uses in the different systems across the organizations.

For example, once you can specify a business term "customer" and establish a common meaning, it would be necessary to identify which business processes, applications, tables, and data elements art related to the business concept "customer." Your metadata inventory can be adapted for this purpose by instituting a process for mapping the common concepts to their systemic instantiations.

Semantic Hierarchy Management

The next level of business metadata complexity centers on the organization of business concepts within the contexts of their use. We can return to the previously mentioned automobile example from: "car" and "auto" may be defined as equivalent terms, but the particular class of car ("SUV," "minivan," or "truck") might be categorized as subsidiary to "car" in a conceptual hierarchy.

The hierarchical relationship implies inheritance – the child in the hierarchy shares the characteristics of the parent in the hierarchy. That basically means that any SUV is also a car (although not the other way around), and like a car it will have brakes and a rear-view mirror. On the other hand, the descendants in the hierarchy may have characteristics that are neither shared with the parent nor with other siblings. The hierarchy is expandable (you could have a "4WD SUV" and a "2WD SUV" subsidiary to an "SUV"). It is also not limited to a single-parent relationship – you could have a hybrid SUV that inherits from both hybrid cars and SUVs.

The hierarchies lay out the aggregation points along the dimensions. Continuing the example, an auto manufacturer might count the total number of cars sold, but also might want that broken down by the different subsidiary categories in the hierarchy.

Considerations: Entity Concepts and Master Dimensions

All of these metadata ideas converge when lining up the information in the analytical environment with that of the other data sources across the organization, especially when it comes to key master concepts that are relevant for transactional, operational, and analytical applications. The master entity concepts (such as "product") are associated with master dimensions (such as the automobile hierarchy), but the value is the semantic alignment that allows the business analyst reading the report to be confident that the count of sold SUVs is consistent with the operational reporting coming out of the sales system. These aspects of semantic metadata enable that level of confidence.

Data Profiling Activities

You use the data profiling process to evaluate the quality of business data. The data profiling process consists of multiple analyses that investigate the structure and content of business data and make inferences about business data. After an analysis completes, you can review the results and accept or reject the inferences. The data profiling process consists of multiple analyses that work together to evaluate business data.

Column Analysis

Column analysis is a prerequisite to all other analyses except for cross-domain analysis. During a column analysis job, the column or field data is evaluated in a table or file and a frequency distribution is created. A frequency distribution summarizes the results for each column such as statistics and inferences about the characteristics of business data. You review the frequency distribution to find anomalies in business data. When you want to remove the anomalies in business data, you can use a data cleansing tool such as IBM® Info Sphere® Quality Stage® to remove the values.

A frequency distribution is also used as the input for subsequent analyses such as primary key analysis and baseline analysis.

The column analysis process incorporates four analyses:

- Domain analysis: Identifies invalid and incomplete data values. Invalid and incomplete values impact the quality of business data by making the data difficult to access and use. You can use the results from domain analysis when you want to use a data cleansing tool to remove the anomalies.
- Data classification analysis: Infers a data class for each column in business data. Data classes categorize data. If business data is classified incorrectly, it is difficult to compare the data with other domains of data. You compare domains of data when you want to find data that contains similar values.
- Format analysis: Creates a format expression for the values in business data. A format expression is a pattern that contains a character symbol for each distinct character in a column. For example, each alphabetic character might have a character symbol of A and numeric characters might have a character symbol of 9. Accurate formats ensure that business data is consistent with defined standards.

- Data properties analysis: Data properties analysis compares the accuracy of defined properties about business data before analysis to the system-inferred properties that are made during analysis. Data properties define the characteristics of data such as field length or data type. Consistent and well-defined properties help to ensure that data is used efficiently.

Key and Cross-domain Analysis

During a key and cross-domain analysis job, business data is assessed for relationships between tables. The values in business data are evaluated for foreign key candidates, and defined foreign keys. A column might be inferred as a candidate for a foreign key when the values in the column match the values of an associated primary or natural key. If a foreign key is incorrect, the relationship that it has with a primary or natural key in another table is lost.

After a key and cross-domain analysis job completes, you can run a referential integrity analysis job on business data. Referential integrity analysis is an analysis that you use to fully identify violations between foreign key and primary or natural key relationships. During a referential integrity analysis job, foreign key candidates are investigated at a concise level to ensure that they match the values of an associated primary key or natural key.

A key and cross-domain analysis job will also help you to determine whether multiple columns share a common domain. A common domain exists when multiple columns contain overlapping data. Columns that share a common domain might signal the relationship between a foreign key and a primary key, which you can investigate further during a foreign key analysis job. However, most common domains represent redundancies between columns. If there are redundancies in business data, you might want to use a data cleansing tool to remove them because redundant data can take up memory and slow down the processes that are associated with them.

Baseline Analysis

You run a baseline analysis job to compare a prior version of analysis results with the current analysis results for the same data source. If differences between both versions are found, you can assess the significance of the change, such as whether the quality has improved.

The following figure shows how data profiling analyses work together:

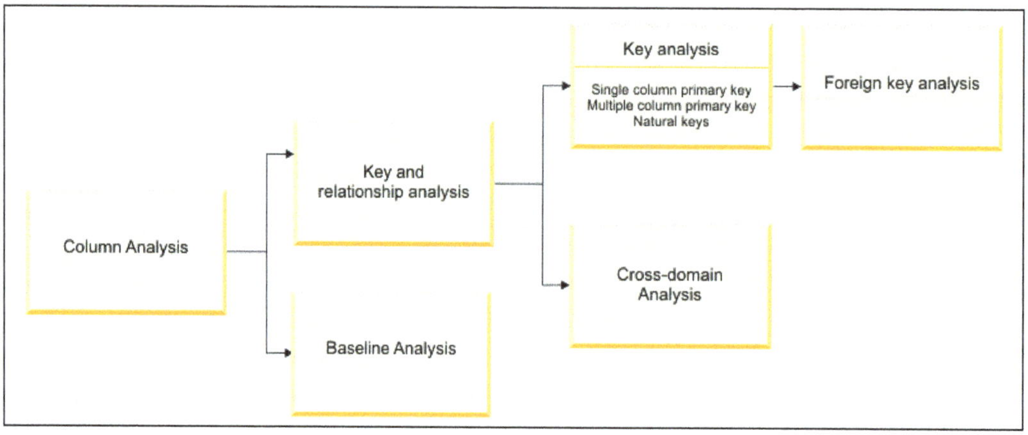

Figure: Data profiling analyses

Types of Data Profiling

There are three main types of data profiling:

1. Structure discovery: Validating that data is consistent and formatted correctly, and performing mathematical checks on the data (e.g. sum, minimum or maximum). Structure discovery helps understand how well data is structured—for example, what percentage of phone numbers do not have the correct number of digits.

2. Content discovery: Looking into individual data records to discover errors. Content discovery identifies which specific rows in a table contain problems, and which systemic issues occur in the data (for example, phone numbers with no area code).

3. Relationship discovery: Discovering how parts of the data are interrelated. For example, key relationships between database tables, references between cells or tables in a spread sheet. Understanding relationships is crucial to reusing data; related data sources should be united into one or imported in a way that preserves important relationships.

Data Profiling Steps

Ralph Kimball, a father of data warehouse architecture, suggests a four-step process for data profiling:

1. Use data profiling at project start to discover if data is suitable for analysis—and make a "go/no go" decision on the project.

2. Identify and correct data quality issues in source data, even before starting to move it into target database.

3. Identify data quality issues that can be corrected by Extract-Transform-Load (ETL), while data is moved from source to target. Data profiling can uncover if additional manual processing is needed.

4. Identify unanticipated business rules, hierarchical structures and foreign key / private key relationships use them to fine-tune the ETL process.

Data Profiling and Data Quality Analysis Best Practices

Basic data profiling techniques:

1. Distinct count and percent—identifies natural keys, distinct values in each column that can help process inserts and updates. Handy for tables without headers.

2. Percent of zero/blank/null values—identifies missing or unknown data. Helps ETL architects setup appropriate default values.

3. Minimum / maximum/average string length—helps select appropriate data types and sizes in target database. Enables setting column widths just wide enough for the data, to improve performance.

Advanced Data Profiling Techniques

1. Key integrity—ensures keys are always present in the data, using zero/blank/null analysis. Also, helps identify orphan keys, which are problematic for ETL and future analysis.
2. Cardinality—checks relationships like one-to-one, one-to-many, many-to-many, between related data sets. This helps BI tools perform inner or outer joins correctly.
3. Pattern and frequency distributions—checks if data fields are formatted correctly, for example if emails are in a valid format. Extremely important for data fields used for outbound communications (emails, phone numbers, addresses).

Business Rules

In an environment devoid of clear rules or guidance on what business actions are allowed or not allowed, employees would make decisions on the fly. Decisions would be made without consulting company policies/guidelines, leading to complete chaos. Business rules are the conditions or constraints that define how the business operates and should be analysed alongside business requirements.

A business rule is a specific, actionable, testable directive under the control of an organization, which supports a business policy. Business rules are derivable from business policies. A business policy on the other hand, is a non-actionable directive that supports a business goal. Business rules come from different components: Terms, facts and rules. Terms represent definition; facts build on terms while rules build on facts.

Business rules are a combination of guidelines and inferences that direct how we do business. They are often referred to as "first class" citizens of the requirements world though they are different from, and documented separately from requirements. Business rules are often referenced in requirements documents; managing them in a separate document prevents the need to modify separate portions of the requirements document if changes are made to the business rules. Though business rules are not requirements, they can imply requirements and do constrain the proposed solution.

Forms of Business Rules

Business Rules are stated explicitly for the understanding of all parties to a process or business. Complex business rules are usually documented using decision tables. Business rules may also be implemented in a rules engine or expert system. Though they are mostly implemented through technology, they are not the result of the hardware or software that supports them.

Business rules can relate to:

1. Access Control Issue: Only the Marketing Director can approve sales forecasts.

2. Policy: Eliminate any product with < 5% contribution to the business after its first 5 years.
3. Calculation: Minimum buffer stock is calculated as 10% of monthly sales forecast.

Qualities Every Business Rule should have

1. Business rules should be atomic. They should be expressed in a format as granular and declarative as possible. A business rule should be framed as an atomic statement that defines a term, fact, constraint or derivation.
2. Business rules guide the flow of the process or how the system works. A business rule should be separated from the process that implements it. Roger Burlton recommends that BAs should "separate the flow from the know", meaning the process should be separated from the business rules. This ensures that changes to a business rule can be made without changing the associated process. Rules are not process or procedure and should not be contained in them.
3. Business rules only become active or legit when stated explicitly. They should not reside in a person's head but be clearly stated using an understandable format.
4. Business rules should be actively managed. They are vital business assets and should be ready for re-use when needed.
5. Business rules should be documented independently of the who, when, where and how of their enforcement.
6. Business rules should be numbered for easy identification and traceability.
7. Business rules should be documented with attributes such as: Name/description, example, source, related rules, revision history and version number, where available.
8. Each business rule should be about only one thing – that is, it must be cohesive.

Example of a business rule:

Business Rule	Only the Marketing Director can approve sales forecasts
Process	Forecast sales
Identifier	BR/SL02
Relevance/Description	For effective monitoring and controal, only the Marketing Director can approve the Sales forecasts generated by the planning unit. The marketing department owns all the products and are in the best position to predict demand
Source	Planning Unit
Related Rules	BR/SL01, BR/SL03
Last Updated	11/05/2013

Business Rules Analyst

Business analysts may be required to elicit and analyze business rules. There is however, a specialist business analyst role dedicated to business rules management and analysis: Business Rules Analyst.

A Business Rules Analyst may be required to:

1. Analyze, design and implement business rules that drive an organization and its operations.
2. Understand how business rules are determined, enforced, documented and managed.
3. Map business rules to the processes guided by them.
4. Update business rules to reflect organizational changes.
5. Verify which rules will be affected by certain organizational changes.
6. Manage risks that may interfere with the implementation of business rules.

Business Rule Management Systems

A business rule management system (BRMS) is a software system that is designed to automate the implementation of a business rule. A business rule is a rule that defines some operation of a business and always evaluates true or false. With a BRMS, companies can quickly adapt to new operating conditions without having to involve IT staff.

A business rule management system is a software package that allows businesses to deploy new business rules across an entire enterprise. Business rules may be based on company policies or laws and regulations that a company or industry operates under.

A BRMS can reduce the time it takes to implement new business rules by automating changes to IT systems such as databases without the IT department having to manually reconfigure these systems. The downside is that because defining business rules requires a lot of knowledge about a company, industry and regulations, a BRMS is often difficult to implement.

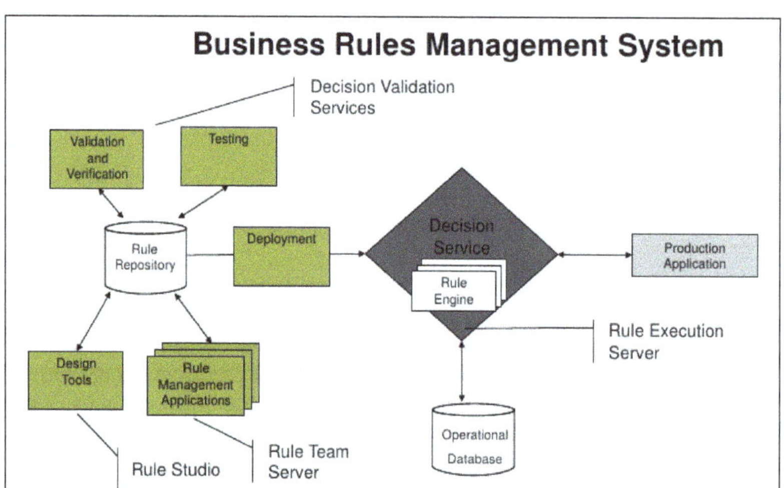

Benefits of Business Rules Management System

A BRMS delivers a number of key benefits:

1. Provides safeguards to protect the integrity of decision logic.

2. Identifies incomplete, conflicting or circular rule logic.
3. Compiles rules down to an executable (.exe) for open standards integration into apps calling Web or REST services.
4. Scales endlessly, regardless of the number or complexity of rules.
5. Promotes fast, easy and accurate rules changes, highlighting dependencies so each affected rule is identified.

Who Needs a Business Rules Management System?

Rules—in some form or fashion—govern every vertical, sector and industry, so it's not surprising that there are strong application scenarios for a BRMS in nearly every enterprise. This includes:

1. Any business, organization or government entity that is governed by rules.
2. Organizations with internal policies that affect staff, customers or vendors.
3. Businesses wanting to improve decision making efficiency or accuracy.
4. Entrepreneurs who want to respond quickly to market segment opportunities.
5. Companies wanting to reduce exposure to regulatory fines.

Sources of Business Rules

The main sources of business rules are company managers, policy makers, department managers, and written documentation such as a company's procedures, standards, and operations manuals. A faster and more direct source of business rules is direct interviews with end users. Unfortunately, because perceptions differ, end users are sometimes a less reliable source when it comes to specifying business rules. For example, a maintenance department mechanic might believe that any mechanic can initiate a maintenance procedure, when actually only mechanics with inspection authorization can perform such a task. Such a distinction might seem trivial, but it can have major legal consequences. Although end users are crucial contributors to the development of business rules, it pays to verify end-user perceptions. Too often, interviews with several people who perform the same job yield very different perceptions of what the job components are. While such a discovery may point to "management problems," that general diagnosis does not help the database designer. The database designer's job is to reconcile such differences and verify the results of the reconciliation to ensure that the business rules are appropriate and accurate.

The process of identifying and documenting business rules is essential to database design for several reasons:

1. They help to standardize the company's view of data.
2. They can be a communications tool between users and designers.

3. They allow the designer to understand the nature, role, and scope of the data.
4. They allow the designer to understand business processes.
5. They allow the designer to develop appropriate relationship participation rules and constraints and to create an accurate data model.

Of course, not all business rules can be modeled. For example, a business rule that specifies "no pilot can fly more than 10 hours within any 24-hour period" cannot be modeled. However, such a business rule can be enforced by application software.

Data Quality

Data quality is a perception or an assessment of data's fitness to serve its purpose in a given context. The quality of data is determined by factors such as accuracy, completeness, reliability, relevance and how up to date it is. As data has become more intricately linked with the operations of organizations, the emphasis on data quality has gained greater attention.

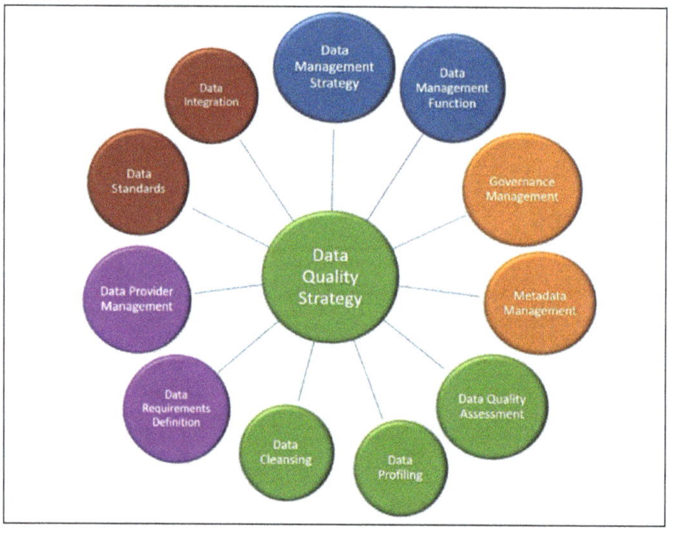

Importance of Data Quality

Poor-quality data is often pegged as the source of inaccurate reporting and ill-conceived strategies in a variety of companies, and some have attempted to quantify the damage done. Economic damage due to data quality problems can range from added miscellaneous expenses when packages are shipped to wrong addresses, all the way to steep regulatory compliance fines for improper financial reporting.

An oft-cited estimate originating from IBM suggests the yearly cost of data quality issues in the U.S. during 2016 alone was about $3.1 trillion. Lack of trust by business managers in data quality is commonly cited among chief impediments to decision-making.

The demon of poor data quality was particularly common in the early days of corporate computing, when most data was entered manually. Even as more automation took hold, data quality issues rose in prominence. For a number of years, the image of deficient data quality was represented in stories of meetings at which department heads sorted through differing spread sheet numbers that ostensibly described the same activity.

Determining Data Quality

Aspects, or dimensions, important to data quality include: accuracy, or correctness; completeness, which determines if data is missing or unusable; conformity, or adherence to a standard format; consistency, or lack of conflict with other data values; and duplication, or repeated records.

As a first step toward data quality, organizations typically perform data asset inventories in which the relative value, uniqueness and validity of data can undergo baseline studies. Established baseline ratings for known good data sets are then used for comparison against data in the organization going forward.

Methodologies for such data quality projects include the Data Quality Assessment Framework (DQAF), which was created by the International Monetary Fund (IMF) to provide a common method for assessing data quality. The DQAF provides guidelines for measuring data dimensions that include timeliness, in which actual times of data delivery are compared to anticipated data delivery schedules.

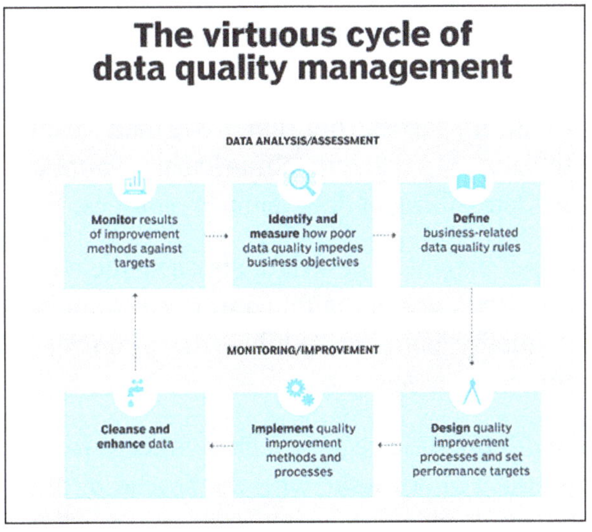

Data Quality Management

Several steps typically mark data quality efforts. In a data quality management cycle identified by data expert David Loshin, data quality management begins with identifying and measuring the effect of business outcomes. Rules are defined, performance targets are set, and quality improvement methods as well as specific data cleansing, or data scrubbing, and enhancement processes are put in place. Results are then monitored as part of ongoing measurement of the use of the data in the organization. This virtuous cycle of data quality management is intended to assure consistent improvement of overall data quality continues after initial data quality efforts are completed.

Software tools specialized for data quality management match records, delete duplicates, establish remediation policies and identify personally identifiable data. Management consoles for data quality support creation of rules for data handling to maintain data integrity, discovering data relationships and automated data transforms that may be part of quality control efforts.

Collaborative views and workflow enablement tools have become more common, giving data stewards, who are charged with maintaining data quality, views into corporate data repositories. These tools and related processes are often closely linked with master data management (MDM) systems that have become part of many data governance efforts.

Data quality management tools include IBM InfoSphere Information Server for Data Quality, Informatica Data Quality, Oracle Enterprise Data Quality, Pitney Bowes Spectrum Technology Platform, SAP Data Quality Management and Data Services, SAS DataFlux and others.

Emerging Data Quality Challenges

Over time, the burden of data quality efforts centered on the governance of relational data in organizations, but that began to change as web and cloud computing architectures came into prominence. Unstructured data, text, natural language processing and object data became part of the data quality mission. The variety of data was such that data experts began to assign different degrees of trust to various data sets, forgoing approaches that took a single, monolithic view of data quality.

Also, the classic issues of garbage in/garbage out that drove data quality efforts in early computing resurfaced with artificial intelligence (AI) and machine learning applications, in which data preparation often became the most demanding of data teams' resources.

The higher volume and speed of arrival of new data also became a greater challenge for the data quality steward. Expansion of data's use in digital commerce, along with ubiquitous online activity, has only intensified data quality concerns. While errors from rekeying data are a thing of the past, dirty data is still a common nuisance.

Protecting the privacy of individuals' data became a mild concern for data quality teams beginning in the 1970s, growing to become a major issue with the spread of data acquired via social media in the 2010s. With the formal implementation of the General Data Protection Regulation (GDPR) in the European Union (EU) in 2018, the demands for data quality expertise were expanded yet again.

Fixing Data Quality Issues

With GDPR and the risks of data breaches, many companies find themselves in a situation where they must fix data quality issues.

The first step toward fixing data quality requires identifying all the problem data. Software can be used to perform a data quality assessment to verify data sources are accurate, determine how much data there is and the potential impact of a data breach. From there, companies can build a data quality program, with the help of data stewards, data protection officers or other data management professionals. These data management experts will help implement business processes that ensure future data collection and use meets regulatory guidelines and provides the value that businesses expect from data they collect.

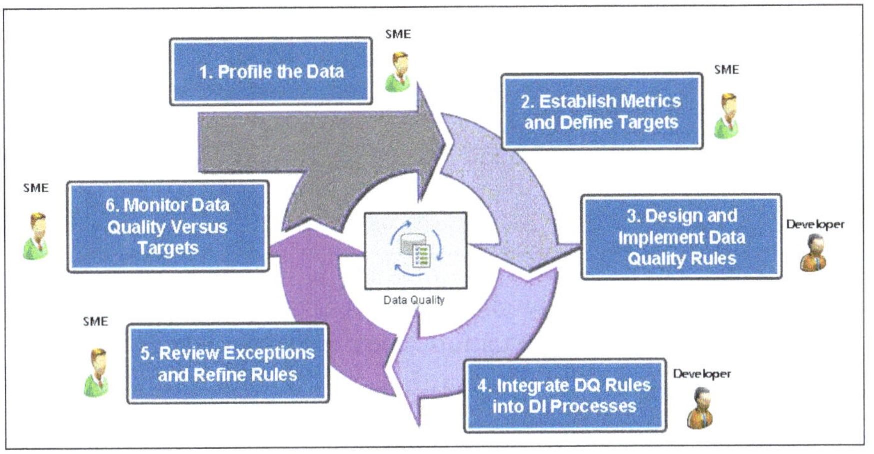

Virtuous Cycle of Data Quality

Data quality management incorporates a "virtuous cycle" in which continuous analysis, observation, and improvement lead to overall improvement in the quality of organizational information across the board. The objective of this cycle is to transition from being an organization in which the data stewards react to acute data failures into an organization that proactively controls and limits the introduction of data flaws into the environment.

In turn, this virtuous cycle incorporates five fundamental data quality management practices, which are ultimately implemented using a combination of core data services. Those practices are:

1. Data quality assessment, as a way for the practitioner to understand the scope of how poor data quality affects the ways that the business processes are intended to run, and to develop a business case for data quality management;

2. Data quality measurement, in which the data quality analysts synthesize the results assessment and concentrate on the data elements that are deemed critical based on the selected business users' needs. This leads to the definition of performance metrics that feed management reporting via data quality scorecards;

3. Integrating data quality into the application infrastructure, by way of integrating data requirements analysis across the organization and by engineering data quality into the system development life cycle;

4. Operational data quality improvement, where data stewardship procedures are used to manage identified data quality rules, conformance to acceptability thresholds.

5. Data quality incident management, which allows the data quality analysts to review the degree to which the data does or does not meet the levels of acceptability, report, log, and track issues, and document the processes for remediation and improvement.

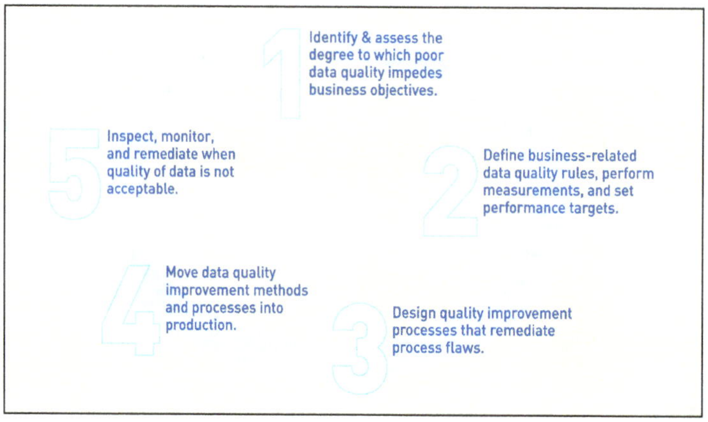

Together, these practices establish the foundation of the data quality management program, since they enable a repeatable process for incrementally accumulating metrics for data quality that will contribute to populating a data quality scorecard, a data quality dashboard, as well as driving proactive data quality management. In turn, trained staff must employ core data services to make these practices operational.

Data Quality Assessment

Smart organizations want to maximize their investment in data quality management, and this means understanding how poor data quality negatively impacts the achievement of business objectives. By quantifying that value gap, the data quality practitioner can determine the cost- effectiveness, feasibility, and speed of any proposed data quality improvement. Understanding the impacts of data flaws within the context of the business helps provides a yardstick to measure and prioritize emergent data issues.

As an example, there may be some suspicion of increased mailing and shipping costs due to inaccurate or invalid addresses. This suspicion may be introduced by a perception of a large number of undelivered shipped items returned. However, invalid or incorrect addresses not Only incurs direct costs associated with returned items; analytical applications used to profile customer purchase patterns by region are skewed, which can impact the effective execution of marketing campaigns and regional sales promotions. The data quality assessment process can be used to quantify those costs and impacts and determine what percentage of those costs is directly attributed to addresses that can be corrected.

This practice incorporates processes for identifying, assessing, quantifying, and prioritizing data quality issues:

- Business Impact Analysis – This process is intended to guide the analysts by noting any potential data-related issues that increase costs, reduce revenues, impact margins, or introduce inefficiencies or delays in business activities. In essence, the objective is to identify any negative business impacts that can be attributed to data of unacceptable quality. Identifying the location and magnitude of critical paint points in the various business processes helps to scope the business requirements for information for the assessment, narrow the list of data sets that will be examined, and guide the identification of data quality requirements.

- Data Quality Assessment using Data Profiling – This process performs a bottom-up review of the actual data as a way to isolate apparent anomalies that may be real data flaws. Using data profiling and other statistical and analysis techniques, the analysts can identify these apparent anomalies, which can be subjected to further scrutiny when reviewed with business data consumers.
- Data Quality Assessment Anomaly Review – During this process, the data quality analysts review the discovered apparent anomalies with business data consumers to see if there are any links between the data errors and any potential business impacts. By distinguishing those data errors that have material impact from the irrelevant ones, the team can prioritize issues based on business impact, and explore ways that the issues can be resolved.
- Define Measures of Data Quality – Correlating business impacts to data issues through defined business rules provides the method of measurement, and these measures can be used to baseline levels of data quality as well as continuous observation and inspection within an information production flow. This process guides the consideration of data measures to be performed and the technology requirements for collecting those measurements.
- Prepare DQ Assessment Report – The process of documenting the correlation of business impacts with data anomalies along with potential methods of measurement all within a single report provides a "fix-point" for the business data consumers regarding the current state of data quality, and provides the baseline for considering target levels for improvement.

Data Quality Measurement and Metrics

Having used an assessment to identify areas for data quality improvement, the next step is to synthesize the results of the assessment to narrow the scope by concentrating on the data elements that are deemed critical based on the business users' needs. Defining performance metrics for reporting using a data quality scorecard requires processes for the determination of dimensions and corresponding units of measure and acceptability thresholds, and the presentation of quantifiable metrics that are relevant to the business data consumers.

To continue our example, once we have determined using the data quality assessment process that problems with addresses impacts the ability to optimally deliver shipped items, we can narrow the focus for data quality measurements to specific metrics associated with the critical data elements that contribute to the delivery failures. Some items might not be delivered due to missing street information, while others might have incorrect ZIP codes. The first problem is one of completeness, while the second of consistency with defined reference data. Measurements associated with the data quality dimensions of completeness and consistency can be defined using data quality validation rules for each address, and the resulting measures can be presented as metrics to the business users in the fulfillment department to estimate how invalid addresses are related to increased costs.

Aspects of this Practice Include:

- Select Dimensions of Data Quality – A dimension of data quality describes a context and a frame of reference for measurement along with suggested units of measurement. Commonly measured dimensions of data quality include completeness, consistency, timeliness, and uniqueness, although the range of possible dimensions is only limited by the ability to provide a method for measurement. During this process, the data quality analysts select the dimensions that are to be measured and consider the tools, techniques, and skills needed to capture the measurements. The result of this process is a collection of specific measures that can be combined to contribute to qualitative data quality metrics.

- Define Data Quality Metrics – Having identified the dimensions of data quality that are relevant to the business data consumers as well as the dimensions and the specific measures, the analyst can create specific reportable metrics that can be presented to the business data stewards. These may be basic metrics composed of directly measured rules, or may be more complex metrics that are composed as weighted averages of collected scores. Other aspects include reporting schemas and methods for drilling into flawed data for root cause analysis.

- Define Data Validity Rules – The assessment process will expose potential anomalies, which are reviewed with the business users to identify data quality measures and, ultimately, data quality metrics. Yet in order to transition away from a reactive approach that seeks to remediate data quality issues once they are manifested at the end-user interface, the organization must engineer data controls into the application development process so that data errors can be identified and addressed as they occur. This process has the data quality analysts developing data validity rules; these rules can be integrated into the business applications as controls to verify that data meet expectations throughout the information flow.

- Set Acceptability Thresholds – Once the data quality dimensions and metrics have been validated, the business users are consulted to express their acceptability thresholds. When a metric score is below the acceptability threshold, it means that the data does not meet business expectations. Integrating these thresholds with the methods for measurement completes the construction of the data quality metric.

- Devise Data Quality Scorecard – A data quality scorecard presents metric scores to the data stewards observing the business data sets. Metrics scores can be captured within a repository over a long time period to enable trending and demonstrate continuous improvement or (conversely) show that progress is not being made. The process of devising the scorecard include managing the metrics definitions, measurement processes, weightings, how the scores are captured and stored, as well as composing the tools and technologies for delivery and presentation.

Data Quality and the System Development Life Cycle

Too often, data quality becomes an afterthought, with staff members reacting to discovered errors instead of proactively rooting out the causes of data flaws. Because data quality cannot just be an afterthought, once there are processes for identifying the business impact of data quality as well as the capability to define rules for inspection and monitoring, the next step is to integrate that inspection directly into the business applications. In essence, the next practice is to establish the means by which data quality management is designed and engineered across the enterprise application architecture.

However, because traditional approaches to system requirements analysis and design have concentrated on functional requirements for transactional or operational applications, the information needs of downstream business processes are ignored until long after the applications are put into production. Instead, engineering data quality management into the enterprise requires reformulating the view to requirements analysis, with a new focus on horizontal and downstream information requirements instead of solely addressing immediate functional needs.

To continue our example, with the understanding that invalid addresses lead to increased shipping costs, there are two approaches for remediation. The reactive approach is to subject all addresses to a data cleansing and enhancement process prior to generating a shipping label as a way of ensuring the best addresses. While this may result in reducing some of the increased costs, there may be records that are not correctable, or are not properly corrected. Yet if the data validity rules are known, they can be integrated directly into the application when the location data is created. In other words, validating and correcting the address when it is entered by the customer prevents invalid addresses from being introduced into the environment altogether.

Processes that Contribute to this Practice

Data Quality Requirements Analysis – During this process, the data quality analysts will synthesize data quality expectations for consumed data sets based on the business impact analysis, the determination of data quality dimensions, and aspects of prioritization related to feasibility as well as systemic impact. For each business application, the information flow is traversed backwards to the points where data is created or acquired, and the end-to-end map is investigated to determine the most appropriate points for inserting data inspection routines. At the points where data sets are extracted, transformed, or exchanged, the analysts can propose data controls that will trigger notification events when downstream expectations are violated.

Enhancing the SDLC for DQ – Incorporating data validation and data quality inspection and reporting into business processes and the corresponding business application by adjusting the general system development life cycle (SDLC) so that organizational data requirements can be solicited and integrated into the requirements phase of system development. This process looks at business ownership of data, and how business process modeling can be used to elaborate on the information needs in addition to functional requirements for business operations. Since downstream users such as business intelligence reporting consumers will depend on the data collected during operational activities, there is a need to formally collect data requirements as part of the SDLC process.

Integrate data quality improvement methods – Capturing the organization's data quality requirements as part of the requirements and design phases of a development life cycle empower the development team in integrating data quality and data correction directly into the application. This includes the ability to validate data values and records at their entry into the environment (either through acquisition or creation) or at any hand-off between processing stages, verify acceptability, and either push invalid data back to the provider for resolution or to apply adjustments or corrections on the fly.

Operational Data Quality Improvement

Having collected data quality requirements, defined data validation rules and recommended methods for measuring conformance, the next step is to establish the contract between data suppliers and data consumers as to the service level for maintaining high quality data.

In our example, addresses are validated against a set of defined data standards, either specifically managed by postal agencies in different countries, or "de facto" standards employed by delivery practitioners to ensure proper distribution. These data standards define reference tables and other metadata artifacts that can be used to actively ensure that the validity of a delivery location specification.

Combining the data validity rules and the documented metadata, the data quality analysts can document the level of acceptability for location data expected by the business users. In turn, the performance of any remediation activities can be measured to guarantee that the data is of acceptable quality.

The practice of establishing a data quality service level agreement incorporates these tasks:

Data Standards Management – The absence of a common frame of reference, as well as common business term definitions and an agreed-to format for exchange makes it difficult for parties to understand each other. This is acutely true with respect to data when specific pieces of information need to be shared across two or more business applications. This suggests the need for a normalized standard for data sharing. A data standard is an agreement between collaborating parties on the definitions of common business terms, the ways those terms are named and represented in data, and a set of rules that may describe how data are stored, exchanged, formatted, or presented. This process describes the policies and procedures for defining rules and reaching agreement about standard data elements.

Active Metadata Management – Because the use of the data elements and their underlying concepts drive how the business applications will ultimately execute, an enterprise metadata repository can be used as a "control center" for driving and managing how those business applications use common data concepts. Aside from the need to collect standard technical details regarding the numerous data elements that are potentially available, a metadata repository can help when there is a need to:

- Determine business uses of each data element,
- Determine which data element definitions refer to similar concepts,
- Identify the applications that refer to those data concepts,
- Review how each data element and associated concepts are created, read, modified, or retired by different applications,
- Document the data quality characteristics, note the inspection and monitoring locations within the business process flow, and
- Summarize how all the uses are tied together.

Therefore, a valuable component of an information architecture is an enterprise business metadata management program to facilitate the desired level of standards across the organization.

Data Quality Inspection and Monitoring

The availability of data validation rules is the basis for data quality inspection and monitoring. Inserting inspection probes and monitoring the quality of data provides the means for identifying data flaws and for notifying the appropriate people when those data flaws are discovered so that any agreed-to remediation tasks can be initiated. Mechanisms for data inspection and monitoring and the corresponding process workflows must be defined for the purposes of inspecting data and ensuring that the data elements, records, and data sets meet downstream requirements.

This process involves defining the data quality inspection routines, which may include both automated and manual processes. Automated processes may include the results of edit checks executed during application processing, data profiling or data analysis automation, ETL tools, or customized processing. Manual inspection may require running queries or reports on data sources or even obtaining samples of data which are then examined Inspection procedures are defined for each relevant data quality dimension. The inspection methods are customized for each system as appropriate.

Data Quality Service Level Agreements

A service level agreement is a contract between a service provider and that provider's consumers that specifies the service provider's responsibilities with respect to different measurable aspects of what is being provided, such as availability, performance, response time for problems, etc. A data quality service level agreement, or DQ SLA, is an agreement that specifies data consumer expectations in terms of data validity rules and levels of acceptability, as well as reasonable expectations for response and remediation when data errors and corresponding process failures are discovered. DQ SLAs can be expressed for any situation in which a data supplier provides data to a data consumer.

This process is to specify expectations regarding measurable aspects relating to one or more dimensions of data quality (such as accuracy, completeness, consistency, timeliness, etc.), as suggested by other processes already described. Then, the service level agreement specifies what is meant by conformance to those expectations, and describes the workflow that is performed when those expectations are not met. Reported issues will be prioritized and the appropriate people in the organization will be notified to take specific actions to resolve issues before any negative business impacts can occur.

Issue Tracking, Remediation and Improvement

Operationalizing the data quality service level agreement means that there are processes for reporting, logging, and tracking emergent or discovered data quality issues. Incident reporting frameworks can be adapted to this purpose, which allows the data stewards to concentrate on evaluating the root causes of data issues and proposing a remediation plan, ranging from process reengineering to simple data corrections.

Issues tracking, logging, and management ensures that any discovered issues don't fall through the cracks. In our example, any time a shipment is returned due to a data quality problem, a data analyst will review the error to determine the source of the problem, consider whether it was due to a validation step that was not taken, or determine that there is a new root cause that can lead to defining additional validation rules that can be integrated into the business process flow.

This practice incorporates these tasks:

- Data Quality Issue Reporting and Tracking: Enforcing a data quality service level agreement requires the processes for reporting and tracking data quality issues as well as any follow-on activities. Using a system to log and track data quality issues encourages more formal evaluation and initial diagnosis of "bad data," and the availability of a data quality issue tracking system helps staff members be more effective at identifying and consequently fixing data-related problems. Incident tracking can also feeds performance reporting such as mean-time-to-resolve issues, frequency of occurrence of issues, types of issues, sources of issues, and common approaches for correcting or eliminating problems.

- Root Cause Analysis: Data validation rules used as data controls integrated within business applications can trigger notifications that a data error has occurred. At that point it is the role of the data stewards to not just correct the data, but also identify the source of the introduction of the errors into the data. The root cause analysis process employs inspection and monitoring tools and techniques to help isolate the processing phase where the error actually occurred and to review the business processes to determine the ultimate root cause of any errors.

- Data Cleansing: Remedying data errors is instinctively reactive, incorporating processes to correct errors in order to meet acceptability limits, especially when the root cause cannot be determined or if it is beyond the administrative domain of the data stewards to influence a change to the process. Corrections must be socialized and synchronized with all data consumers and data suppliers, especially when the data is used in different business contexts. For example, there must be general agreement for changes when comparing reported data and rolled-up aggregate results to operational systems, because different numbers that have no explanation will lead to extra time spent attempting to reconcile the variant results.

- Process Remediation: Despite the existence of a governed mechanism for correcting bad data, the fact that errors occur implies that flawed processes must be reviewed and potentially corrected. Process correction encompasses governed process for evaluating the information production flow, business process work flow, and the determination of how processes can be improved so as to reduce or eliminate the introduction of errors.

Data Quality Practices and Core Data Services

Instituting a data quality management program means more than just purchasing data cleansing tools or starting a data governance board, and establishing a good data management program takes more than just documenting a collection of processes. An iterative cycle of assessment, planning, execution, and performance management for data quality requires repeatable processes that join people with the right sets of skills with the most appropriate tools, and the staff members who are to take part in the program need to have the right kinds of tools at their disposal in order to transition from theory to actual practice. This suggests a combination of the right technology and the proper training in the use of technology, employing data services such as:

- Data integration, to ensure suitable means for extracting and transforming data between different kinds of systems.
- Data profiling, used for data quality assessment, data validation, and inspection and monitoring.
- Parsing and standardization and identity resolution, which is used for data validation, identification of data errors, normalization, and data correction.
- Record Linkage and merging, also used to identify data errors and for resolving variance and subsequent data correction.

These are a subset of the core data services for standardizing sound data management practices. Standardizing the way data quality is deployed and using the right kinds of tools will ensure predictable information reliability and value. When developing or reengineering the enterprise architecture, implementing the fundamental data quality practices will ultimately reduce the complexity of the data management framework, thereby reducing effort, lowering risk, and leading to a high degree of trust in enterprise information.

Data Flaws

With the advent of data socialisation and data democratisation, many organisations are organising, sharing and making available the information in an efficient manner to all the employees. While most organisations are profiting by the liberal usage of such mine of information at their employees' fingertips, others are facing problems with the quality of data being used by them.

As most organisations also look at implementing systems with artificial intelligence or connecting their business via internet of things, this becomes especially important.

Business analysts determine market trends, performance data, and even present insights to executives that will help direct the future of the company. And as the world becomes even more data-driven, it is vitally important for business and data analysts to have the right data, in the right form, at the right time so they can turn it into insight.

However, many times, business analysts end up spending the majority of their time focused on data quality. This is a problem because data preparation and management isn't the business analyst's' primary responsibility.

The basic model that a company follows when implementing data socialisation is:

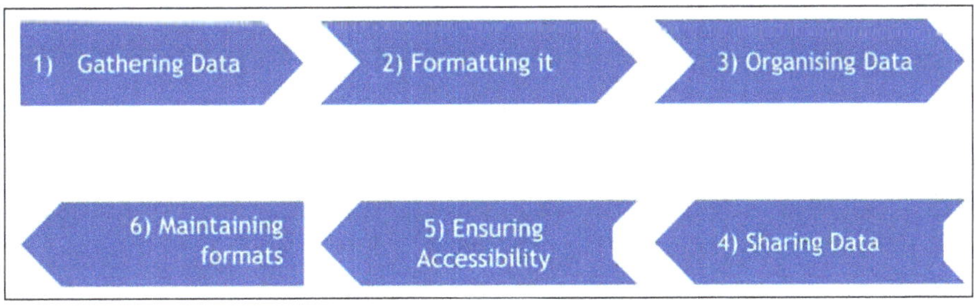

Some of the most common data quality-related issues faced by analysts and organisations in general are:

1. Duplicates: Multiple copies of the same records take a toll on the computation and storage, but may also produce skewed or incorrect insights when they go undetected. One of the key problems could be human error — someone simply entering the data multiple times by accident — or it can be an algorithm that has gone wrong.

   A remedy suggested for this problem is called "data deduplication". This is a blend of human insight, data processing and algorithms to help identify potential duplicates based on likelihood scores and common sense to identify where records look like a close match.

2. Incomplete Data: Many a times because the data has not been entered in the system correctly, or certain files may have been corrupted, the remaining data has several missing variables. For example, if an address does not include a zip code at all, the remaining information can be of little value, since the geographical aspect of it would be hard to determine.

3. Inconsistent Formats: If the data is stored in inconsistent formats, the systems used to analyse or store the information may not interpret it correctly. For example, if an organisation is maintaining the database of their consumers, then the format for storing basic information should be pre-determined. Name (first name, last name), date of birth (US/UK style) or phone number (with or without country code) should be saved in the exact same format. It may take data scientists a considerable amount of time to simply unravel the many versions of data saved.

4. Accessibility: The information which most data scientists use to create, evaluate, theorise and predict the results or end products often gets lost. The way data trickles down to business analysts in big organisations — from departments, sub-divisions, branches, and finally the teams who are working on the data — leaves information that may or may not have complete access to the next user.

   The method of sharing and making available the information in an efficient manner to all the employees in an organisation is the cornerstone in sharing corporate data.

5. System upgrades: Every time the data management system gets an upgrade or the hardware is updated, there are chances of information getting lost or corrupt. Making several back-ups of data and upgrading the systems only through authenticated sources is always advisable.

6. Data Purging and Storage: With every management level in an organisation, there are chances that locally saved information could be deleted — either by mistake or deliberately. Therefore, saving the data in a safe manner, and sharing only a mirror copy with the employees is crucial.

"As business users grow frustrated that they can't get answers when they need them, they may give up waiting and revert to flying blind without data. Alternatively, they may go rogue and introduce their own analytics tool to get the data they require, which can create a conflicting source of truth. In either scenario data loses its potency," wrote Brent Dykes.

If care isn't taken to avoid incorrect or corrupt data before analysing it for business decisions, the organisation may end up losing opportunities, revenue, suffer from damage to reputation, or even undermine the confidence of the CXOs.

- Technical data not recorded properly: This occurs in research programs when the data are not recorded in accordance with the accepted standards of the particular academic field. This is a very serious matter. Should another researcher wish to replicate the research, improper recording of the original research would make any attempt to replicate the work questionable at best. Also, should an allegation of misconduct arise concerning the research, having the data improperly recorded will greatly increase the likelihood that a finding of misconduct will be substantiated.
- Technical data management not supervised by PI: In this situation the principal investigator might inappropriately delegate his/her oversight responsibilities to someone in his/her lab that is insufficiently trained. Another situation might arise if the principal investigator simply does not dedicate the appropriate time and effort to fulfill responsibilities related to proper data management.
- Data not maintained at the institution: This situation could occur in a collaboration in which all data is maintained by one collaborator. It would be particularly problematical if each collaborator is working under a sponsored project in which their institutions are responsible for data management. In other cases, researchers might maintain data in their homes, and this can also present problems of access.
- Financial or administrative data not maintained properly: This basically means that the information is not maintained in sufficient detail, is inaccurately recorded, or not maintained in identifiable files. External auditors or reviewers would find these matters to be a serious breach of exercising appropriate responsibility regarding the proper stewardship of funds.
- Data not stored properly: This could occur with research, financial, and administrative data. Careless storage of the data that could permit its being destroyed or made unusable is a significant matter. In such case, the institution and/or researcher have acted negligently, have not fulfilled their stewardship duties, and have violated sponsor policies as well as the terms of the sponsored agreement.
- Data not held in accordance with retention requirements: As noted previously, it is absolutely essential that those involved with sponsored projects know how long different kinds of data must be retained to satisfy all compliance requirements as well as to offer appropriate support in the event of lawsuits or disputes over intellectual property.
- Data not retained by the institution: This is a major problem that would occur if a researcher leaves the institution and takes the original research data and does not leave a copy at the institution. In the event access is needed, it places the institution in an untenable position since it has not fulfilled its fiduciary responsibility to the sponsor.

Dimensions of Data Quality

Organisations select the data quality dimensions and associated dimension thresholds based on their business context, requirements, levels of risk etc. Note that each dimension is likely to have a different weighting and in order to obtain an accurate measure of the quality of data, the organisation will need to determine how much each dimension contributes to the data quality as a whole.

A typical Data Quality Assessment approach might be:

1. Identify which data items need to be assessed for data quality, typically this will be data items deemed as critical to business operations and associated management reporting.
2. Assess which data quality dimensions to use and their associated weighting.
3. For each data quality dimension, define values or ranges representing good and bad quality data. Please note, that as a data set may support multiple requirements, a number of different data quality assessments may need to be performed.
4. Apply the assessment criteria to the data items.
5. Review the results and determine if data quality is acceptable or not.
6. Where appropriate take corrective actions e.g. clean the data and improve data handling processes to prevent future recurrences.
7. Repeat the above on a periodic basis to monitor trends in Data Quality.

The outputs of different data quality checks may be required in order to determine how well the data supports a particular business need. Data quality checks will not provide an effective assessment of fitness for purpose if a particular business need is not adequately reflected in data quality rules. Similarly, when undertaking repeat data quality assessments, you should check to determine whether business data requirements have changed since the last assessment.

Whilst most data quality dimensions can be assessed by analysing the data itself, assessing accuracy of data can only be achieved by either:

1. Assessing the data against the actual thing it represents, for example, when an employee visits a property; or

2. Assessing the data against an authoritative reference data set, for example, checking customer details against the official list of voters.

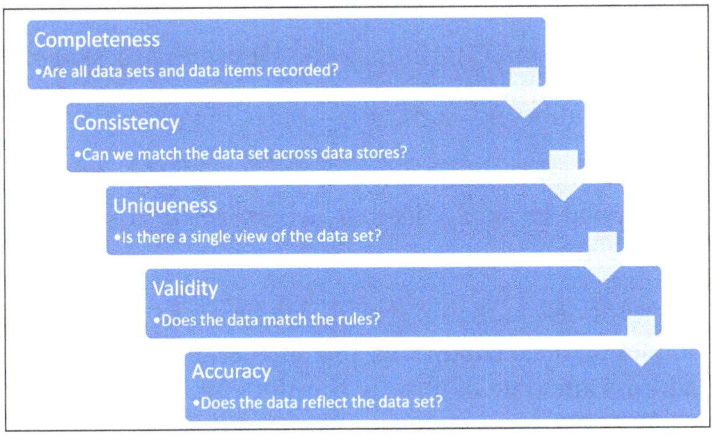

Example of the application of different data quality dimensions to a data set.

Six Core Data Quality Dimensions

The six core dimensions of data quality are:

1. Completeness
2. Uniqueness
3. Timeliness
4. Validity
5. Accuracy
6. Consistency.

Completeness

The proportion of stored data against the potential of "100% complete"

1. Reference: Business rules which define what "100% complete" represents.
2. Measure: A measure of the absence of blank (null or empty string) values or the presence of non-blank values.

3. Scope: 0-100% of critical data to be measured in any data item, record, data set or database.
4. Unit of Measure: Percentage.
5. Type of Measure: Assessment, Continuous and Discrete: Assessment only.
6. Related dimension: Validity and Accuracy.
7. Optionality: If a data item is mandatory, 100% completeness will be achieved, however validity and accuracy checks would need to be performed to determine if the data item has been completed correctly.
8. Example(s): Parents of new students at school are requested to complete a Data Collection Sheet which includes medical conditions and emergency contact details as well as confirming the name, address and date of birth of the student.
9. Scenario: At the end of the first week of the Autumn term, data analysis was performed on the 'First Emergency Contact Telephone Number' data item in the Contact table.

There are 300 students in the school and 294 out of a potential 300 records were populated, therefore 294/300 x 100 = 98% completeness has been achieved for this data item in the Contact table.

Uniqueness

No thing will be recorded more than once based upon how that thing is identified.

1. Reference: Data item measured against itself or its counterpart in another data set or database.
2. Measure: Analysis of the number of things as assessed in the 'real world' compared to the number of records of things in the data set. The real world number of things could be either determined from a different and perhaps more reliable data set or a relevant external comparator.
3. Scope: Measured against all records within a single data set.
4. Unit of Measure: Percentage.
5. Type of Measure: Assessment, Continuous and Discrete.
6. Related dimension: Consistency.
7. Optionality: Dependent on circumstances.
8. Example(s): A school has 120 current students and 380 former students (i.e. 500 in total) however; the Student database shows 520 different student records. This could include Fred Smith and Freddy Smith as separate records, despite there only being one student at the school named Fred Smith. This indicates a uniqueness of 500/520 x 100 = 96.2%.
9. External Validation: IAM Asset Information Quality Handbook Principles of Data Management, Keith Gordon.

Timeliness

The degree to which data represent reality from the required point in time:

1. Reference: The time the real world event being recorded occurred.
2. Measure: Time difference.
3. Scope: Any data item, record, data set or database.
4. Unit of Measure: Time.
5. Type of Measure: Assessment, Continuous and Discrete: Assessment and Continuous.
6. Related dimension: Accuracy because it inevitably decays with time.
7. Optionality: Optional dependent upon the needs of the business.
8. Example(s): Tina Jones provides details of an updated emergency contact number on 1st-June 2013 which is then entered into the Student database by the admin team on 4th June 2013. This indicates a delay of 3 days. This delay breaches the timeliness constraint as the service level agreement for changes is 2 days.

Validity

Data are valid if it conforms to the syntax (format, type, range) of its definition.

1. Reference: Database, metadata or documentation rules as to the allowable types (string, integer, floating point etc.), the format (length, number of digits etc.) and range (minimum, maximum or contained within a set of allowable values).
2. Measure: Comparison between the data and the metadata or documentation for the data item.
3. Scope: All data can typically be measured for Validity. Validity applies at the data item level and record level (for combinations of valid values).
4. Unit of Measure: Percentage of data items deemed Valid to Invalid.
5. Type of Measure: Assessment, Continuous and Discrete: Assessment, Continuous and Discrete.
6. Related dimension: Accuracy, Completeness, Consistency and Uniqueness.
7. Optionality: Mandatory.
8. Example(s): Each class in a UK secondary school is allocated a class identifier; this consists of the 3 initials of the teacher plus a two digit year group number of the class. It is declared as AAA99 (3 Alpha characters and two numeric characters).
9. Scenario 1: A new year 9 teacher, Sally Hearn (without a middle name) is appointed therefore there are only two initials. A decision must be made as to how to represent two initials

or the rule will fail and the database will reject the class identifier of "SH09". It is decided that an additional character "Z" will be added to pad the letters to 3: "SZH09", however this could break the accuracy rule. A better solution would be to amend the database to accept 2 or 3 initials and 1 or 2 numbers.

10. Scenario 2: The age at entry to a UK primary and junior school is captured on the form for school applications. This is entered into a database and checked that it is between 4 and 11. If it were captured on the form as 14 or N/A it would be rejected as invalid.

Accuracy

The degree to which data correctly describes the "real world" object or event being described:

1. Reference: Ideally the "real world" truth is established through primary research. However, as this is often not practical, it is common to use 3rd party reference data from sources which are deemed trustworthy and of the same chronology.
2. Measure: The degree to which the data mirrors the characteristics of the real world object or objects it represents.
3. Scope: Any "real world" object or objects that may be characterised or described by data, held as data item, record, data set or database.
4. Unit of Measure: The percentage of data entries that pass the data accuracy rules.
5. Type of Measure: Assessment, Continuous and Discrete - Assessment, e.g. primary research or reference against trusted data. Continuous Measurement, e.g. age of students derived from the relationship between the students' dates of birth and the current date.

   Discrete Measurement, e.g. date of birth recorded.
6. Related Dimension: Validity is a related dimension because, in order to be accurate, values must be valid, the right value and in the correct representation.
7. Optionality: Mandatory because - when inaccurate - data may not be fit for use.
8. Example(s): A European school is receiving applications for its annual September intake and requires students to be aged 5 before the 31st August of the intake year.
9. In this scenario, the parent, a US Citizen, applying to a European school completes the Date of Birth (D.O.B) on the application form in the US date format, MM/DD/YYYY rather than the European DD/MM/YYYY format, causing the representation of days and months to be reversed.
10. As a result, 09/08/YYYY really meant 08/09/YYYY causing the student to be accepted as the age of 5 on the 31st August in YYYY. The representation of the student's D.O.B.–whilst valid in its US context–means that in Europe the age was not derived correctly and the value recorded was consequently not accurate.

Consistency

The absence of difference, when comparing two or more representations of a thing against a definition.

- Reference: Data item measured against itself or its counterpart in another data set or database.
- Measure: Analysis of pattern and/or value frequency.
- Scope: Assessment of things across multiple data sets and/or assessment of values or formats across data items, records, data sets and databases. Processes including: people based, automated, electronic or paper.
- Unit of Measure: Percentage.
- Type of Measure: Assessment, Continuous and Discrete: Assessment and Discrete.
- Related Dimension(s): Validity, Accuracy and Uniqueness.
- Optionality: It is possible to have consistency without validity or accuracy.
- Example(s): School admin: a student's date of birth has the same value and format in the school register as that stored within the Student database.

Other Data Quality Considerations

It is crucial to understand and manage the six core dimensions. However, there are additional factors which can have an impact on the effective use of data. Even when all six dimensions are deemed to be satisfactory, the data can still fail to achieve the objective.

Data may be perfectly complete, unique, timely, valid, accurate and timely. However if data items are in English and the users don't understand English then it will be useless.

It may be useful to ask these additional questions about your data.

- Usability of the data - Is it understandable, simple, relevant, accessible, maintainable and at the right level of precision?
- Timing issues with the data (beyond timeliness itself) - Is it stable yet responsive to legitimate change requests?
- Flexibility of the data - Is it comparable and compatible with other data, does it have useful groupings and classifications? Can it be repurposed, and is it easy to manipulate?
- Confidence in the data - Are Data Governance, Data Protection and Data Security in place? What is the reputation of the data, and is it verified or verifiable?
- Value of the data - Is there a good cost/benefit case for the data? Is it being optimally used? Does it endanger people's safety or privacy or the legal responsibilities of the enterprise?
- Does it support or contradict the corporate image or the corporate message?

Data Quality Assessment

Data quality assessment (DQA) is the process of scientifically and statistically evaluating data in order to determine whether they meet the quality required for projects or business processes and are of the right type and quantity to be able to actually support their intended use. It can be considered a set of guidelines and techniques that are used to describe data, given an application context, and to apply processes to assess and improve the quality of data.

Data quality assessment (DQA) exposes issues with technical and business data that allow the organization to properly plan for data cleansing and enrichment strategies. This is usually done to maintain the integrity of systems, quality assurance standards and compliance concerns. Generally, technical quality issues such as inconsistent structure and standard issues, missing data or missing default data, and errors in the data fields are easy to spot and correct, but more complex issues should be approached with more defined processes.

DQA is usually performed to fix subjective issues related to business processes, such as the generation of accurate reports, and to ensure that data-driven and data-dependent processes are working as expected.

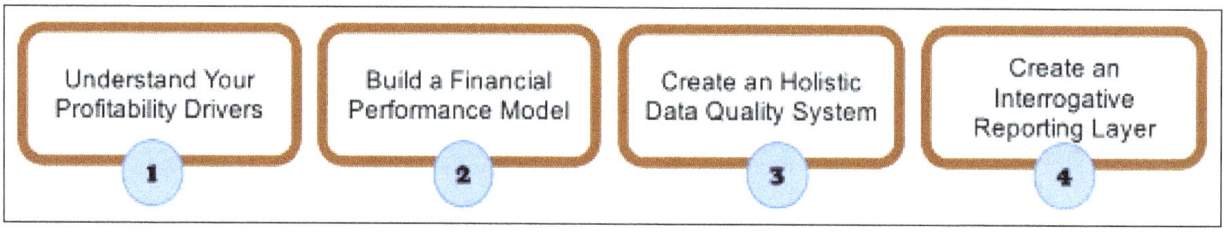

Functional Forms

When performing objective assessments, companies should follow a set of principles to develop metrics specific to their needs. Three pervasive functional forms are simple ratio, min or max operation, and weighted average. Refinements of these functional forms, such as addition of sensitivity parameters, can be easily incorporated. Often, the most difficult task is precisely defining a dimension, or the aspect of a dimension that relates to the company's specific application. Formulating the metric is straightforward once this task is complete.

Simple Ratio

The simple ratio measures the ratio of desired outcomes to total outcomes. Since most people measure exceptions, however, a preferred form is the number of undesirable outcomes divided by total outcomes subtracted from 1. This simple ratio adheres to the convention that 1 represents the most desirable and 0 the least desirable score. Although a ratio illustrating undesirable outcomes gives the same information as one illustrating desirable outcomes, our experience sug- gests managers prefer the ratio showing positive outcomes, since this form is useful for longitudinal comparisons illustrating trends of continuous improvement. Many traditional data quality metrics, such as free-of-error, completeness, and consistency take this form. Other dimensions that can be evaluated using this form include concise representation, relevancy, and ease of manipulation.

The free-of-error dimension represents data correctness. If one is counting the data units in error, the metric is defined as the number of data units in error divided by the total number of data units subtracted from 1. In practice, determining what constitutes a data unit and what is an error requires a set of clearly defined criteria. For example, the degree of precision must be specified. It is possible for an incorrect character in a text string to be tolerable in one circumstance but not in another.

The completeness dimension can be viewed from many perspectives, leading to different metrics. At the most abstract level, one can define the concept of schema completeness, which is the degree to which entities and attributes are not missing from the schema. At the data level, one can define column completeness as a function of the missing values in a column of a table. This measurement corresponds to Codd's column integrity, which assesses missing values. A third type is called population completeness. If a column should contain at least one occurrence of all 50 states, for example, but it only contains 43 states, then we have population incompleteness. Each of the three types (schema completeness, column completeness, and population completeness) can be measured by taking the ratio of the number of incomplete items to the total number of items and subtracting from 1.

The consistency dimension can also be viewed from a number of perspectives, one being consistency of the same (redundant) data values across tables. Codd's Referential Integrity constraint is an instantiation of this type of consistency. As with the previously discussed dimensions, a metric measuring consistency is the ratio of violations of a specific consistency type to the total number of consistency checks subtracted from one.

Min or Max Operation

To handle dimensions that require the aggregation of multiple data quality indicators (variables), the minimum or maximum operation can be applied. One computes the minimum (or maximum) value from among the normalized values of the individual data quality indicators. The min operator is conservative in that it assigns to the dimension an aggregate value no higher than the value of its weakest data quality indicator (evaluated and normalized to between 0 and 1).

The maximum operation is used if a liberal interpretation is warranted. The individual variables may be measured using a simple ratio. Two interesting examples of dimensions that can make use of the min operator are believability and appropriate amount of data. The max operator proves useful in more complex metrics applicable to the dimensions of timeliness and accessibility.

Believability is the extent to which data is regarded as true and credible. Among other factors, it may reflect an individual's assessment of the credibility of the data source, comparison to a commonly accepted standard, and previous experience. Each of these variables is rated on a scale from 0 to 1, and overall believability is then assigned as the minimum value of the three. Assume the believability of the data source is rated as 0.6; believability against a common standard is 0.8; and believability based on experience is 0.7. The overall believability rating is then 0.6 (the lowest number). As indicated earlier, this is a conservative assessment. An alternative is to compute the believability as a weighted average of the individual components.

A working definition of the appropriate amount of data should reflect the data quantity being neither too little nor too much. A general metric that embeds this tradeoff is the minimum of two simple ratios: the ratio of the number of data units provided to the number of data units needed, and the ratio of the number of data units needed to the number of data units provided.

Timeliness reflects how up-to-date the data is with respect to the task it's used for. A general metric to measure timeliness has been proposed by Ballou et al., who suggest timeliness be measured as the maximum of one of two terms: 0 and one minus the ratio of currency to volatility. Here, currency is defined as the age plus the delivery time minus the input time. Volatility refers to the length of time data remains valid; delivery time refers to when data is delivered to the user; input time refers to when data is received by the system; and age refers to the age of the data when first received by the system.

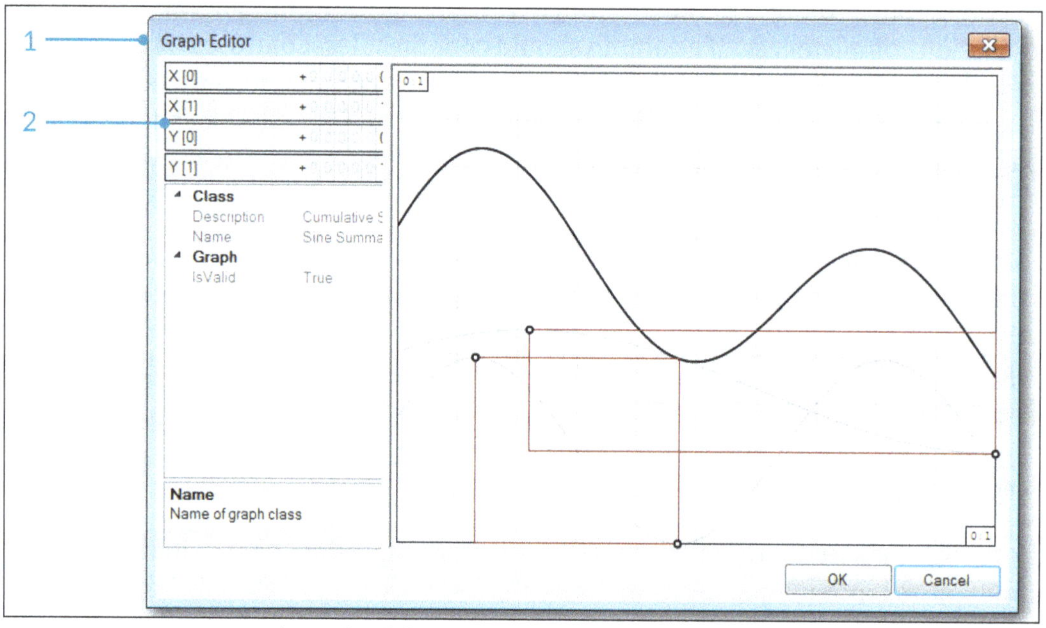

Dimensional data quality assessment across roles.

An exponent can be used as a sensitivity factor, with the max value raised to this exponent. The value of the exponent is task-dependent and reflects the analyst's judgment. For example, suppose the timeliness rating without using the sensitivity factor (equivalent to a sensitivity factor of 1) is 0.81. Using a sensitivity factor of 2 would then yield a timeliness rating of 0.64 (higher sensitivity factor reflects fact that the data becomes less timely faster) and 0.9 when sensitivity factor is 0.5 (lower sensitivity factor reflects fact that the data loses timeliness at a lower rate).

A similarly constructed metric can be used to measure accessibility, a dimension reflecting ease of data attainability. The metric emphasizes the time aspect of accessibility and is defined as the maximum value of two terms: 0 or one minus the time interval from request by user to delivery to user divided by the time interval from request by user to the point at which data is no longer useful. Again, a sensitivity factor in the form of an exponent can be included.

If data is delivered just prior to when it is no longer useful, the data may be of some use, but will not be as useful as if it were delivered much earlier than the cut- off. This metric trades off the time interval over which the user needs data against the time it takes to deliver data. Here, the time to obtain data increases until the ratio goes negative, at which time the accessibility is rated as zero (maximum of the two terms).

In other applications, one can also define accessibility based on the structure and relationship of the data paths and path lengths. As always, if time, structure, and path lengths all are considered important, then individual metrics for each can be developed and an overall measure using the min operator can be defined.

Weighted Average

For the multivariate case, an alternative to the min operator is a weighted average of variables. If a company has a good understanding of the importance of each variable to the overall evaluation of a dimension, for example, then a weighted average of the variables is appropriate. To insure the rating is normalized, each weighting factor should be between zero and one, and the weighting factors should add to one. Regarding the believability example mentioned earlier, if the company can specify the degree of importance of each of the variables to the over-all believability measure, the weighted average may be an appropriate form to use.

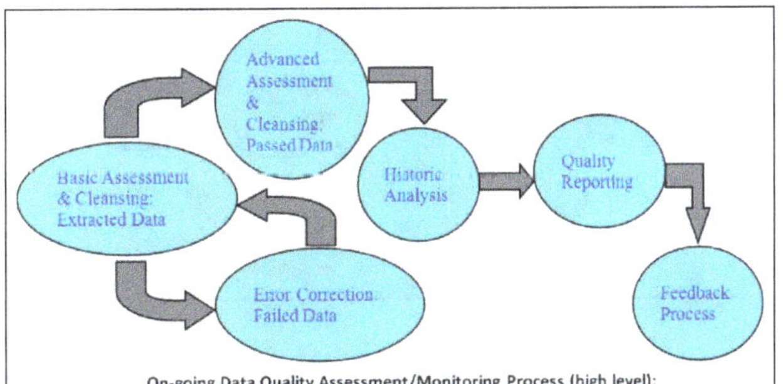

On-going Data Quality Assessment/Monitoring Process (high level):

Data Quality Rules

Data rules can have various designations such as:

- Business rules (in the data modeling),
- Data test,
- Quality screen.

They follow the same concept than the rules from an event driven architecture.

Data quality rules fall into two categories to help on the data cleansing process:

- Data detecting rules which must design the business rules.
- Data correction rules which take place in the data correction process.

Validations Rules

One set of rules, validations, simply asserts what must be true about the data, and is used as a means of validating that data conforms to our expectations. Both data transformation and data profiling products will allow the end client to define validation rules that can be tested against a large set of data instances. For example, having determined through profiling that the values within a specific column should fall within a range of 20-100, one can specify a rule asserting that "all values must be greater than or equal to 20, and less than or equal to 100." The next time data is streamed through the data quality tool, the rule can be applied to verify that each of the values falls within the specified range, and tracks the number of times the value does not fall within that range.

Data Rule Type

The following data rules may be discover or classify through three type of data profiling analysis.

Data Rule Type	Data profiling Analysis	Description	Example
Domain List	Attribute Analysis	A domain list rule defines a list of values that an attribute is allowed to have.	The Gender attribute can have 'M' or 'F'.
Domain Pattern List	Attribute Analysis	A domain pattern list rule defines a list of patterns that an attribute is allowed to conform to. The patterns are defined in the regular expression syntax.	An example pattern for a telephone number is as follows: (^[[::space]]*[0-9]{ 3 } [[::punct|:space:]]?[0-9]{ 4 }[[::space]]*$)
Domain Range	Attribute Analysis	A domain range rule defines a range of values that an attribute is allowed to have.	The value of the salary attribute can be between 100 and 10000.
Common Format / Pattern	Attribute Analysis	A common format rule defines a known common format that an attribute is allowed to conform to.	This rule type has many subtypes: Telephone Number, IP Address, SSN, URL, E-mail Address.
No Nulls	Attribute Analysis	A no nulls rule specifies that the attribute cannot have null values	The department_id attribute for an employee in the Employees table cannot be null.
Functional Dependency	Functional Dependency	A functional dependency defines that the data in the data object may be normalized or derived	

Unique Key	Attribute Analysis	A unique key data rule defines whether an attribute or group of attributes are unique in the given data object.	The name of a department should be unique.
Referential	Referential Analysis	A referential data rule defines the type of a relationship (1:x) a value must have to another value.	The department_id attribute of the Departments table should have a 1:n relationship with the department id attribute of the Employees table.
Name and address	Functional Dependency	A name and address data rule evaluate a group of attributes as a name or address	
Custom	-	A custom data rule applies a SQL expression that you specify to its input parameters.	VALID_DATE with two input parameters, START_DATE and END_DATE. A valid expression for this rule is: "THIS"."END_DATE" > "THIS"."START_DATE

The second set of rules, cleansing or correction rules, identifies a violation of some expectation and a way to modify the data to then meet the business needs.

Data Correction is the second step in a data cleansing process after the detection of values that not meet the business rules (data rules).

For each data values that are not accepted, you can have to choose one of the following actions:

- Ignore: The data rule is ignored and, therefore, no values are rejected based on this data rule.
- Report: The data rule is run only after the data has been loaded for reporting purposes only. It is like the Ignore option, except a report is created that contains the values that did not adhere to the data rules.
- Cleanse: The values rejected by this data rule are moved to an error table where cleansing strategies are applied. When you choose this option, you must specify a cleansing strategy of correction rule.

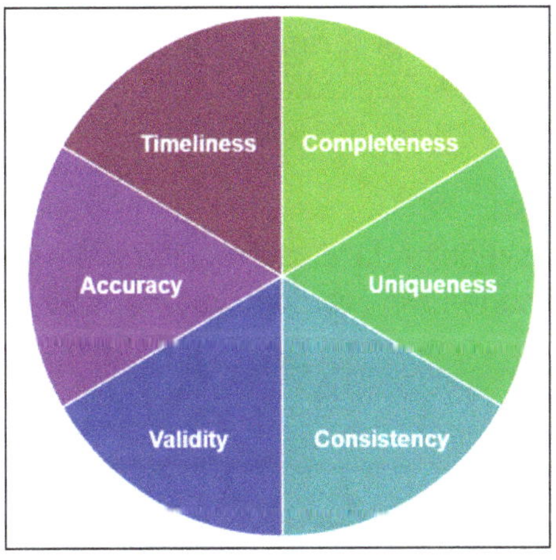

Cleansing Strategy (Data Cleansing Rule)

Cleansing or correction rules, identifies a violation of some expectation and a way to modify the data to then meet the business needs. For example, while there are many ways that people provide telephone numbers, an application may require that each telephone number be separated into its area code, exchange, and line components. This is a cleansing rule, as is shown in the figure below, which can be implemented and tracked using data cleansing tools.

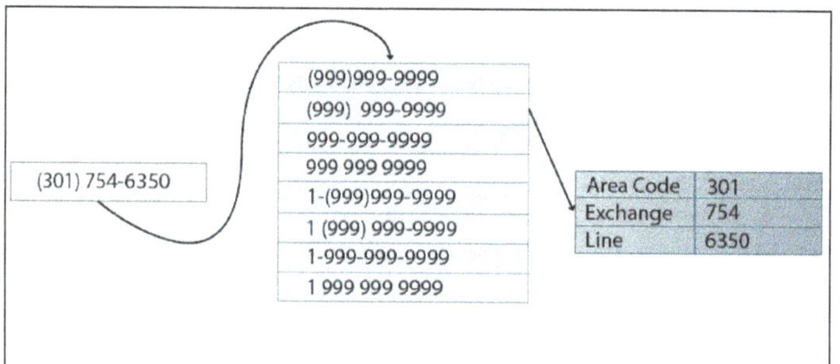

Transforming and standardizing telephone numbers.

Transforming and standardizing telephone numbers.

Cleansing Strategy	Description
Remove	Does not populate the target table with error records
Custom	Custom function in the target table
Set to Min	Sets the attribute value of the error record to the minimum value defined in the data rule.
Set to Max	Sets the attribute value of the error record to the maximum value defined in the data rule.
Similarity	Uses a similarity algorithm based on permitted domain values to find a value that is similar to the error record.
Soundex	Uses a soundex algorithm based on permitted domain values to find a value that is similar to the error record.
Merge	Merge duplicate records into a single row.

Continuous Data Quality Monitoring and Improvement

The key elements of a good data quality program include establishing a baseline, continuous improvement, appropriate metrics, and scorecarding.

Establishing a Baseline

The first step is establishing a baseline of the current state of data quality. This should identify the critical failure points and determine improvement targets. The targets must be tied to business objectives.

Continuous Measurement

Data quality must be tracked, managed, and monitored if it is to improve business efficiency and transparency. Therefore, being able to measure and monitor data quality throughout the lifecycle and compare the results over time is an essential ingredient in the proactive management of ongoing data quality improvement and data governance.

Organizations need a formalized way of setting targets, measuring conformance to those targets, and effectively communicating tangible data quality metrics to senior management and data owners. Standard metrics provide everyone (executives, IT, and line-of-business managers) with a unified view of data and data quality, and can also provide the basis for regulatory reporting in certain circumstances, such as Basel II, where there are specific data quality reporting requirements.

Metrics to Suit the Job

Ultimately, data quality monitoring and reporting based on a well-understood set of metrics provides important knowledge about the value of the data in use, and empowers knowledge workers with the ability to determine how the data can best be used to meet their own business needs.

The critical attributes of data quality (completeness, conformity, consistency, accuracy, duplication, and integrity) should map to specific business requirements. Duplicate records in a data warehouse, for example, make it difficult to analyze customer habits and segment customers in terms of market. Inaccurate data results in poor targeting, budgeting, staffing, unreliable financial projections, and so on. (The Informatica white paper, "Monitoring Data Quality Performance Using Data Quality Metrics," outlines a more comprehensive list of metrics and examples.)

A well-defined set of metrics should be used to get a baseline understanding of the levels of data quality; this baseline should be used to build a business case to justify investment in data quality. Beyond that, the same metrics become central to the ongoing data quality process, enabling business users and data stewards to track progress and quickly identify problem areas that need to be addressed.

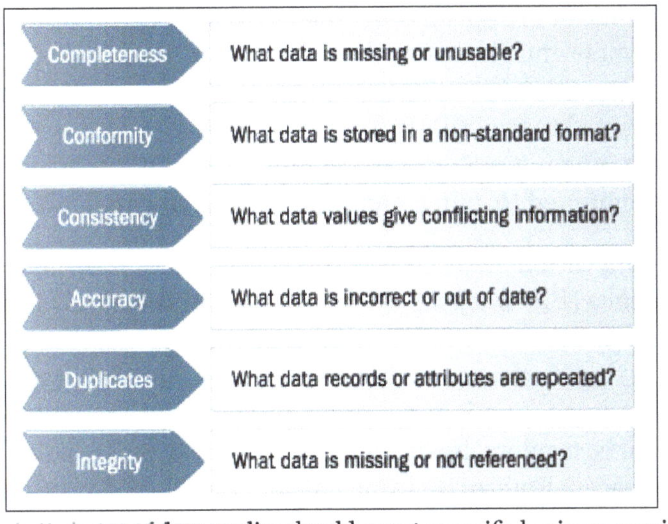

The critical attributes of data quality should map to specific business requirements.

Breaking down data issues into these key measures highlights where best to focus your data quality improvement efforts by identifying the most important data quality issues and attributes based on the lifecycle stage of your different projects. For example, early in a data migration, the focus may be on completeness of key master data fields, whereas the implementation of an e-banking system may require greater concern with accuracy during individual authentication.

Scorecarding

Inherent in the metrics-driven approach is the ability to aggregate company-wide results into data quality scorecards. A scorecard is the key visual aid that helps to drive the data quality process in the right direction, empowering data analysts to set accurate and focused quality targets and to define improvement processes accordingly, including setting priorities for data quality improvement in upstream information systems.

Metrics and scorecards that report on data quality, audited and monitored at multiple points across the enterprise, help to ensure data quality is managed in accordance with real business requirements. They provide both the carrot and the stick to support ownership, responsibility, and accountability. But, beyond the data quality function itself, the metrics used for monitoring the quality of data can actually roll up into higher-level performance indicators for the business as a whole.

Data Integration

In today's business world, it is typical that enterprises run different but coexisting information systems. Employing these systems, enterprises struggle to realize business opportunities in highly competitive markets. In this setting, the integration of existing information systems is becoming more and more indispensable in order to dynamically meet business and customer needs while leveraging long-term investments in existing IT infrastructure.

In general, integration of multiple information systems aims at combining selected systems so that they form a unified new whole and give users the illusion of interacting with one single information system. The reason for integration is twofold: First, given a set of existing information systems, an integrated view can be created to facilitate information access and reuse through a single information access point. Second, given a certain information need, data from different complementing information systems is combined to gain a more comprehensive basis to satisfy the need.

There is a manifold of applications that benefit from integrated information. For instance, in the area of business intelligence (BI), integrated information can be used for querying and reporting on business activities, for statistical analysis, online analytical processing (OLAP), and data mining in order to enable forecasting, decision making, enterprise-wide planning, and, in the end, to gain sustainable competitive advantages. For customer relationship management (CRM), integrated information on individual customers, business environment trends, and current sales can be used to improve customer services. Enterprise information portals (EIP) present integrated company information as personalized web sites and represent single information access points primarily for employees, but also for customers, business partners, and the public. Last, but not least, in the area of e-commerce and e-business, integrated information enables and facilitates business transactions and services over computer networks.

Similar to information, IT services and applications can be integrated, either to provide a single service access point or to provide more comprehensive services to meet business requirements. For instance, integrated workflow and document management systems can be used within enterprises to leverage in traorganizational collaboration. Based on the ideas of business process reengineering (BPR), integrated IT services and applications that support business processes can help to reduce time-to-market and to provide added-value products and services. Thereby, interconnecting building blocks from selected IT services and applications enables supply chain management within individual enterprises as well as cooperation beyond the boundaries of traditional enterprises, as in interorganizational cooperation, business process networks (BPN), and virtual organizations. For instance, in e-procurement, supply and demand for producer goods are provided with integrated information and services to streamline the purchasing process for institutional buyers. Thus, it is possible to bypass intermediaries and to enable direct interaction between supply and demand, as in business-to-business (B2B), business-to-consumer (B2C), and business-to-employee (B2E) transactions. These trends are fueled by XML that is becoming the industry standard for data exchange as well as by web services that provide interoperability between various software applications running on different platforms.

In the enterprise context, the integration problem is commonly referred to as enterprise integration (EI). Enterprise integration denotes the capability to integrate information and functionalities from a variety of information systems in an enterprise. This encompasses enterprise information integration (EII) that concerns integration on the data and information level and enterprise application integration (EAI) that considers integration on the level of application logic.

Problem of Integration

Integration of multiple information systems generally aims at combining selected systems so that they form a unified new whole and give users the illusion of interacting with one single information system. Users are provided with a homogeneous logical view of data that is physically distributed over heterogeneous data sources. For this, all data has to be represented using the same abstraction principles (unified global data model and unified semantics). This task includes detection and resolution of schema and data conflicts regarding structure and semantics.

In general, information systems are not designed for integration. Thus, whenever integrated access to different source systems is desired, the sources and their data that do not fit together have to be coalesced by additional adaptation and reconciliation functionality. Note that there is not the one single integration problem. While the goal is always to provide a homogeneous, unified view on data from different sources, the particular integration task may depend on:

- The architectural view of an information system,
- The content and functionality of the component systems,
- The kind of information that is managed by component systems (alphanumeric data, multimedia data; structured, semi-structured, unstructured data),
- Requirements concerning autonomy of component systems,
- Intended use of the integrated information system (read-only or write access),
- Performance requirements, and the available resources (time, money, human resources, know-how, etc.).

Additionally, several kinds of heterogeneity typically have to be considered. These include differences in:

- Hardware and operating systems,

- Data management software,
- Data models, schemas, and data semantics,
- Middleware,
- User interfaces, and business rules and integrity constraints.

Approaches to Integration

The presented classification is based on and distinguishes integration approaches according to the level of abstraction where integration is performed. Information systems can be described using a layered architecture, On the topmost layer, users access data and services through various interfaces that run on top of different applications. Applications may use middleware – transaction processing (TP) monitors, message-oriented middleware (MOM), SQL-middleware, etc. – to access data via a data access layer. The data itself is managed by a data storage system. Usually, database management systems (DBMS) are used to combine the data access and storage layer.

In general, the integration problem can be addressed on each of the presented system layers. For this, the following principal approaches are available:

- Manual Integration: Here, users directly interact with all relevant information systems and manually integrate selected data. That is, users have to deal with different user interfaces and query languages. Additionally, users need to have detailed knowledge on location, logical data representation, and data semantics.
- Common User Interface: In this case, the user is supplied with a common user interface (e.g., a web browser) that provides a uniform look and feel. Data from relevant information systems is still separately presented so that homogenization and integration of data yet has to be done by the users (for instance, as in search engines).
- Integration by Applications: This approach uses integration applications that access various data sources and return integrated results to the user. This solution is practical for a small number of component systems. However, applications become increasingly fat as the number of system interfaces and data formats to homogenize and integrate grows.

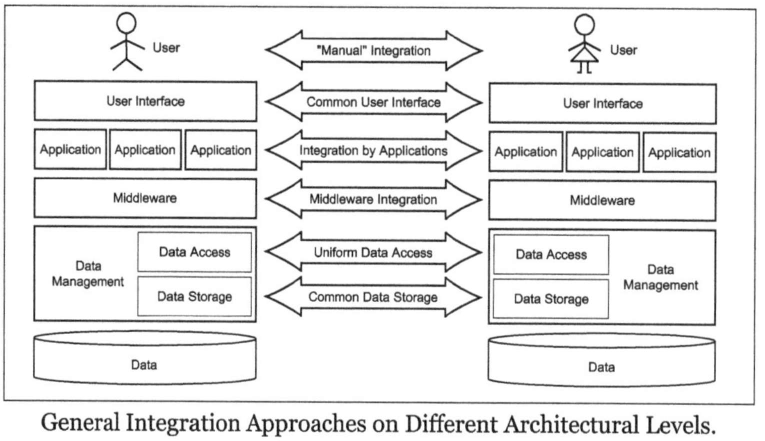

General Integration Approaches on Different Architectural Levels.

- Integration by Middleware: Middleware provides reusable functionality that is generally used to solve dedicated aspects of the integration problem, e.g., as done by SQL-middleware. While applications are relieved from implementing common integration functionality, integration efforts are still needed in applications. Additionally different middleware tools usually have to be combined to build integrated systems.
- Uniform Data Access: In this case, a logical integration of data is accomplished at the data access level. Global applications are provided with a unified global view of physically distributed data, though only virtual data is available on this level. Local information systems keep their autonomy and can support additional data access layers for other applications. However, global provision of physically integrated data can be time-consuming since data access, homogenization, and integration have to be done at runtime.
- Common Data Storage: Here, physical data integration is performed by transferring data to a new data storage; local sources can either be retired or remain operational. In general, physical data integration provides fast data access. However, if local data sources are retired, applications that access them have to be migrated to the new data storage as well. In case local data sources remain operational, periodical refreshing of the common data storage needs to be considered.

In practice, concrete integration solutions are realized based on the presented six general integration approaches. Important examples include:

- Mediated query systems represent a uniform data access solution by pro- viding a single point for read-only querying access to various data sources, e.g., as in TSIMMIS. A mediator that contains a global query processor is employed to send subqueries to local data sources; returned local query results are then combined.
- Portals as another form of uniform data access are personalized doorways to the internet or intranet where each user is provided with information according to his detected information needs. Usually, web mining is applied to determine user-profiles by click-stream analysis; thereby, information the user might be interested in can be retrieved and presented.
- Data warehouses realize a common data storage approach to integration. Data from several operational sources (on-line transaction processing systems, OLTP) are extracted, transformed, and loaded (ETL) into a data warehouse. Then, analysis, such as online analytical processing (OLAP), can be performed on cubes of integrated and aggregated data.
- Operational data stores are a second example of a common data storage. Here, a "warehouse with fresh data" is built by immediately propagating updates in local data sources to the data store. Thus, up-to-date integrated data is available for decision support. Unlike in data warehouses, data is neither cleansed nor aggregated nor are data histories supported.
- Federated database systems (FDBMS) achieve a uniform data access solution by logically integrating data from underlying local DBMS. Federated database systems are fully-fledged DBMS; that is, they implement their own data model, support global queries, global transactions, and global access control. Usually, the five-level reference architecture by is employed for building FDBMS.

- Workflow management systems (WFMS) allow to implements business processes where each single step is executed by a different application or user. Generally, WFMS support modeling, execution, and maintenance of processes that are comprised of interactions between applications and human users. WFMS represent an integration-by-application approach.
- Integration by web services performs integration through software components (i.e., web services) that support machine-to-machine interaction over a network by XML-based messages that are conveyed by internet protocols. Depending on their offered integration functionality, web services either represent a uniform data access approach or a common data access interface for later manual or application-based integration.
- Model management introduces high-level operations between models (such as database schemas, UML models, and software configurations) and model mappings; such operations include matching, merging, selection, and composition. Using a schema algebra that encompasses all these operations, it is intended to reduce the amount of hand-crafted code required for transformations of models and mappings as needed for schema integration. Model management falls into the category of manual integration.
- Peer-to-peer (P2P) integration is a decentralized approach to integration between distributed, autonomous peers where data can be mutually shared and integrated through mappings between local schemas of peers. P2P integration constitutes, depending on the provided integration functionality, either a uniform data access approach or a data access interface for sub- sequent manual or application-based integration.
- Grid data integration provides the basis for hypotheses testing and pattern detection in large amounts of data in grid environments, i.e., interconnected computing resources being used for high-throughput computing. Here, often unpredictable and highly dynamic amounts of data have to be dealt with to provide an integrated view over large (scientific) data sets. Grid data integration represents an integration by middleware approach. Personal data integration systems are a special form of manual integration. Here, tailored integrated views are defined (e.g., by a declarative integration language), either by users themselves or by dedicated integration engineers. Each integrated view precisely matches the information needs of a user by encompassing all relevant entities with real-world semantics as intended by the particular user; thereby, the integrated view reflects the user's personal way to perceive his application domain of interest.
- Collaborative integration, another special form of manual integration, is based on the idea to have users to contribute to a data integration system for using it. Here, initial partial schema mappings are presented to users who answer questions concerning the mappings; these answers are then taken to refine the mappings and to expand the system capabilities. Similar to folksonomies, where data is collaboratively labeled for later retrieval, the task of schema mapping is distributed over participating users.
- In Data space systems co-existence of all data (i.e., both structured and unstructured) is propagated rather than full integration. A data space system is used to provide the same basic functionality, e.g., search facilities, over all data sources independently of their degree

of integration. Only when more sophisticated services are needed, such as relational-style queries, additional efforts are made to integrate the required data sources more closely. In general, data space systems may simultaneously use every one of the presented six general integration approaches.

From Structural to Semantic Integration

Database technology was introduced in enterprises since the late 1960s to sup- port (initially rather simple) business applications. As the number of applications and data repositories rapidly grew, the need for integrated data became apparent. As a consequence, first integration approaches in the form of multi- database systems were developed around 1980. This was a first cornerstone in a remarkable history of research in the area of data integration. The evolution continued over mediators and agent systems to ontology-based, peer-to-peer (P2P), and web service-based integration approaches. Recently, tailored personal data integration, collaborative integration, and data space systems are being addressed by the research community. In general, early integration approaches were based on a relational or functional data model and realized rather tightly-coupled solutions by providing one single global schema. To overcome their limitations concerning the aspects of abstraction, classification, and taxonomies, object-oriented integration approaches were adopted to perform structural homogenization and integration of data. With the advent of the internet and web technologies, the focus shifted from integrating purely well-structured data to also incorporating semi-and unstructured data while architecturally, loosely-coupled mediator and agent systems became popular.

However, integration is more than just a structural or technical problem. Technically, it is rather easy to connect different relational DBMS (e.g., via ODBC or JDBC). More demanding is to integrate data described by different data models; even worse are the problems caused by data with heterogeneous semantics. For instance, having only the name “loss” to denote a relation in an enterprise information system does not provide sufficient information to doubtlessly decide whether the represented loss is a book loss, a realized loss, or a future expected loss and whether the values of the tuples reflect only a roughly estimated loss or a precisely quantified loss. Integrating two “loss” relations with (implicit) heterogeneous semantics leads to erroneous results and completely senseless conclusions. Therefore, explicit and precise semantics of integratable data are essential for semantically correct and meaningful integration results. Note that none of the principal integration approaches helps to resolve semantic heterogeneity; neither is XML that only provides structural information a solution.

In the database area, semantics can be regarded as people’s interpretation of data and schema items according to their understanding of the world in a certain context. In data integration, the type of semantics considered is generally real-world semantics that are concerned with the “mapping of objects in the model or computational world onto the real world and the issues that involve human interpretation, or meaning and use of data and information”. In this setting, semantic integration is the task of grouping, combining or completing data from different sources by taking into account explicit and precise data semantics in order to avoid that semantically in- compatible data is structurally merged. That is, semantic integration has to ensure that only data related to the same or sufficiently3 similar real-world entity or concept is merged. A prerequisite for this is to resolve semantic ambiguity concerning integratable data by explicit metadata to elicit all relevant implicit assumptions and underlying context information.

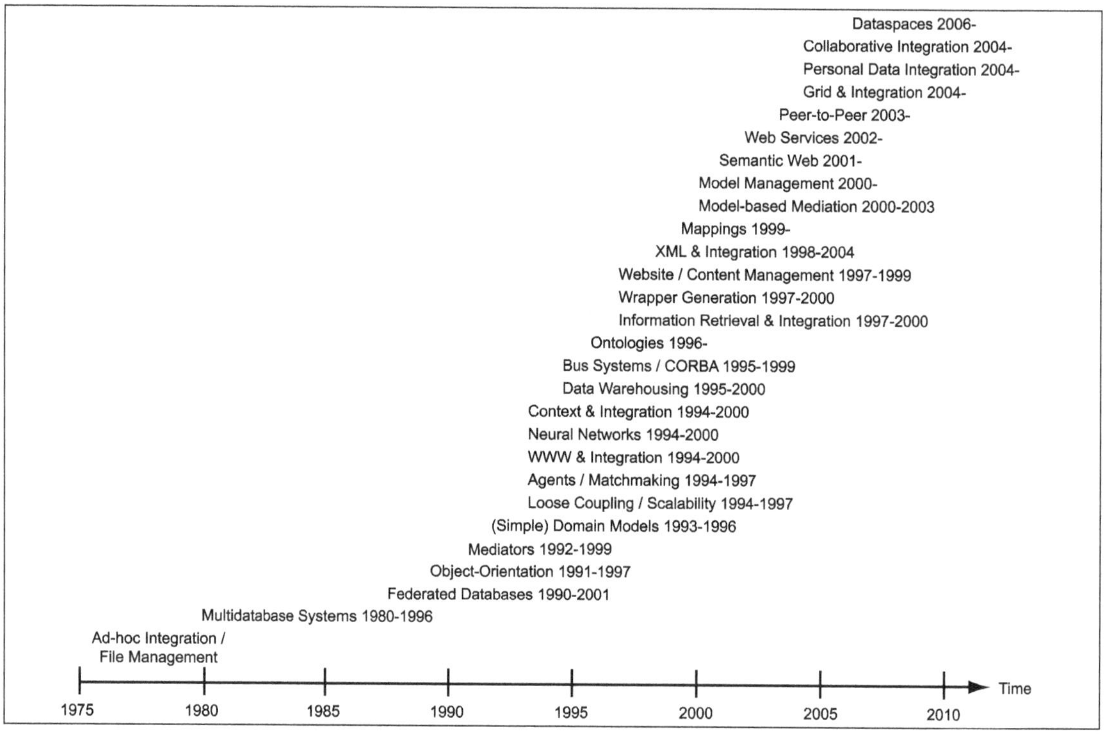

Figure: Data Integration Research Trends over Time.

One idea to overcome semantic heterogeneity in the database area is to exhaustively specify the intended real-world semantics of all data and schema elements. Unfortunately, it is impossible to completely define what a data or schema element denotes or means in the database world. Therefore, database schemas do typically not provide enough explicit semantics to interpret data always consistently and unambiguously. These problems are further worsened by the fact that semantics may be embodied in data models, conceptual schemas, application programs, the data itself, and the minds of users. Moreover, there are no absolute semantics that are valid for all potential users; semantics are relative. These difficulties concerning semantics are the reason for many still open research challenges in the area of data integration.

Ontologies — which can be defined as explicit, formal descriptions of concepts and their relationships that exist in a certain universe of discourse, together with a shared vocabulary to refer to these concepts — can contribute to solve the problem of semantic heterogeneity. Compared with other classification schemes, such as taxonomies, thesauri, or keywords, ontologies allow more complete and more precise domain models. With respect to an ontology a particular user group commits to, the semantics of data pro- vided by data sources for integration can be made explicit. Based on this shared understanding, the danger of semantic heterogeneity can be reduced. For instance, ontologies can be applied in the area of the Semantic Web to explicitly connect information from web documents to its definition and con- text in machine processable form; thereby, semantic services, such as semantic document retrieval, can be provided.

In database research, single domain models and ontologies were first applied to overcome semantic heterogeneity. As in SIMS, a domain model is used as a single ontology to which the contents of data sources are mapped. Thus, queries expressed in terms of the global ontology can be asked. In general, single-ontology approaches are useful for integration problems where all information sources to be integrated provide nearly the same view on a domain. In case the domain views of the sources differ, finding a common view becomes difficult. To overcome this problem, multi-ontology approaches like OBSERVER describe each data source with its own ontology; then, these local ontologies have to be mapped, either to a global ontology or between each other, to establish a common understanding. Thus, it is now state of the art that information systems "carry with them an explicit model of the world that they operate in, a model of what the data that they carry stand for.

Personal Semantic Data Integration in the SIRUP Approach

Mapping all data to one single domain model or ontology forces users to adapt to one single conceptualization of the world. This contrasts to the fact that receivers of integrated data widely differ in their conceptual interpretation of and preference for data — they are generally situated in various real-world contexts and have different conceptual models of the world in mind. These models do not only vary between different people in the same domain, but even for the same individual over time. COIN was one of the first research projects to consider the different contexts data providers and data receivers are situated in.

In our own research, we continue the trend of taking into account user- specific aspects in the process of semantic integration. We address the problem how individual mental domain models and personal semantics of concepts can be reflected in data integration to provide tailor-made integration for personal information needs. In the SIRUP (Semantic Integration Reflecting User-specific semantic Perspectives) approach, we investigate how data — equipped with explicit, queryable semantics — can be effectively pre- integrated on a conceptual level. Thereby, we aim at enabling users to perform declarative data integration by conceptual modeling of their individual ways to perceive a domain of interest.

Origin of our research is the observation that different users often have diverse views of reality — i.e., they perceive and conceptualize the same real- world part differently, according to their relative points of view, their information needs, and expectations. Additionally, none of these co-existing views of the real world can be regarded as being more correct than another because each view is intended for a worthy purpose. In general, we refer to this phenomenon as data receiver heterogeneity. Imposing a single global schema for all users can have severe limitations that seriously interfere with the users' individual work because thereby, data receiver sovereignty is violated. Sovereignty of data receivers refers to the fact that using integrated data must be non-intrusive; i.e., users should not be forced to adapt to any standard concerning structure and semantics of data they desire. Therefore, to take a "one integrated schema fits all" approach is definitely not a satisfactory solution. We generally subsume problems that cause a single global schema to be inappropriate for particular users as perspectual integration mistakes. These include:

- Data selection mistakes are caused when data that is available through the global schema is, from the users' perspective, inappropriately collected and selected from a given data source — for example, by only including particular local relations in the global schema.
- Source selection mistakes occur when the decision of the global schema designer, which data sources to incorporate into the global schema, differs from individual users' preferences for data from various origins (e.g., due to quality or reliability).

- Entity granularity mistakes refer to the fact that the degree of granularity in which information is represented in the global schema can be too coarse-grained (general) or too fine-grained (specialized) according to the requirements of individual users — e.g., by integrating a "seminar" and a "colloquium" relation into a general global "course" relation.
- Attribute granularity mistakes are problems of inadequate granularity concerning attributes of entities in the global schema.
- Data semantics mistakes arise when the global schema provides an integrated view on data that is semantically not related according to the individual perception of specific users. For instance, data concerning lectures and seminars may be globally merged since both represent similar forms of teaching. However, this is not useful for people who are only interested in seminars because seminar information is blurred with lectures.
- Last, but not least, data taxonomy mistakes occur when generalization/specialization hierarchies given by the global schema do not fit the perspective of the particular domain according to individual users.

In general, all six integration mistakes presented can be independently combined to form combined perspectual integration mistakes. To avoid perspectual integration mistakes, we advocate user-specific, personal semantic data integration. However, to be suitable for this, data integration approaches have to meet certain requirements. We summarize these requirements with the ASME criteria:

- Abstraction refers to shielding users from low-level heterogeneities of underlying data sources;
- Selection means the possibility of user-specific selection of data and data sources for individual integration;
- Modeling corresponds to the availability of means to incorporate user- specific perception of the domain for which integrated data is desired in the process of data integration.

Explicit semantics refers to means for explicitly representing the intended real-world semantics of data.

Current data integration approaches fail to completely meet these requirements. In response to this, we propose the SIRUP approach to personal semantic data integration to fulfill all the ASME criteria entirely. In SIRUP, data providers declaratively link groups of attributes representing alphanumeric data for particular real-world concepts (e.g., "database lecture at University of Zurich") to so-called IConcepts (short for "Intermediate Concept"). Each IConcept represents a single, distinct concept of the real world, and for each real-world concept, there is only one single IConcept in a SIRUP integration system. To make its meaning explicit for both, humans and computers, every IConcept is connected to an ontological concept (through the SOQA ontology API) that precisely represents its intended semantics. Thus, by connecting attribute data from diverse data sources to IConcepts, data from these sources is pre-integrated on a conceptual level and its in- tended semantics made explicit. In order to allow more than one data source to provide data concerning a particular concept of the real world and to distinguish the origin of data, all the attributes from each data source are organized as separate attribute groups in their respective IConcept. In addition, data providers annotate all attributes they provide for IConcepts so that metadata on attribute meaning, data types, key constraints, measurement units, etc. is explicitly available for users.

Based on these foundations, we provide a declarative integration and query language so that users, equipped with suitable IConcept search tool, can derive user-specific concepts (User Concepts) that are tailored to their information needs from the available set of IConcepts. These User Concepts can be organized in hierarchies so that individually integrated, virtual views (so-called Semantic Perspectives) representing user-specific conceptual domains models to precisely meet personal information needs can be built. In the whole process of User Concept modeling and combination, all available metadata including ontology links is automatically maintained and propagated; thus, Semantic Perspectives are annotated individual schemas over diverse data sources with explicit semantics. Finally, queries against Semantic Perspectives can be formulated that are processed by the respective SIRUP integration system. If desired, resulting data can be exported in a variety of formats, such as XML documents, relational tuples (through JDBC), and Excel spreadsheets.

Outlook

Albeit there is a remarkable history of research in the field of data integration and in spite of significant progress that has been made since the mid-1990s, ranging from concepts and algorithms to systems and commercial aspects, significant challenges still remain.

First of all, dynamic markets and increased competition demand for higher degrees of flexibility concerning data access and interoperability in the business domain. Thus, enterprises are faced with the requirement to provide multiple co-existing integrated views on their distributed corporate data sources to flexibly support different information needs. For instance, to enable banks to precisely assess credit risks according to the Basel II standard for risk management, a comprehensive and sound basis of integrated customer data is necessary. While in most banks, the needed data is available, it is often scattered over distributed sources, can be inconsistent and partially available only in hard paper copies. This alone is a challenging integration task for many banks; however, it is aggravated by the fact that alternative ways to organize the integrated data can simultaneously be necessary to support distinct information needs (e.g., categorization of credit risks according to geographical criteria or based on customer types). Here, personal data integration approaches like SIRUP can contribute.

Fostering agile cross-enterprise cooperation is another area that imposes challenges for data integration. For example, for virtual organizations as sets of organizational units that work towards a common goal, on-the-fly data integration is extremely important due to their dynamic nature. To effectively provide the needed information by all the cooperating partners in a timely manner, each of them being situated in a different real-world context having his own conceptual model of the world in mind, flexible and tailored data integration is a prerequisite. Based on adequately integrated data, required applications like supply chain management (SCM), enterprise resource planning (ERP), and customer relationship management (CRM) can be realized. Another area of inter-organizational cooperation between organizational units is e-science. Here, virtual experiments based on intensive computations and huge amounts of data are performed in grid environments, as, for example, in earth sciences, particle physics, and bioinformatics. Not only is data integration in this field required to meet diverse scientific information needs, but also scalability and manageability issues rise due to the fact that masses of data need to be handled efficiently. A key factor for interdisciplinary multi-national e-science projects is the ability to precisely satisfy the data integration and sharing needs of the involved research groups from diverse disciplines. Similarly, successful work in life sciences and e-health relies on integrated access to disparate forms of data that are spread over many biological and medical institutions by taking into account local data semantics. For these areas, user and group-specific integration approaches like SIRUP can be useful.

As one of the goals of data integration is the provision of unified access to multiple data sources, privacy and security are important issues. Thus, flexible yet effective means for access control in integrated systems are necessary. Despite the fact that integration can provide many benefits, data integration and data sharing are often hampered by privacy concerns. For instance, companies abstain from exchanging data because of fear to be exploited by competitors or regulatory institutions. Similarly, integrated access to patient data can advance medical research but may be impossible without proven measures for privacy protection and access control. Therefore, the development of techniques to guarantee data integration and data sharing without loss of privacy is essential.

Data quality, that can be characterized through accuracy, completeness, timeliness, and consistency of data, is of major interest for the usability of integrated data. In the realm of data integration, however, often complex data flows between data producers, data integrators, and consumers of integrated data have to be taken into account to provide appropriate data quality solutions. Fortunately, ontology-enhanced schemas, as used in semantic data integration, represent an important prerequisite for high quality integrated data and can thus ease quality related issues. In particular, the possibility for users to verify where data originates from and how it was combined and converted into its current form are central in enabling users to distinguish between facts and beliefs and, in consequence, to establish trust in integrated data. Therefore, data lineage and traceability issues are likely to play an important role in future integrations systems, especially when complex data transformations over widely distributed data sources are involved. In addition, globally enforcing integrity constraints can help users to trust integrated data from diverse sources.

In our own work in the SIRUP project, we focus on personal semantic integration of structured and annotated alphanumeric data. However, un- structured data, such as letters, reports, presentations, emails, and web pages constitute about 80-90% of all the data in enterprises according to current estimates by analyst firms, such as Gartner. Thus, there is a big challenge to transform this into valueable integrated information that precisely serves the needs in a dynamic business world. One approach to manage this may be provided by the emerging concept of dataspaces that postulates co-existing structured and unstructured data sets without initially requiring to integrate all data. Similar loosely-coupled approaches to data integration are represented by social networks and data sharing communities who collaboratively and incrementally contribute to building an integrated set of data. Here, the vision is to provide ease of use in community data sharing so that also non- expert users can manage and share their diverse data with minimal effort. However, the future needs to show to what extent these approaches can contribute to reach the grand challenge as formulated in the Asilomar report on database research, i.e., to make it easy for everyone to store, organize, access, and analyze the majority of human information online.

References

- Data-Requirements-Analysis: academia.edu, Retrieved 18 April, 2019
- Data-modeling-examples-for-analytics, analytics-stack-guide: panoply.io, Retrieved 21 July, 2019
- Data-warehousing: guru99.com, Retrieved 24 March , 2019
- Analytics-platform, definition: techopedia.com, Retrieved 13 July, 2019
- Operational-data-store-ods, definition: techopedia.com, Retrieved 3 June, 2019
- Metadata-definition-and-examples: lifewire.com, Retrieved 12 April, 2019
- Types, metadatabasics: marciazeng.slis.kent.edu, Retrieved 21 March , 2019
- Data-profiling-best-practices, analytics-stack-guide: panoply.io, Retrieved 23 June, 2019
- Business-rule-analysis, ba-techniques: businessanalystlearnings.com, Retrieved 17 March, 2019
- Business-rule-management-system-brms, definition: techopedia.com, Retrieved 13 February, 2019
- What-is-a-business-rules-management-system, corticon-faqs, faqs: progress.com, Retrieved 7 May, 2019
- Data-rule, quality, data: gerardnico.com, Retrieved 13 July, 2019
- Data-quality-monitoring-the-basis-for-ongoing-information-quality-management: tdwi.org, Retrieved 10 May, 2019

4

Utilization of Business Data

The usage of business data involves the extraction of business intelligence from unstructured data, drawing insights from the collection of data and reusing data. These diverse uses of business data as well as the use of data mining for the purpose of predictive analysis have been thoroughly discussed in this chapter.

Deriving Business Intelligence from Unstructured Data

Data warehouse is a subject-oriented, integrated, time-variant, and non-volatile collection of data which helps in decision-making process. According to Kimball, a data warehouse is designed for querying and analysing structured data which can be divided into facts and dimensions. Structured data has a pre-defined schema and is record oriented whereas Unstructured Data (USD) is vast, freeform and exists in variety of forms. It poses difficulty in querying and analysis due to lack of well- defined schema.

The organizations successfully apply the Data Warehouse and OLAP technologies to build decision support systems for organizing and analyzing the huge amounts of structured data that companies store in their databases. Whereas the need of the hour lies in the discovery of such methodologies and tools that can deal with the massive storage and retrieval of documents with large text-rich sections and hence cater to BI applications. Companies and enterprises also circulate an enormous amount of information as text-rich documents – pdf, word files, e-mails, chat files, blogs, organization forums and many other. Nowadays, World Wide Web has become the greatest source of information, organizations can now find highly valuable information about their business environment on the Internet, which is a benefit although but has created around 80% of the data floating to be in unstructured format which is difficult to analyze and store in data warehouse. Data warehouses are the huge data repositories which stores historical and current data of enterprise worlds and thus keep all the data at one place. Structured data is stored easily into the data warehouse but unstructured data poses problem in such storage. But actionable knowledge is pertinent in unstructured textual documents. The need to manage unstructured data arises due to the fact that more than three-fourth of information on internet is unstructured. The advantages one can get out of Unstructured Data management is Business Value, Better information, Timely information, Relevant Information.

Traditional unstructured data sources are very high in volume. So, the challenges facing data are as follows: getting the right information from it, transforming it into knowledge, analyzing it to find patterns & trends, storing information for fast & efficient access, managing the workflow and finally, making useful BI reports.

To investigate any fact or incident, we need to analyze multi format data from multiple sources in different time frames. The integrated information architecture facilitates better insight of multi-dimensional information for the targeted entities. It also provides better insight, more powerful statistical, semantic, co-relational and reporting capabilities. Faster read and write ability provides collected data in near real time analytical capabilities. The requirement is to make the warehouse capable of handling large data sets that are challenging to store, analyze, search, visualize, share, and manage.

Total Data Warehouse (TDW) using Text Annotation

The process of capturing intelligent information from unstructured data is performed in two phases. In the first phase, structure is added to the unstructured data via named entity extraction. After that results are integrated with structured data. The output obtained from phase 1(that will be TDW), acts as an input to phase 2, in which BI application requirements are catered by the TDW.

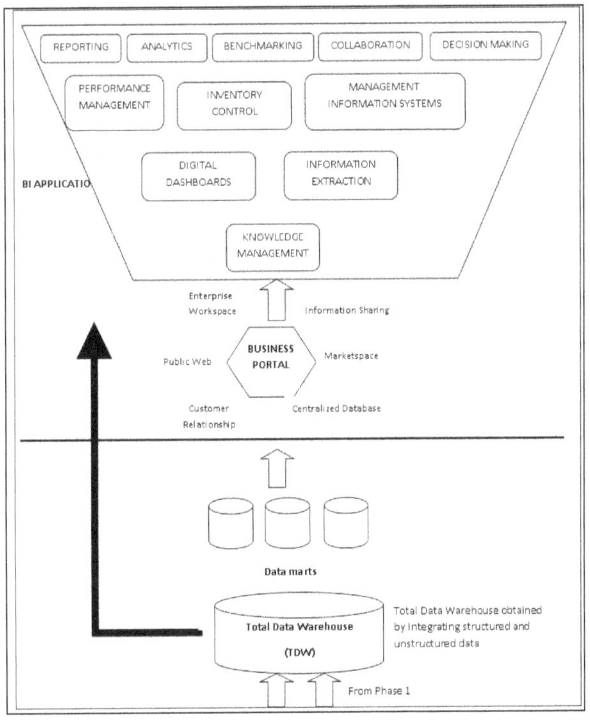

ETL, text tagging, and annotation are used to build the total data warehouse (phase 1).

As shown in figure, data within an enterprise can come from traditional transactional sources such as an RDBMS, legacy systems, and repositories of enterprise applications, and from unstructured data sources such as file systems, document and content management systems, and mail systems.

To build an effective decision-support backbone, this data must be moved into the TDW. An ETL process executes the required formatting, cleansing, and modification before moving data from transactional systems to the TDW. In the case of unstructured data sources, the tagging and annotation platform extracts information based on domain ontology into an XML database. As in figure, extraction of data from an XML database into the TDW is accomplished with an ETL tool. This materializes the unified data creation into the TDW—the foundation for the organization's decision-support and BI needs.

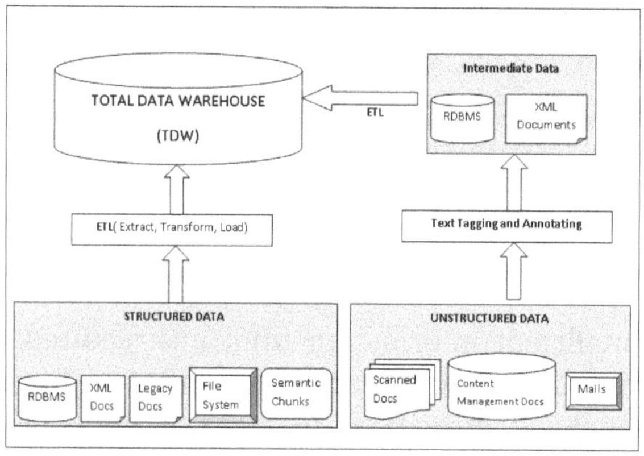

Building business intelligence applications from the TDW: phase 2.

Product Performance Insights from Customer Warranty Claims Data

An example of BI application is to analyze warranty claims data in case of a product's failure or defect. Warranty claims have some structured and some unstructured content. These claim forms constitute warranty data that is to be analysed for gaining business intelligence, and moreover diagnosing the problem in the company product. A claim form has details such as product id, product name, model number, date and time of purchase, customer name and address, defects encountered etc. These forms are appended into a database (may be as BLOB). Some of these entered information is structured data which is in defined format and has finite answers in defined fields. But the comments section in the form has freeform English language text which is unstructured and the most important information for understanding and analyzing the defect encountered. The huge number of claim forms renders the manual reading of all comments time-consuming and practically difficult. The idea is to automate text analysis that collects claim form information by extracting information from unstructured data and linking it with an external knowledge base.

Figure illustrates a claim form entered by a customer and received by a company repair center. The form is partially structured for the reason that some fields have a defined format. Other fields allow the user to enter paragraph form text. The user provides details that describe the technical defect in the product. The text of the user's comments contains many domain specific entities. For example, camera is an entity of type "Computer Parts", crashed is a "Defect" entity. Similarly technician's problem analysis is also written in a natural language text, from which many real world business entities can be derived. The basic technology used to tag and annotate the text can be based on a dictionary lookup created from an external knowledge base.

As depicted on the right side of figure the output of the text tagging and annotation process is in XML file format containing the extracted entities enclosed within XML tags. The XML file produced by the text tagging process is in a form amenable to query, search, and integration with other structured data sources.

The first step in gathering business intelligence from these claim forms is to tag and annotate the text—this is the named entity extraction. In the second step, the tagged data is combined and analyzed with an external structured data repository. The output of text tagging can also be imported into a relational database.

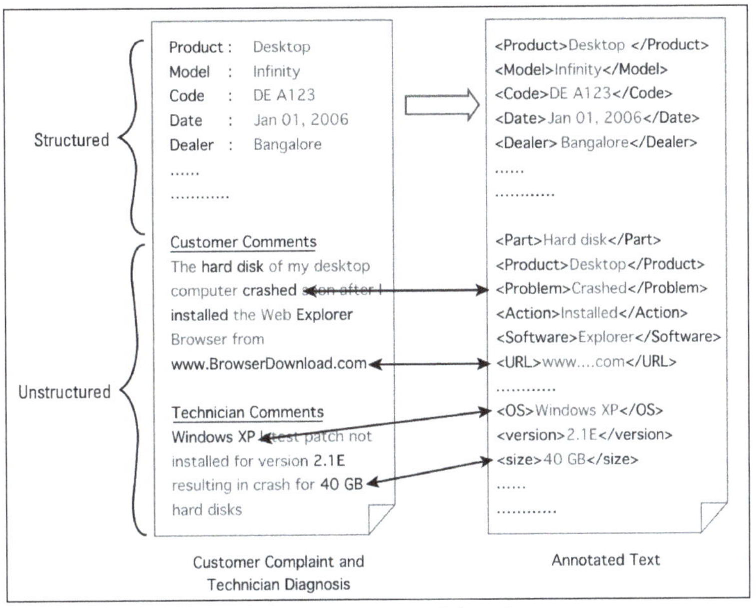

Annotating warranty claims data.

Text tagging and text annotation plays efficient role to integrate structured and unstructured data. The resulting total data warehouse becomes the basic framework for BI applications. The BI benefits of deploying a text analytics methodology speeds up the identification of product defects and their consequent repairmen or replacement by integrating the unstructured data entered by customers and technical assistant with the structured data stored in a relational database. As shown, the methodology can be applied to help an enterprise gather intelligent information from meetings text or gain intelligence about product performances from customer warranty claim forms. The total data warehouse can be employed as a framework for efficient and accurate business decisions.

Drawing Insights from Collection of Data

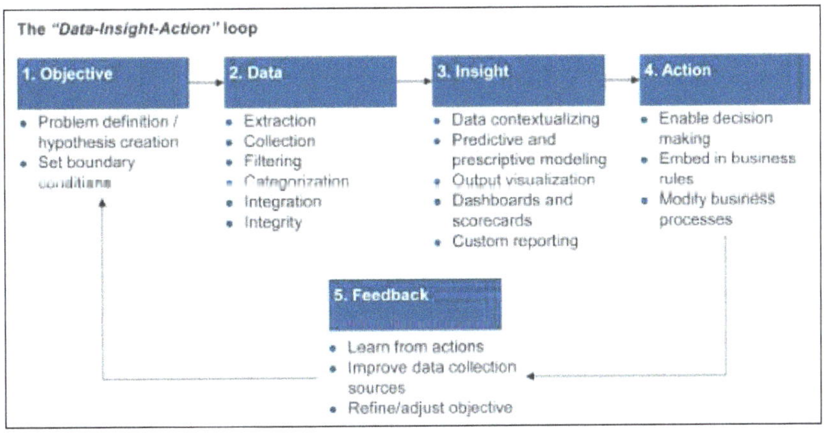

Customer Profiling

Customer profiling is a way to create a portrait of your customers to help you make design decisions concerning your service. Your customers are broken down into groups of customers sharing similar goals and characteristics and each group is given a representative with a photo, a name, and a description. A small group of customer profiles or 'personas' are then used to make key design decisions with, e.g. "which of these features will help Mary achieve her goals most easily?

Customer Profiles are a useful Design Tool

Customer profiles are 'customer types', which are generated to represent the typical users of a product or service, and are used to help the project team make customer centred decisions without confusing the scope of the project with personal opinion.

Also known as personas, customer profiles are created from an understanding of the typical audience generated from customer research, and focus on the different goals and scenarios the customers might and themselves in when interacting with a specific touch-point (website, catalogue, shop etc.). Unlike typical demographics or segmentation, differences in geography, income, status, etc. do not necessarily split customers into different groups. For example, when looking to buy the latest CD by The Kooks for a nephew, a 24 year old single mother of three living in the south of England will use Amazon in the same way that a married 53 year old senior executive living in the north of England would do. Their goal is the same, to buy a specific CD online quickly and easily.

When creating a profile the critical information needed for each user is their goals (why are they interacting with the touch-point? – to buy a CD), their tasks (what will they be doing when they interact with the touch-point – browse for The Kooks CDs, purchase the latest CD, arrange delivery to a different address?), and the touch-point goals (to sell a CD, clearly show which of The Kooks CDs is the latest, cross and up sell, etc.). For the example above very loose manner you might create a profile called Jane, who is 31, married, has three young children, is time poor, and needs to buy The Kooks CD online, but doesn't know who The Kooks are or what their latest CD is called. Jane will represent all the users who want to buy a specific product but are unsure of all the details.

Advantages of Customer Profiling

Most projects evolve from an idea, and grow through the opinions of influential members of the project team. The trouble is that these influential members of the project team are rarely the end user or customer. This often results in a product or service that doesn't quite meet customer expectations or needs, and the interaction with it might be clumsy. Similarly, the decision-making process can be delayed due to a clash of different opinions, with no member of the project team able to make a definite agreement on whether X or Y is best for this project.

So when the project team is discussing the scope, or making design decisions, they can talk about whether Jane's needs and expectations are being met, regardless of what the influential project team member might deem as a 'cool' piece of functionality.

Disadvantages of Customer Profiling

Traditional marketers often react negatively to the suggestion of customer profiling because it does not cater for the standard demographics that are traditionally used and taught. However, in this situation it is important to explain that profiles are not designed to replace general marketing demographics, which are used for Macro marketing and advertising campaigns, but are created for the specific touch point (website, kiosk, catalogue, etc.) as a design tool for the project team to make better decisions.

Customer Knowledge

A company must have customer knowledge. Why – simply because by definition this knowledge is about understanding customers in totality – their needs, goals, wants, emotional reasons for buying, and other such aspects. Without this knowledge, it would be impossible for a company to provide top class customer service, ensure customized products and services, and align its business processes and operations such that it is able to forge strong relationships with customers. Customer knowledge is about collecting, collating, and using the data that customer's leave online – data such as browsing history, buying patterns, search behaviour, and other analytical pieces of information with regard to their preferences.

Companies must know as much as possible about their customers, however, the information customers leave is scattered and difficult to use unless companies collect it and make some sense from all of it. In addition, customer knowledge should be visible, shareable, and possible to be analysed by those teams that directly and indirectly serve customers, in order to ensure that the company is able to hear and respond to whatever the customers say and need. Despite understanding the importance of customer knowledge, several companies fail to provide what customers need and are unable to comprehend their preferences. This, according to research, happens because companies often turn complacent, taking their understanding of customers to be absolute based on historical data and their accomplishments with regard to customer needs. The fact is that customers change – their needs alter over time, and their expectations develop depending on the market conditions and their business needs. Hence, what may have been relevant for a customer in the past may be obsolete in their current situation, and unless companies have the most current customer knowledge, the gap the between actual needs of customers and what they provide, will continue to exist and widen. When this gap becomes too large customers often turn away from a company and seek another company with which to engage in business.

Customer knowledge is extremely beneficial for any company. If a company accurately captures customer data, it would be easier to organize and share this data within the company for use in various departments. Obviously, the customer service teams would need access in order to enhance their interactions with customers, the sales and marketing teams would be able to prepare customized content and pitches for customers, the accounts teams would have better control over payments and refunds, and other uses for teams. It would also enable the leadership of the company to understand buying patterns, 'visit' behaviour of customers on the website and social media sites, sudden changes in buying behaviour, reasons for complaints, and other such crucial quantifiable factors.

As customer knowledge becomes deeper, a company would be able to build better and more emotional connections and rapport with their customers. This of course, is an on-going process since needs and expectations of customers change continually, and as long as a company can keep pace, the relationships with customers would sustain. Smart companies understand that they must not limit customer knowledge to their own relationship with the customers. A company must also have information on what customers spend with competitors and their relationship with them. This would enable a company to find ways and formulate strategies to outdo their competitors, such that customers spend more on the company rather than elsewhere. Of course, it would be impractical to expect that a company is able to collect every single piece of information on their customers, but whatever data it may have, should be useful and such that a company is able to make things easier for its customers.

Since businesses exist for and because of customers, the aim of collecting customer knowledge should be develop and sustain robust customer relationships, with an eye on customer loyalty. This knowledge should be the guiding factor for companies to know which offerings to give customers, when to give them, and at what rate. In addition, customer knowledge would enable a company to mould and monitor customer behaviour to advantage, and help the company with designing future products and services, and compete in new markets successfully. Customer knowledge would also help a company to know the reasons for which customers may stay or defect and whether lowered pricing by a competitor could be one of the reasons leading the company's customers away.

Many companies skimp on collecting and analysing customer knowledge simply because it requires a great deal of effort and cost. Hence, some companies tend to collect such knowledge only for larger accounts in the B2B realm, where the value they get would justify the costs they would incur on collecting and analysing huge amounts of customer data. This may not be a sensible approach for most companies – customer knowledge should be aimed at getting an all-round and overall view of all the customers of a company, in order to improve sales, profits, and gain customer loyalty. Customer knowledge must not however, be confused with other systems of customer data management – CRM for example. According to experts, while there may be some factors that overlap, CRM is more structured but has a lesser variety of information to build insights leading to stronger ties with customers.

Experts also add that customer knowledge if collected correctly would include information about individual customers that would tell the company who they are and, what they do, and what their expectations would be from the association with the company. In addition, customer knowledge would enable a company to analyse all the customers as a whole, in order to put together behaviour patterns, needs, and allow the company to customize its offerings based on individual customer requirements. Customer knowledge would therefore, have both qualitative insights – preferences, likes, and dislikes, and quantitative insights – number of orders, total value of the customer's business. With an all-round view of customers, a company would be better equipped at preparing targeted communication and content, enabling an even stronger bond and relationship with each customer.

Customer-focused companies understand how to use customer knowledge. This means that they know how and when to address concerns that customers may have with regard to the safety and privacy of their information. These companies are constantly aware that every customer is a live person and are careful not to treat any customer as data or a number, but with a lot of respect and care. It is advisable for companies to be completely honest and transparent about why they collect customer knowledge, the manner in which it is stored, and how it is used. This is reassuring for customers, knowing that their data is being used to make things easier for them and in their best interest, and that the company would never use the data to manipulate them in any manner. The better a company can do this, the more trust and reliability it would build among customers and in the market, thereby increasing customer loyalty and market share.

Developing Consumer Behavior Models

Customer Behavior Modeling is the creation of a mathematical construct to represent the common behaviors observed among particular groups of customers in order to predict how similar customers will behave under similar circumstances. Customer behavior models are typically based on data mining of customer data, and each model is designed to answer one question at one point in time. For example, a customer model can be used to predict what a particular group of customers will do in response to a particular marketing action. If the model is sound and the marketer follows the recommendations it generated, then the marketer will observe that a majority of the customers in the group responded as predicted by the model.

Difficulty of Customer Behavior Modeling

Unfortunately, building customer behavior models is typically a difficult and expensive task. This is because the smart and experienced customer analytics experts who know how to do it are expensive and difficult to find, and because the mathematical techniques they need to use are complex and risky. Furthermore, even once a model has been built, it is difficult to manipulate it for the purposes of the marketer, i.e., to determine exactly what marketing actions to take for each customer or group of customers.

Finally, despite their mathematical complexity, most customer models are actually relatively simple. Because of this necessity, most customer behavior models ignore so many pertinent factors that the predictions they generate are generally not very reliable.

RFM Approach to Customer Behavior Analysis

Many customer behavior models are based on an analysis of Recency, Frequency and Monetary Value (RFM). This means that customers who have spent money at a business recently are more likely than others to spend again, that customers who spend money more often at a business are more likely than others to spend again and that customers who have spent the most money at a business are more likely than others to spend again.

RFM is popular because it is easy to understand by marketers and business managers, it does not require specialized software and it holds true for customers in almost every business and industry.

Unfortunately, RFM alone does not deliver the level of accuracy that marketers require. Firstly,

RFM models only describe what a customer has done in the past and cannot accurately predict future behaviors. Secondly, RFM models look at customers at a particular point in time and do not take into account how the customer has behaved in the past or in what lifecycle stage the customer is currently found. This second point is critical because accurate customer modeling is very weak unless the customer's behavior is analyzed over time.

Better Approach to Customer Behavior Modeling

Optimove introduces customer behavior modeling methods which are far more advanced and effective than conventional methods. By combining a number of technologies into an integrated, closed-loop system, marketers enjoy highly accurate customer behavior analysis in an easy-to-use application.

Optimove achieves market-leading predictive customer behaviour modeling with the combination of the following capabilities:

1. Segmenting customers into small groups and addressing individual customers based on actual behaviors – instead of hard-coding any pre-conceived notions or assumptions of what makes customers similar to one another, and instead of only looking at aggregated/ averaged data which hides important facts about individual customers.
2. Tracking customers and how they move among different segments over time (i.e., dynamic segmentation), including customer lifecycle context and cohort analysis – instead of just determining in what segments customers are now without regard for how they arrived there.
3. Accurately predicting the future behaviors of customers (e.g., convert, churn, spend more, spend less) using predictive customer behavior modeling techniques – instead of just looking in the rear-view mirror of historical data.
4. Using advanced calculations to determine the customer lifetime value (LTV) of every customer and basing decisions on it – instead of looking only at the short-term revenue that a customer may bring the company.
5. Knowing, based on objective metrics, exactly what marketing actions to do now, for each customer, in order to maximize the long-term value of every customer – instead of trying to figure out what to do based on a dashboard or pile of reports.
6. Employing marketing machine learning technologies that can reveal insights and make recommendations for improving customer marketing that human marketers are unlikely to spot on their own.

One way to think of the difference between conventional approaches and the Optimove approach is that the former is like a customer snapshot whereas the latter is a customer animation. The animated view of the customer is far more revealing, allowing much more accurate customer behavior predictions.

Customer Lifetime Value

Customer lifetime value (CLV) is gaining increasing importance as a marketing metric in both academia and practice. Companies such as Harrah's, IBM, Capital One, LL Bean, ING, and others are routinely using CLV as a tool to manage and measure the success of their business. Academics have written scores of articles and dozens of books on this topic in the past decade. There are several factors that account for the growing interest in this concept.

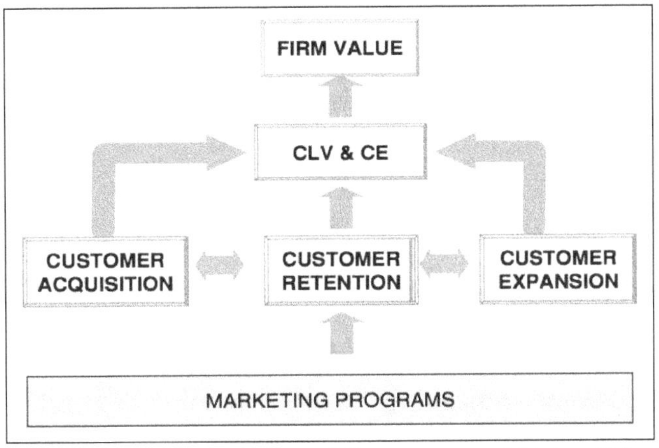

Conceptual Framework for Modeling Customer Lifetime Value.

First, there is an increasing pressure in companies to make marketing accountable. Traditional marketing metrics such as brand awareness, attitudes, or even sales and share are not enough to show a return on marketing investment. In fact, marketing actions that improve sales or share may actually harm the long-run profitability of a brand.

Second, financial metrics such as stock price and aggregate profit of the firm or a business unit do not solve the problem either. Although these measures are useful, they have limited diagnostic capability. Recent studies have found that not all customers are equally profitable. Therefore, it may be desirable to "fire" some customers or allocate different resources to different group of customers. Such diagnostics are not possible from aggregate financial measures. In contrast, CLV is a disaggregate metric that can be used to identify profitable customers and allocate resources accordingly. At the same time, CLV of current and future customers (also called customer equity or CE) is a good proxy of overall firm value.

Third, improvements in information technology have made it easy for firms to collect enormous amount of customer transaction data. This allows firms to use data on revealed preferences rather than intentions. Furthermore, sampling is no longer necessary when you have the entire customer base available. At the same time, sophistication in modeling has enabled marketers to convert these data into insights. Current technology makes it possible to leverage these insights and customize marketing programs for individual customers.

Approaches to Modeling

Fundamentals of CLV Modeling

CLV is generally defined as the present value of all future profits obtained from a customer over his or her life of relationship with a firm. CLV is similar to the discounted cash flow approach used in finance. However, there are two key differences. First, CLV is typically defined and estimated at an individual customer or segment level. This allows us to differentiate between customers who are more profitable than others rather than simply examining average profitability. Second, unlike finance, CLV explicitly incorporates the possibility that a customer may defect to competitors in the future.

CLV for a customer (omitting customer subscript) is,

$$CLV = \sum_{t=0}^{T} \frac{(p_t - c_t) r_t}{(1 + i)^t} - AC$$

Where,

P_t = price paid by a consumer at time t,

C_t = direct cost of servicing the customer at time t,

i = discount rate or cost of capital for the firm,

r_t= probability of customer repeat buying or being "alive" at time t,

AC = acquisition cost, and

T = time horizon for estimating CLV.

In spite of this simple formulation, researchers have used different variations in modeling and estimating CLV. Some researchers have used an arbitrary time horizon or expected customer lifetime whereas others have used an infinite time horizon. Gupta and Lehmann showed that using an expected customer lifetime generally overestimates CLV, sometimes quite substantially.

Gupta and Lehmann also showed that if margins (p – c) and retention rates are constant over time and we use an infinite time horizon, then CLV simplifies to the following expression:

$$CLV = \sum_{t=0}^{\infty} \frac{(p_t - c_t) r^t}{(1 + i)^t} = m \frac{r}{(1+i-r)}.$$

In other words, CLV simply becomes margin (m) times a margin multiple ($r/1 + i - r$). When retention rate is 90% and discount rate is 12%, the margin multiple is about four. Gupta and Lehmann showed that when margins grow at a constant rate "g," the margin multiple becomes $r/[1 + i - r(1 + g)]$.

It is also important to point out that most modeling approaches ignore competition because of the lack of competitive data. Finally, how frequently we update CLV depends on the dynamics of a particular market. For example, in markets where margins and retention may change dramatically over a short period of time (e.g., due to competitive activity), it may be appropriate to reestimate CLV more frequently.

Researchers either build separate models for customer acquisition, retention, and margin or sometimes combine two of these components. For example, and Reinartz, Thomas, and Kumar simultaneously captured customer acquisition and retention. Fader, captured recency and frequency in one model and built a separate model for monetary value. However, the approaches for modeling these components or CLV differ across researchers.

RFM Models

RFM models have been used in direct marketing for more than 30 years. Given the low response rates in this industry (typically 2% or less), these models were developed to target marketing programs (e.g., direct mail) at specific customers with the objective to improve response rates. Prior to these models, companies typically used demographic profiles of customers for targeting purposes. However, research strongly suggests that past purchases of consumers are better predictors of their future purchase behavior than demographics.

RFM models create "cells" or groups of customers based on three variables—Recency, Frequency, and Monetary value of their prior purchases. The simplest models classify customers into five groups based on each of these three variables. This gives 5 × 5 × 5 or 125 cells. Studies show that customers' response rates vary the most by their recency, followed by their purchase frequency and monetary value. It is also common to use weights for these cells to create "scores" for each group. Mailing or other marketing communication programs are then prioritized based on the scores of different RFM groups.

Whereas RFM or other scoring models attempt to predict customers' behavior in the future and are therefore implicitly linked to CLV, they have several limitations. First, these models predict behavior in the next period only. However, to estimate CLV, we need to estimate customers' purchase behavior not only in Period 2 but also in Periods 3, 4, 5, and so on. Second, RFM variables are imperfect indicators of true underlying behavior, that is, hey are drawn from a true distribution. This aspect is completely ignored in RFM models. Third, these models ignore the fact that consumers' past behavior may be a result of firm's past marketing activities. Despite these limitations, RFM models remain a mainstay of the industry because of their ease of implementation in practice.

How Well do RFM Models do?

Several recent studies have compared CLV models with RFM models and found CLV models to be superior. used a catalog retailer's data of almost 12,000 customers over 3 years to compare CLV and RFM models. They found that the revenue from the top 30% of customers based on the CLV model was 33% higher than the top 30% selected based on the RFM model. also compared several competing models for customer selection. Using data on almost 2,000 customers from a business-to-business (B2B) manufacturer, they found that the profit generated from the top 5% customers as selected by the CLV model was 10% to 50% higher than the profit generated from the top 5% customers from other models (e.g., RFM, past value, etc).

Incorporating RFM in CLV Models

One key limitation of RFM models is that they are scoring models and do not explicitly provide a dollar number for customer value. However, RFM are important past purchase variables that should be good predictors of future purchase behavior of customers. Fader, Hardie, and Lee (2005) showed how RFM variables can be used to build a CLV model that overcomes many of its limitations. They also showed that RFM are sufficient statistics for their CLV model. One interesting result of their approach is the iso-CLV curves, which show different values of R, F, or M that produce the same CLV of a customer.

Probability Models

A probability model is a representation of the world in which observed behavior is viewed as the realization of an underlying stochastic process governed by latent (unobserved) behavioral characteristics, which in turn vary across individuals. The focus of the model-building effort is on telling a simple paramorphic story that describes (and predicts) the observed behavior instead of trying to explain differences in observed behavior as a function of covariates (as is the case with any regression model). The modeler is typically quite happy to assume that consumers' behavior varies across the population according to some probability distribution. For the purposes of computing CLV, we wish to be able to make predictions about whether an individual will still be an active customer in the future and, if so, what his or her purchasing behavior will be. One of the first models to explicitly address these issues is the Pareto/NBD model developed by Schmittlein, Morrison, and Colombo, which describes the flow of transactions in noncontractual setting. Underlying this model is the following set of assumptions:

- A customer's relationship with the firm has two phases: He or she is "alive" for an unobserved period of time, and then becomes permanently inactive.
- While "alive," the number of transactions made by a customer can be characterized by a Poisson process.
- Heterogeneity in the transaction rate across customers follows a gamma distribution.
- Each customer's unobserved "lifetime" is distributed exponential.
- Heterogeneity in dropout rates across customers follows a gamma distribution.
- The transaction rates and the dropout rates vary independently across customers.

The second and third assumptions result in the NBD, whereas the next two assumptions yield the Pareto (of the second kind) distribution. This model requires only two pieces of information about each customer's past purchasing history: his or her "recency" (when his or her last transaction occurred) and "frequency" (how many transactions he or she made in a specified time period). The notation used to represent this information is (x, t_x, T), where x is the number of transactions observed in the time period $(0, T]$ and t_x $(0 < t_x \le T)$ is the time of the last transaction. Using these two key summary statistics, Schmittlein, Morrison, and Colombo derived expressions for a number of managerially relevant quantities, including (a) P(alive | x, tx, T), the probability that an individual with observed behavior (x, tx, T) is still an active customer at time T, and (b) E[$Y(t)$ | x, tx, T], the expected number of transactions in the period $(T, T + t]$ for an individual with observed behavior (x, tx, T).

This basic model has been used by Reinartz and Kumar as an input into their lifetime value calculations. However, rather than simply using it as an input to a CLV calculation, it is possible to derive an expression for CLV directly from this model. As an intermediate step, it is necessary to augment this model for the flow of transactions with a model for the value of each transaction. Schmittlein and Peterson, Colombo and Jiang, and Fader, Hardie, and Berger have all proposed models based on the following story for the spend process:

- The dollar value of a customer's given transaction varies randomly around his mean transaction value.

- Mean transaction values vary across customers but do not vary over time for any given individual.

Fader, Hardie, and Berger are able to derive the following explicit formula for the expected lifetime revenue stream associated with a customer (in a noncontractual setting) with "recency" t_x, "frequency" x (in a time period of length T), and an average transaction value of m_x, with continuous compounding at rate of interest δ:

$$\mathrm{CLV}(\delta \mid r, \alpha, s, \beta, p, q, \gamma, x, t_x, T)$$
$$= \frac{\alpha^r \beta^s \delta^{s-1} \Gamma(r + x\_1)\Psi(s, s; \delta(\beta + T))}{\Gamma(r)(\alpha + T)^{r+x+1} L(r, \alpha, s, \beta \mid x, t_x, T)}$$
$$\times \frac{(\gamma + m_x x)p}{px + q - 1}$$

where (r, α, s, β) are the Pareto/NBD parameters, (p, q, γ) are the parameters of the transaction value model, $\psi(\cdot)$ is the confluent hypergeometric function of the second kind, and $L(\cdot)$ is the Pareto/NBD likelihood function.

The Pareto/NBD model is a good benchmark model when considering noncontractual settings where transaction can occur at any point in time. It is not an appropriate model for any contractual business settings. Nor is it an appropriate model for noncontractual settings where transactions can only occur at fixed (discrete) points in time, such as attendance at annual academic conferences, arts festivals, and so on, as in such settings, the assumption of Poisson purchasing is not relevant. Thus, models such as Fader, beta-binominal/beta-geometric (BG/BB) model or Morrison et al.'s brand loyal with exit model would be appropriate alternatives. Several researchers have also created models of buyer behavior using Markov chains.

Econometric Models

Many econometric models share the underlying philosophy of the probability models. Specifically, studies that use hazard models to estimate customer retention are similar to the NBD/Pareto models except for the fact that the former may use more general hazard functions and typically incorporate covariates. Generally these studies model customer acquisition, retention, and expansion (cross-selling or margin) and then combine them to estimate CLV.

Customer Acquisition

Customer acquisition refers to the first-time purchase by new or lapsed customers. Research in this area focuses on the factors that influence buying decisions of these new customers. It also attempts to link acquisition with customers' retention behavior as well as CLV and CE. The basic model for customer acquisition is a logit or a probit. Specifically, customer j at time t (i.e., $Z_{jt} = 1$) is modeled as follows:

$$Z^*_{jt} = \alpha_j X_{jt} + \varepsilon_{jt}$$
$$Z_{jt} = 1 \ if \ Z^*_{jt} > 0$$
$$Z_{jt} = 0 \ if \ Z^*_{jt} \le 0,$$

where Xjt are the covariates and αj are consumer-specific response parameters. Depending on the assumption of the error term, one can obtain a logit or a probit model.

Although intuition and some case studies suggest that acquisition and retention should be linked, early work in this area assumed these two outcomes to be independent. Later, indirectly linked acquisition and retention by using a logit model for acquisition and a right-censored Tobit model for CLV. More recently, several authors have explicitly linked acquisition and retention.

Using data for airline pilots' membership, Thomas showed the importance of linking acquisition and retention decisions. She found that ignoring this link can lead to CLV estimates that are 6% to 52% different from her model. Thomas, Blattberg, and Fox found that whereas low price increased the probability of acquisition, it reduced the relationship duration. Therefore, customers who may be inclined to restart a relationship may not be the best customers in terms of retention. Thomas, Reinartz, and Kumar empirically validated this across two industries. They also found that customers should be acquired based on their profitability rather than on the basis of the cost to acquire and retain them.

Lewis showed how promotions that enhance customer acquisition may be detrimental in the long run. He found that if new customers for a newspaper subscription were offered regular price, their renewal probability was 70%. However, this dropped to 35% for customers who were acquired through a $1 weekly discount. Similar effects were found in the context of Internet grocery where renewal probabilities declined from 40% for regular-priced acquisitions to 25% for customers acquired through a $10 discount. On average, a 35% acquisition discount resulted in customers with about half the CLV of regularly acquired customers. In other words, unless these acquisition discounts double the baseline acquisition rate of customers, they would be detrimental to the CE of a firm. These results are consistent with the long-term promotion effects found in the scanner data.

In contrast, Anderson and Simester conducted three field studies and found that deep price discounts have a positive impact on the long-run profitability of first-time buyers but negative long-term impact on established customers. The dynamics of pricing was also examined by Lewis using a dynamic programming approach. He found that for new customers, price sensitivity increases with time lapsed, whereas for current customers, it decreases with time. Therefore, the optimal pricing involves offering a series of diminishing discounts (e.g., $1.70 per week for new newspaper subscribers, $2.20 at first renewal, $2.60 at second renewal, and full price of $2.80 later) rather than a single deep discount.

Customer Retention

Customer retention is the probability of a customer being "alive" or repeat buying from a firm. In contractual settings (e.g., cellular phones, magazine subscriptions), customers inform the firm when they terminate their relationship. However, in noncontractual settings (e.g., buying books from Amazon), a firm has to infer whether a customer is still active. For example, as of October 2005, eBay reported 168 million registered customers but only 68 million active customers. Most companies define a customer as active based on simple rules of thumb. For example, eBay defines a customer to be active if she or he has bid, bought, or listed on its site during the past 12 months. In contrast, researchers rely on statistical models to assess the probability of retention.

There are two broad classes of retention models. The first class considers customer defection as permanent or "lost for good" and typically uses hazard models to predict probability of customer defection. The second class considers customer switching to competitors as transient or "always a share" and typically uses migration or Markov models. We briefly discuss each class of models.

Hazard models fall into two broad groups—accelerated failure time (AFT) or proportional hazard (PH) models. The AFT models have the following form.

$$\ln\left(t_j\right) = \beta_j X_j + \sigma\mu_j,$$

where t is the purchase duration for customer j and X are the covariates. If $\sigma = 1$ and μ has an extreme value distribution, then we get an exponential duration model with constant hazard rate. Different specifications of σ and μ lead to different models such as Weibull or generalized gamma, and Venkatesan and Kumar used a generalized gamma for modeling relationship duration. For the k th interpurchase time for customer j, this model can be represented as follows:

$$f\left(t_{jk}\right) = \frac{\gamma}{\Gamma(\alpha)\lambda_j^{\alpha\gamma}} t_{jk}^{\alpha\gamma-1}\, e^{-(tjj/\lambda j\,)\gamma}$$

where α and γ are the shape parameters of the distribution and λ_j is the scale parameter for customer j. Customer heterogeneity is incorporated by allowing λ_j to vary across consumers according to an inverse generalized gamma distribution.

Proportional hazard models are another group of commonly used duration models. These models specify the hazard rate (λ) as a function of baseline hazard rate (λ_o) and covariates (X),

$$\lambda(t;\, X) = \lambda_0(t)\exp(\beta X)$$

Different specifications for the baseline hazard rate provide different duration models such as exponential, Weibull, or Gompertz. This approach was used by Bolton.

Instead of modeling time duration, we can model customer retention or churn as a binary outcome (e.g., the probability of a wireless customer defecting in the next month). This is a form of discrete-time hazard model. Typically the model takes the form of a logit or probit. Due to its simplicity and ease of estimation, this approach is commonly used in the industry. Neslin et al. (in press) described these models which were submitted by academics and practitioners as part of a "churn tournament."

In the second class of models, customers are allowed to switch among competitors and this is generally modeled using a Markov model. These models estimate transition probabilities of a customer being in a certain state. Using these transition probabilities, CLV can be estimated as follows:

$$V' = \sum_{t=0}^{T} \left[(1 + i)^{-1}\ P\right]^{t} R$$

where V′ is the vector of expected present value or CLV over the various transition states; P is the transition probability matrix, which is assumed to be constant over time; and R is the reward or margin vector, which is also assumed to be constant over time. defined transition states based on RFM measures. defined them based on customers' recency of purchases as well as an additional state for new or former customers. Rust, Lemon, and Zeithaml defined P as brand switching probabilities that vary over time as per a logit model. Furthermore, they broke R into two components—customer's expected purchase volume of a brand and his or her probability of buying a brand at time t.

Rust et al. argued that the "lost for good" approach understates CLV because it does not allow a defected customer to return. Others have argued that this is not a serious problem because customers can be treated as renewable resource and lapsed customers can be reacquired. It is possible that the choice of the modeling approach depends on the context. For example, in many industries (e.g., cellular phone, cable, and banks), customers are usually monogamous and maintain their relationship with only one company. In other contexts (e.g., consumer goods, airlines, and business-to-business relationship), consumers simultaneously conduct business with multiple companies, and the "always a share" approach may be more suitable.

The interest in customer retention and customer loyalty increased significantly with the work of Reichheld and Sasser, who found that a 5% increase in customer retention could increase firm profitability from 25% to 85%. Reichheld also emphasized the importance of customer retention. However, Reinartz and Kumar argued against this result and suggested that "it is the revenue that drives the lifetime value of a customer and not the duration of a customer's tenure". Reinartz and Kumar further contradicted Reichheld based on their research findings of weak to moderate correlation (.2 to .45) between customer tenure and profitability across four data sets. However, a low correlation can occur if the relationship between loyalty and profitability is nonlinear.

What drives customer retention? In the context of cellular phones, found that customers' satisfaction with the firm had a significant and positive impact on duration of relationship. She further found that customers who have many months of experience with the firm weigh prior cumulative satisfaction more heavily and new information relatively less heavily. After examining a large set of published studies, concluded that there is a strong correlation between customer satisfaction and customer retention.

In their study of the luxury car market, Yoo and Hanssens found that discounting increased acquisition rate for the Japanese cars but increased retention rate for the American brands. They also found product quality and customer satisfaction to be highly related with acquisition and retention effectiveness of various brands. Based on these results, they concluded that if customers are satisfied with a high-quality product, their repeat purchase is less likely to be affected by that brand's discounting. They also found that advertising did not have any direct significant impact on retention rates in the short term.

Venkatesan and Kumar found that frequency of customer contacts had a positive but nonlinear impact on customers' purchase frequency. found that face-to-face interactions had a greater impact on duration, followed by telephones and e-mails. Reinartz and Kumar found that duration was positively affected by customers' spending level, cross-buying, number of contacts by the firm, and ownership of firm's loyalty instrument.

Customer Margin and Expansion

The third component of CLV is the margin generated by a customer in each time period t. This margin depends on a customer's past purchase behavior as well as a firm's efforts in cross-selling and up-selling products to the customer. There are two broad approaches used in the literature to capture margin. One set of studies model margin directly while the other set of studies explicitly model cross-selling. We briefly discuss both approaches.

Several authors have made the assumption that margins for a customer remain constant over the future time horizon. used average contribution margin of a customer based on his or her prior purchase behavior to project CLV. Gupta, Lehmann, and Stuart also used constant margin based on history. Gupta and Lehmann showed that in many industries this may be a reasonable assumption used a simple regression model to capture changes in contribution margin over time. Specifically, they suggested that change in contribution margin for customer *j* at time *t* is:

$$\Delta CM_{jt} = \beta X_{jt} + e_{jt}.$$

Covariates for their B2B application included lagged contribution margin, lagged quantity purchased, lagged firm size, lagged marketing efforts, and industry category. This simple model had an R^2 of .68 with several significant variables.

Thomas, Blattberg, and Fox modeled the probability of reacquiring a lapsed newspaper customer. One of the key covariates in their model was price, which had a significant impact on customers' reacquisition probability as well as their relationship duration. Price also has a direct impact on the contribution margin of a customer. This allowed Thomas, Blattberg, and Fox to estimate the expected CLV for a customer at various price points.

The second group of studies has explicitly modeled cross-selling, which in turn improves customer margin over time. With the rising cost of customer acquisition, firms are increasingly interested in cross-selling more products and services to their existing customers. This requires a better understanding of which products to cross-sell, to whom, and at what time.

In many product categories, such as books, music, entertainment, and sports, it is common for firms to use recommendation systems. A good example of this is the recommendation system used by Amazon. Earlier recommendation systems were built on the concept of collaborative filtering. Recently, some researchers have used Bayesian approach for creating more powerful recommendation systems.

In some other product categories, such as financial services, customers acquire products in a natural sequence. For example, a customer may start her or his relationship with a bank with a checking and/or savings account and over time buy more complex products such as mortgage and brokerage service. Kamakura, Ramaswami, and Srivastava argued that customers are likely to buy products when they reach a "financial maturity" commensurate with the complexity of the product. Recently, Li, Sun, and Wilcox used a similar conceptualization for cross-selling sequentially ordered financial products. Specifically, they used a multivariate probit model where consumer *i* makes binary purchase decision (buy or not buy) on each of the *j* products. The utility for consumer *i* for product *j* at time *t* is given as:

$$U_{ijt} + \beta_i \left| O_j - DM_{it-1} \right| + \gamma_{ij} X_{it} + \varepsilon_{ijt},$$

where O_j is the position of product j on the same continuum as demand maturity DM_{it-1} of consumer *i*. *X* includes other covariates that may influence consumers' utility to buy a product. They further model demand or latent financial maturity as a function of cumulative ownership, monthly balances, and the holding time of all available J accounts (covariates *Z*), weighted by the importance of each product (parameters λ):

$$DM_{it-1} = \sum_{j=1}^{J} \left[O_j D_{ijt-1} \left(\lambda_k Z_{ijk-1} \right) \right].$$

Verhoef, Franses, and Hoekstra used an ordered probit to model consumers' cross-buying. Knott, Hayes, and Neslin used logit, discriminant analysis, and neural networks models to predict the next product to buy and found that all models performed roughly the same and significantly better (predictive accuracy of 40% to 45%) than random guessing (accuracy of 11% to 15%). In a field test, they further established that their model had a return on investment (ROI) of 530% compared to the negative ROI from the heuristic used by the bank that provided the data. Knott, Hayes, and Neslin complemented their logit model, which addresses what product a customer is likely to buy next, with a hazard model, which addresses the question of when customers are likely to buy this product. They found that adding the hazard model improves profits by 25%. Finally, Kumar, Venkatesan, and Reinartz showed that cross-selling efforts produced a significant increase in profits per customer when using a model that accounts for dependence in choice and timing of purchases.

Persistence Models

Like econometric models of CLV, persistence models focus on modeling the behavior of its components, that is, acquisition, retention, and cross-selling. When sufficiently long-time series are available, it is possible to treat these components as part of a dynamic system. Advances in multivariate time-series analysis, in particular vectorautoregressive (VAR) models, unit roots, and cointegration, may then be used to study how a movement in one variable (say, an acquisition campaign or a customer service improvement) impacts other system variables over time. To date, this approach, known as persistence modeling, has been used in a CLV context to study the impact of advertising, discounting, and product quality on customer equity and to examine differences in CLV resulting from different customer acquisition methods.

The major contribution of persistence modeling is that it projects the long-run or equilibrium behavior of a variable or a group of variables of interest. In the present context, we may model several known marketing influence mechanisms jointly; that is, each variable is treated as potentially endogenous. For example, a firm's acquisition campaign may be successful and bring in new customers (consumer response). That success may prompt the firm to invest in additional campaigns (performance feedback) and possibly finance these campaigns by diverting funds from other parts of its marketing mix (decision rules). At the same time, the firm's competitors, fearful of a decline in market share, may counter with their own acquisition campaigns (competitive reaction). Depending on the relative strength of these influence mechanisms, a long-run outcome will emerge that may or may not be favorable to the initiating firm. Similar dynamic systems may be developed to study, for example, the long-run impact of improved customer retention on customer acquisition levels, and many other dynamic relationships among the components of customer equity.

The technical details of persistence modeling are beyond the scope of this article and may be found, for example, in Dekimpe and Hanssens. Broadly speaking, persistence modeling consists of three separate steps:

1. Examine the evolution of each system's variable over time: This step distinguishes between temporary and permanent movements in that variable. For example, are the firm's retention rates stable over time, are they improving or deteriorating? Similarly, is advertising spending stable, growing, or decreasing? Formally, this step involves a series of unit-root tests and results in a VAR model specification in levels (temporary movements only) or changes (permanent or persistent movements). If there is evidence in favor of a long-run equilibrium between evolving variables (cointegration test), then the resulting system's model will be of the vector-error correction type, which combined movements in levels and changes.

2. Estimate the VAR model, typically with leastsquares methods: As an illustration, consider the customer-acquisition model in Villanueva, Yoo, and Hanssens:

$$\begin{pmatrix} AM_t \\ AW_t \\ V_t \end{pmatrix} = \begin{pmatrix} a_{10} \\ a_{20} \\ a_{30} \end{pmatrix} + \sum_{l=1}^{P} \begin{pmatrix} a_{11}^l & a_{12}^l & a_{13}^l \\ a_{21}^l & a_{22}^l & a_{23}^l \\ a_{31}^l & a_{32}^l & a_{33}^l \end{pmatrix} \begin{pmatrix} AM_{t-l} \\ AW_{t-l} \\ V_{t-l} \end{pmatrix} + \begin{pmatrix} e_{1t} \\ e_{2t} \\ e_{3t} \end{pmatrix}$$

   where *AM* stands for the number of customers acquired through the firm's marketing actions, *AW* stands for the number of customers acquired from word of mouth, and *V* is the firm's performance. The subscript *t* stands for time, and *p* is the lag order of the model. In this VAR model, $(e_{1t}, e_{2t}, e_{3t})'$ are white-noise disturbances distributed as $N(0, \Sigma)$. The direct effects of acquisition on firm performance are captured by a_{31}, a_{32}. The cross effects among acquisition methods are estimated by a_{12}, a_{21}; performance feedback effects by a_{13}, a_{23}; and finally, reinforcement effects by a_{11}, a_{22}, a_{33}. As with all VAR models, instantaneous effects are reflected in the variancecovariance matrix of the residuals (Σ).

3. Derive the impulse response functions: The parameter estimates of VAR models are rarely interpreted directly. Instead, they are used in obtaining estimates of short- and long-run impact of a single shock in one of the variables on the system. These "impulse response" estimates and their standard errors are often displayed visually, so that one can infer the anticipated short-term and long-run impact of the shock. In the illustration above, Villanueva, Yoo, and Hanssens found that marketing-induced customer acquisitions are more profitable in the short run, whereas word-of-mouth acquisitions generate performance more slowly but eventually become twice as valuable to the firm.

In conclusion, as customer lifetime value is de facto a long-term performance metric, persistence models are well suited in this context. In particular, they can quantify the relative importance of the various influence mechanisms in long-term customer equity development, including customer selection, method of acquisition, word of mouth generation, and competitive reaction. With only two known applications, this approach to CLV modeling is early in its development, in part because the demands on the data are high, for example, long time series equal-interval observations. It would be useful to explore models such as fractionally differenced time series models or Markov switching modes and extensions to duration dependent Markov switching models in CLV analysis.

Computer Science Models

The marketing literature has typically favored structured parametric models, such as logit, probit, or hazard models. These models are based on theory (e.g., utility theory) and are easy to interpret. In contrast, the vast computer science literature in data mining, machine learning, and nonparametric statistics has generated many approaches that emphasize predictive ability. These include projection-pursuit models; neural network models; decision tree models; spline-based models such as generalized additive models (GAM), multivariate adaptive regression splines (MARS), classification and regression trees (CART); and support vector machines (SVM).

Many of these approaches may be more suitable to the study of customer churn where we typically have a very large number of variables, which is commonly referred to as the "curse of dimensionality." The sparseness of data in these situations inflates the variance of the estimates, making traditional parametric and nonparametric models less useful. To overcome these difficulties, Hastie and Tibshirani proposed generalized additive models where the mean of the dependent variable depends on an additive predictor through a nonlinear, nonparametric link function. Another approach to overcome the curse of dimensionality is MARS. This is a nonparametric regression procedure that operates as multiple piecewise linear regression with breakpoints that are estimated from data.

More recently, we have seen the use of SVM for classification purposes. Instead of assuming that a linear function or plane can separate the two (or more) classes, this approach can handle situations where a curvilinear function or hyperplane is needed for better classification. Effectively the method transforms the raw data into a "featured space" using a mathematical kernel such that this space can classify objects using linear planes. In a recent study, Cui and Curry conducted extensive Monte Carlo simulations to compare predictions based on multinomial logit model and SVM. In all cases, SVM outpredicted the logit model. In their simulation, the overall mean prediction rate of the logit was 72.7%, whereas the hit rate for SVM was 85.9%. Similarly, Giuffrida, Chu, and Hanssens reported that a multivariate decision tree induction algorithm outperformed a logit model in identifying the best customer targets for cross-selling purposes.

Predictions can also be improved by combining models. The machine learning literature on bagging, the econometric literature on the combination of forecasts, and the statistical literature on model averaging suggest that weighting the predictions from many different models can yield improvements in predictive ability. Neslin et al. (in press) described the approaches submitted by various academics and practitioners for a "churn tournament." The winning entry used the power of combining several trees, each tree typically no larger than two to eight terminal nodes, to improve prediction of customer churn through a gradient tree boosting procedure.

Recently, Lemmens and Croux (in press) used bagging and boosting techniques to predict churn for a U.S. wireless customer database. Bagging (Bootstrap AGGregatING) consists of sequentially estimating a binary choice model, called base classifier in machine learning, from resampled versions of a calibration sample. The obtained classifiers form a group from which a final choice model is derived by aggregation. In boosting, the sampling scheme is different from bagging. Boosting essentially consists of sequentially estimating a classifier to adaptively reweighted versions of the initial calibration sample. The weighting scheme gives misclassified customers an increased weight in the next iteration. This forces the classification method to concentrate on hard-to-classify customers. Lemmens and Croux compared the results from these methods with the binary logit model and found the relative gain in prediction of more than 16% for the gini coefficient and 26% for the top-decile lift. Using reasonable assumptions, they showed that these differences can be worth more than $3 million to the company. This is consistent with the results of Neslin et al. (in press), who also found that the prediction methods matter and can change profit by hundreds of thousands of dollars.

These approaches remain little known in the marketing literature, not surprisingly because of the tremendous emphasis that marketing academics place on a parametric setup and interpretability. However, given the importance of prediction in CLV, these approaches need a closer look in the future.

Diffusion/Growth Models

CLV is the long-run profitability of an individual customer. This is useful for customer selection, campaign management, customer segmentation, and customer targeting. Whereas these are critical from an operational perspective, CLV should be aggregated to arrive at a strategic metric that can be useful for senior managers. With this in mind, several researchers have suggested that we focus on CE, which is defined as the CLV of current and future customers.

Forecasting the acquisition of future customers is typically achieved in two ways. The first approach uses a disaggregate customer data and builds models that predict the probability of acquiring a particular customer. Examples of this approach include Thomas and Thomas, Blattberg, and Fox. These models were discussed earlier.

An alternative approach is to use aggregate data and use diffusion or growth models to predict the number of customers a firm is likely to acquire in the future. and Libai, Muller, and Peres followed this approach. For example, Gupta, Lehmann, and Stuart suggested the following model for forecasting the number of new customers at time t:

$$n_t = \frac{\alpha\gamma ex\,p\left(-\beta - \gamma t\right)}{\left[1 + \exp\left(-\beta - \gamma t\right)\right]^2}$$

where α, β, and γ are the parameters of the customer growth curve. It is also possible to include marketing mix covariates in this model as suggested in the diffusion literature. Using this forecast of new customers, they estimated the CE of a firm as:

$$CE = \int_{k=0}^{\infty}\int_{t=k}^{\infty} n_k m_{t-k}\, e^{-ik}\, e^{-\left(\frac{1+i-r}{r}\right)(t-k)}\, dt\, dk - \int_{k=0}^{\infty} n_k c_k e^{-ik} dk$$

where n_k is the number of newly acquired customers for cohort k, m is the margin, r is the retention rate, i is the discount rate, and c is the acquisition cost per customer. Rust et al. used a simpler approach where they estimated CLV for an average American Airlines customer and then multiplied it by the number of U.S. airline passengers to arrive at its CE.

Using data for five companies, Gupta, Lehmann, and Stuart showed that CE approximates firm market value quite well for three of the five companies (exceptions were Amazon and eBay). In addition, they assessed the relative importance of marketing and financial instruments by showing that 1% change in retention affected CE by almost 5%, compared to only a 0.9% impact by a similar change in discount rate. Rust et al. estimated CE for American Airlines as $7.3 billion, which compared favorably with its market capitalization of $9.7 billion. They also found that if American Airlines could increase its quality by 0.2 rating points on a 5-point scale, it would increase its customer equity by 1.39%. Similarly, a $45 million expenditure by Puffs facial tissues to increase its ad awareness by 0.3 ratings points would result in an improvement of $58.1 million in CE.

Hogan, Lemon, and Libai also used a diffusion model to assess the value of a lost customer. They argued that when a firm loses a customer it not only loses the profitability linked directly to that customer (his or her CLV) but also the word-of-mouth effect that could have been generated through him or her. Using their approach, they estimated that in the online banking industry the direct effect of losing a customer is about $208, whereas the indirect effect can be more than $850.

Demographic Characteristics in Consumer Profile

The characteristics of the customers are defined by the demographics. To be successful, every business owner has to know the demographics that describe the customers and what trends or changes are happening in those specific characteristics.

Primary Demographic Characteristics

A demographic profile is generally defined by the following categories:

- Age,
- Gender,
- Income,
- Education,
- Marital Status,
- Employment,
- Home Ownership,
- Geographical location,
- Race or Ethnicity.

Effect of Age on Consumer Behavior

Age has a major effect on consumer behavior. People's needs change as they grow older. Age leads to changes in lifestyle, personal values and health needs. Younger consumers are healthy, and will spend more on fun, fashion, entertaining and movies. Older people spend less on these things; they are less active, they stay indoors more and they have more needs for medical treatments.

Age Defines Market Segments

Age also defines market segments. For example, digital products, such as *iPhones*, are marketed more toward millennials than toward the elderly. According to a study from Pew Research Center, while older people are using technology more, they are still less digitally inclined than millennials and buy fewer digital products.

Consumer Preferences Change with Age

Consumers' preference for certain products and brands change with age. For instance, young people like to drink La Croix sparkling water and post selfie pictures on Instagram of themselves having a Starbucks Pumpkin Spice latte with its orange sweater insulation. Elderly people are more interested in things that make their daily lives easier, such as TV remotes with large buttons, folding seats to rest when walking, clip-on book lights and large key holders to stop fumbling with keys.

Gender Needs and Preferences

Males and females have entirely different needs and preferences that affect their buying selections of lifestyle products and fashion. Products are made to appeal to specific genders. Macys, Nordstrom and The Gap all have departments that carry clothing aimed at teenage girls. Seiko has a line of diver watches for men.

Sometimes products are targeted toward both genders, as with retired couples. Travel and Leisure magazine has a list of recommended vacations for retirees; they suggest trips to Ireland, Sicily, Thailand and Costa Rica. And Costco Travel has a website designed to put a vacation package together. Both young males and females may like the same fast foods and movies.

Effect of Income on Buying Decisions

Income has a significant effect on consumer behavior and product decisions. Middle-income consumers make their buying decisions with due consideration to the utility of money. They don't have unlimited funds, so the money for one purchase may be at the expense of not buying something else. Take the family to dinner at Applebee's or put some money aside for the kids' college fund?

On the other hand, consumers with higher incomes don't have to fret about taking the entire family out to dinner at an expensive restaurant, such as *Le Bernardin* in Manhattan. Buyers with higher incomes spend more money on luxury items, vacations, jewelry and cars.

Education Influencing Perceptions

The level of education influences consumers' perceptions of the things around them and affects the degree of research before making a purchase. Higher educated people will take more time to become better informed before spending their money. Education affects choices in fashion, movies and TV programs. Highly educated consumers are more skeptical of advertisements and question the information being presented.

Marital Status Influencing Mindsets

The mindsets of singles versus married couples are different. Ferrari will target its red model 458 Italia at up-and-coming single guys, while John Deere wants to sell riding lawn mowers to young married couples who just bought their first home.

Role of Employment

The consumer's occupation plays a major role in the products they buy. Their jobs give insights into the type of person they are:

- Farmers are interested in any kind of tool or machine that will make their work easier or more productive. For example, Tractor Supply Company sells to farmers and has locations in the South and Midwest selling fencing, pumps, sprayers, chemicals and tractor parts, of course.
- Home Depot and Lowes sell construction supplies to building contractors, and Michael's has just about everything a teacher could want for the classroom.

Differing Needs according to Home Ownership

Renters and home owners have different motivations. Home owners are willing to invest and make improvements in their property. As an example, they represent a good market for lawn and garden supplies, such as flower seeds from Burpee or outdoor furniture from Wayfair. Renters, on the other hand, don't want to damage their apartments so they can get their deposit back.

Effect of Geographic Location

The geographic location of the consumer makes a difference. People who live in New York City don't buy the same products as someone who lives in Austin, Texas. A haberdashery in New York would not be wise to carry a large stock of cowboy hats. A restaurant selling fried catfish will do better in Macon, Georgia, than in San Francisco.

Race or Ethnicity

Kids grow up with their parents and absorb a certain culture and environment with traits that will follow them into adulthood. Asians, for example, have their own style of clothing and like for certain foods; Italians certainly have their own favorite recipes. A retailer of hoodies, for instance, needs to take stock of the race and ethnicity of the people living in a neighborhood before opening a new store.

Changes in Customer Demographics

The factors that make up the demographics of a consumer market are constantly changing. They never stay the same, and marketers must be aware of these changes and adapt to them.

Effect of Change in Population Growth Rate

One trend that is affecting consumer demographics is the change in population. According to Forbes magazine, the rate of US population growth is the lowest it has been since the 1930s. The factors affecting the growth rate are fewer births, a lower death rate and the decline in the number of immigrants.

All of these factors will change the composition of demographic groups. A lower death rate means elderly people will live longer and need more health care. The declining birth rate means that married couples will not be forming families as early as before. Marketers to these groups may need to make changes to their product lines and sales projections.

Middle Class is Less Prosperous

Studies from the Pew Research Center show that the number of middle-class households has been in a steady decline for the past 40 years. Even worse, their share of total national income has dropped from 62 percent in 1970 to 43 percent in 2014. As a result, middle-class workers have less money to spend.

Retailers who sell products to the middle class have a smaller number of possible consumers with less income. This situation has led to an increase in the number of dollar stores, off-price stores and warehouse clubs.

Composition of Households

According to the article in Forbes magazine, more people are living in households with more than one generation. One in five Americans, about 60 million people, now reside in multigenerational households. One in 10 children lives with a grandparent as head of the household.

One effect of this trend is the impact on types of housing. The demand will increase for homes with more square feet, bedrooms and baths. The sizes of garages may even be affected.

Psychographics

Marketing concept seeks to divide customers into groups according to their psychological or lifestyle characteristics. Done properly, psychographic analysis can answer such questions as — Why are consumers choosing Product A over Product B? Why does this product have a higher brand value in the customer's eyes? What marketing messages will match the customer's values in life?

Segmentation in Marketing

Trying to be all things to all people is a dead end in the marketing world. Trying to sell a new luxury car to everyone, for instance, will do little more than blow your marketing budget. That's because people buy luxury cars for all sorts of reasons: The perceived quality, the state-of-the-art technology, its resale value, its function as a status symbol. Some people will not be in the market for a luxury car at all due to income or other restrictions.

Because customers have different motivations, virtually all marketing strategies start by splitting the customer base into groups or segments based on their similar characteristics. Grouping similar consumers together means you can send the right messages to the right group, so you get far more bang for your marketing buck.

To be effective, a market segment usually features three aspects:

1. Homogeneity: The consumers in the segment have common needs.
2. Distinctiveness: Some characteristic of this consumer group makes it different other groups, for example, these consumers are younger or based in a different region.
3. Reaction: Consumers in this segment will have a similar response to the marketing messages you put out.

Here's an example of segmentation. Suppose you perform some market research and learn that *a* large percentage of car buyers choose the luxury model over the value model because it is perceived to be more comfortable. You can be assured that every person in this market segment will react positively to advertising that highlights you product's heated seats, leather interior and remote-start feature.

Types of Market Segmentation

While it is possible to group consumers together by any characteristic, the following four segments are considered to be the richest descriptors of people's buying patterns:

1. Demographic Segmentation: The simplest and most widely used type of segmentation, demographics divides the purchasing population by age, gender, income, occupation, family size, race, religion and nationality. For example, you might define a group as -"men aged 18-35 who earn between $30,000 and $50,000 per year."

2. Behavioral Segmentation: Behavioral segmentation divides the population on the basis of their buying behavior as customers. How frequently do they purchase a product? Are they early adopters or do they wait for a product to have mass appeal before making an investment? How loyal are they to a product or brand?

3. Psychographic Segmentation: Psychographic segmentation is tied into behavior, but this time we're looking more closely at someone's lifestyle and opinions to define a target market. What is the consumer's political opinion? How environmentally conscious is he? Is he the life and soul of the party or an introvert? What activities does he enjoy? What are his hobbies? Understanding these lifestyle influences means you can customize your marketing campaigns so that they appeal more specifically to the customer's motivations.

4. Geographic Segmentation: Dividing people based on where they live is called geographical

segmentation. Your customers will have different needs based on their location: rural versus urban, big city versus small town, hot country versus cold country and so on. You probably won't sell many air conditioners to customers who live in Iceland, but there's scope for market growth in southern Spain.

Types of Psychographic Segmentation

The list of lifestyle variables is as long as it is broad but generally, when marketers talk about psychographic segmentation, they mean one or more of the following characteristics:

1. Stage of Life: Where does the customer sit in her life cycle? Does she still live at home with parents? Is she pre-family, with her own household but no children? Does she have dependent children? Is she an empty nester or one-half of an older, childless couples? Two people of the same age, location and gender may have different buying habits depending on their life stage.

2. Opinions, Interests and Hobbies: This category covers a huge area and includes consumers' sporting activities, views on the environment, cultural issues, reading habits, political opinions, what interests them and what they do in their spare time. Anything that the customer holds close to his heart, regardless of whether her heart values yoga or junk car racing, this will have a material impact on the products they buy.

   A good example here is the upsurge in demand for "free-from" products (gluten free, dairy free, preservative free and so on). These products appeal to a specific consumer group who are concerned about their health and where their food comes from.

3. Personality: How self-confident, dominant or sociable is the consumer? How traditional or avant-garde is he in his tastes? These variables are important because people buy products that match up to their concept of themselves.

   To see how this might play out, Hilton Worldwide commissioned a study that identified consumers with various personality traits. These people were then shown them a series of Facebook ads. Some ads were matched to a particular personality preference — ads aimed at extroverts spoke of "good vibes" and "fun," for example, while ads aimed at the conscientious contained messages of hard work and organization. Some ads were mismatched. The researchers wanted to find out whether the targeted ads would perform better than those without a personality correlation.

   The results were striking, with personality-matched ads getting at least twice the click-through rates of the mismatched ads.

4. Brand Loyalty: Some customers buy the same brand all the time; others will swap out brands according to offers and availability. It is often said that finding new customers is ten-times harder than keeping your old ones, so there are considerable savings to be made if a company can focus its efforts on an existing, loyal customer base.

5. Events and Occasions: This segment identifies when customers consume a product or service. For instance, some people will buy red roses only on Valentine's Day, and

jewelry only for Christmas and birthdays, whereas other consumers will purchase these products more regularly. Now that you understand these motivations, could you develop a strategy to change the consumers' perception of the product as a special-occasion treat?

Advantages of Consumer Psychographics

For many years, marketers have concentrated predominantly on demographics to figure out customers' motivations. Psychographics divides customers on the basis of finer characteristics. Adding lifestyle factors into the mix can leave you one step ahead of the competition.

Apart from the obvious advantage of increased sales, there are several other benefits associated with psychographic customer segmentation:

- Increased perception of the brand in the eyes of the customer.
- Better inputs for the development of new products that the customer will enjoy.
- Simpler to create and more efficient marketing strategies.
- Higher degree of customer loyalty, resulting in repeat business.
- Less cash spent on marketing, since your messages are more specific.

When you introduce psychographics into your market segmentation, you're drilling right down into lifestyle of your consumer group, such as whether they like to work out or eat healthy. It's much more specific that the generalizations of age or gender. In this era of authenticity, exposing the customer's psycho-social motives for purchasing may well signal the difference between acceptance and rejection of your brand.

Customer Knowledge to Insights

Applied customer insight helps companies understand and anticipate customer expectations, and then tailor the customer experience to profitably deliver against these expectations. The real lesson from Macy's Santa is that a company can not truly be customer-driven without the benefit of customer insight.

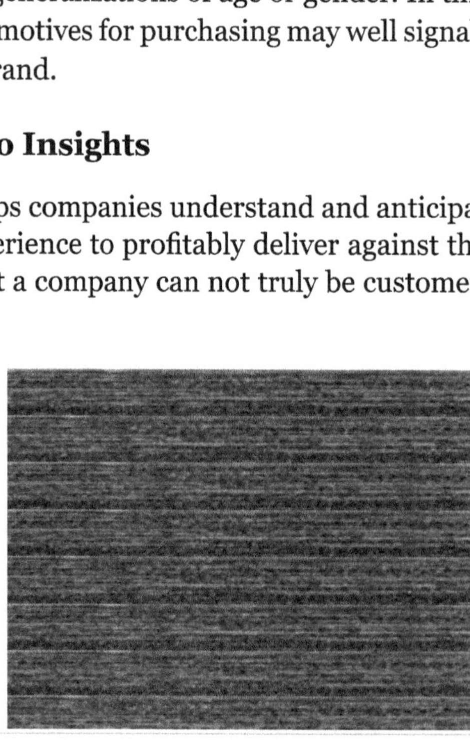

Companies collect customer information at a much faster rate than they apply it.

Customer insight is an ongoing process that applies a unique, fact-based understanding of customer needs, expectations and value potential to personalize customer offers and experiences. By personalizing products, pricing, promotion and message content through appropriate channels, companies can optimize customer acquisition, development and retention. When customer insight is applied effectively, the results are powerful. For instance:

- A French energy retailer stemmed customer defections by anticipating service delivery problems and proactively recommending individualized relationship programs to address them. A six-month pilot of the program led to a 50 percent reduction in the customer defection rate and projected a $30 million net profit increase.
- An automobile manufacturer employed customer insight to identify prospective buyers and then deliver individualized sales and marketing experiences. The program earned 30,000 purchase commitments prior to advertising, and saved $800 in marketing expenditures per vehicle sale.
- Internet merchants like Amazon.com and CDNow analyze a customer's profile and buying habits and use recommendation engines to suggest complementary items. Many Internet merchants are even positioning themselves against bricks and mortar competitors based on their ability to know the customer as an individual and serve as a trusted advisor.

Knowledge is Power

Knowing the customer is paramount in today's marketplace where the customer has more options, greater flexibility and higher expectations. The power shift from seller to customer is forcing companies to treat each customer as an individual, both from a marketing and a service delivery standpoint. Armed with customer insight, a company can understand individual customer expectations, preferences and value potential and use this knowledge to shape the customer relationship.

While traditional marketing skills focusing on brand continue to be important, they will need to encompass the "new world" that is virtual, multichannel and increasingly customer-driven. The one-time use of customer research to drive just strategic decisions needs to be replaced by a continuous, real-time use to drive both strategic and tactical decisions.

For instance, USAA Insurance has developed an intimate understanding of its customers' behaviors and the critical events in their lives. USAA uses this insight to drive its cross-selling efforts. Instead of barraging its customers with a constant stream of solicitations, USAA uses customer insight to drive a lifecycle marketing program that communicates a personalized marketing message when that message is believed to be more relevant. USAA increased its response rates dramatically. Because the marketing message is timely and tailored, customers see USAA's marketing activity as a service rather than a solicitation.

USAA is an example of a company that disseminates customer knowledge across the organization and employs it in real time at multiple points of customer inter- action. USAA is thriving because it anticipates individual customer needs and tailors its marketing messages and service delivery processes accordingly.

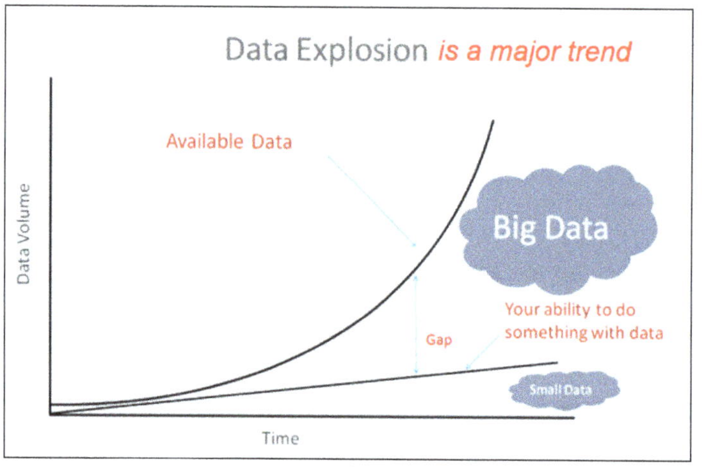

Customer insight capabilities.

In a world where customers order off the Web, dial into VRUs, and zealously use their loyalty cards, companies are awash in customer information. The challenge is to use this data effectively. Companies are collecting customer information at a much faster rate than they are applying it.

Furthermore, the technology capabilities at the point of customer interaction have improved dramatically as well. Today's technology enables companies to move from mass-producing one-size-fits-all customer relationships to relating to customers as individuals.

The advent of e-commerce and rapid evolution of database technology provides the means to collect volumes of customer information, while technology at the point of customer interaction makes it possible to tailor each customer relationship. Customer insight is a critical element of this dynamic; customer insight makes customer data useful by providing an understanding of how to profitably customize the relationship. The Economist Intelligence Unit found that 83 percent of companies already have in place or are developing data warehouses.

Simply having a data warehouse and accessing customer data only brings a company to competitive parity. Competitive advantage will be gained based on the quality of the insight a company gleans from its warehouse and the ability of the company to apply that insight to add value to each customer experience.

Leveraging knowledge to create a valuable customer experience is highly dependent on a tight integration of customer insight capabilities. There are three customer insight capabilities that create value: establishing a single view of the customer, generating insight and applying insight to personalize the customer experience.

Capability One: Create a One-customer View

Companies must be selective about what customer data to collect, how to collect it, maintain and access it, and how to leverage it to anticipate customer behavior. Customer insight flows from the underlying customer data, which may include transactions, preferences, service history, and demographic information. The first step in generating insight is to transform customer data into a customer knowledge base. A customer knowledge base provides a mechanism for developing a holistic view of the customer base at both an aggregate and an individual level – which is often termed "one-customer view."

Customer insight can be applied across broad groups of customers to make strategic marketing decisions and used real-time to drive the interaction with a single customer. When building this "one-customer view", it is important for companies to design their knowledge base around how customer insight will be applied. These applications include: business planning; formulating segment-specific strategies and value propositions; and anticipating and differentiating customer interactions across all touch points.

Building a customer knowledge base can be a difficult undertaking. Customer data is often scattered among disparate databases across the organization. Click stream information is not stored in a way that is relevant to the customer relationship. While revenues may be available by customer, the cost to service the customer may not be. There may be few mechanisms in place to measure a customer's potential value.

An effective view of the customer requires a knowledge base that accomplishes three things:

- Continuously captures customer data.
- Refines the data to assure its integrity.
- Provides an "engine" that supports analysis at both the aggregate level and for an individual customer.

Capability Two: Generate Insight

It is not enough to collect and analyze customer data. What differentiates winning companies is the ability to draw customer insights from collected data to describe customer needs and expectations, anticipate customer behavior to shape interactions accordingly, and measure performance in terms of customer value and profitability.

The value equation is a two-way street. On the one hand, companies must understand what a customer needs and expects. On the other hand, they must balance the cost to deliver against these needs and expectations with the profitability a customer generates. Continual analysis and segmentation is necessary to group customers according to expectations. Companies must further equate the cost to meet customer expectations relative to customer value to understand which customers they can satisfy profitability

Armed with a single view of the customer, companies are in a position to generate three types of insight:

- Insight that is descriptive of customer behaviors, to understand what drives customer desires and behaviors.
- Insight that is predictive, to forecast and anticipate future behavior.
- Insight that is performance-based, which guides a company in evaluating performance of its customers.

Capability Three: Apply Insight

Customer insight guides the company as to which customers to focus on and how much can be invested in each customer relationship. Customer insight also provides a company with a picture of a customer's history, expectations, preferences and value. To be useful, insight must be applied across multiple points of customer interaction, to personalize the experience and deliver consistently differentiated treatment.

The application of customer insight is important to both the strategy and execution of the marketing agenda. Some examples of applied customer insight include:

- Driving marketing planning through strategic segmentation, media planning and effectiveness, and a customer profitability analysis.
- Using insight in multichannel marketing campaigns to identify the target audience and determine the offer to be presented, what the optimal time is to deliver that offer, what the best medium is to convey the offer, and how best to explain it.
- Personalizing customer service and support through, for example, a call center representative using a company's service history and profile to recognize a pattern of performance failure and to then recommend a maintenance program that will head off subsequent problems.
- Driving real-time product configuration and pricing, on a Web site, at a call center or even on a sales representative's laptop.

Value Payoff

Ours is an age of unprecedented choice and constantly rising customer expectations. In the days of Miracle on 34th Street, being a customer-driven company was a refreshing anomaly. Today, customers expect companies to do whatever it takes to satisfy them – if they don't there is a competitor across the street or just a mouse click away. Customer insight provides an understanding of what customers expect and then guides the company in aligning its marketing, service delivery and organizational resources with those expectations.

By applying customer insight across multiple points of customer interaction, companies can better understand customer expectations, determine how to accommodate them and customize the relationship accordingly. Ideally, insight-driven relationships move an organization from a one-size-fits-all customer approach to one that treats customers as individuals, based upon their needs and preferences. Ultimately, this results in greater customer satisfaction, increased profitability per customer, and longer-term customer relationships.

Behavior Analysis

Behavioral analytics is a tool that reveals the actions users take within a digital product. It organizes raw event data such as clicks into a timeline of each user's behavior, also known as a user journey. Teams use behavioral analytics to determine what users like and don't like and, by inference, what adjustments can make the product more valuable.

Behavioral Data

Behavioral data is the raw event data that's generated when users click, swipe, and navigate a site or app. Teams can view the data in aggregate to understand which behaviors are most common, or look at journeys, also called user flows, which show the order in which users took the actions. Behavioral analysis relies on behavioral data.

Why should Companies use Behavioral Analytics?

Most product, marketing, and analytics teams live in constant pursuit of the question, "How are customers using the product, if at all?" Behavioral analytics software provides concrete answers with a visual interface where teams can segment users, run reports, and deduce customers' needs and interests.

Without behavioral analytics, teams are stuck using insufficiently detailed demographic data and so-called vanity metrics. As Streaming, Sharing, Stealing co-author Michael D. Smith explained to The Signal, if a company wants to personalize its service to users, it needs their behavior data. A streaming movie platform can't know that a user loves horror films, for instance, simply based on their age, gender, or nationality.

Behavioral analytics can provide user-level data so teams can answer questions like:

- What do users click within the product?
- Where do users get stuck?
- How do users react to feature changes?
- How long do users take from first click to conversion?
- How do users react to marketing messages?
- Which ads are the most effective?
- Can the team nudge users to be more successful?

Conducting behavioral analysis is more complicated than simply running reports in the analytics tool. "Analyzing generic data doesn't magically produce answers to unidentified problems. Teams must first identify what they want to achieve and write down the paths they expect users to take. Only with preset expectations can teams identify whether users are deviating from the ideal path and redirect them.

The tech-driven insurance provider Lemonade, for instance, adjusted its user paths to increase revenue. The team knew their goal was to convert more website and app visitors into paying customers and with Mixpanel analytics, they noticed a "staggering drop-off" in user flow right before the point of purchase. By analyzing the page where the drop-off occurred, the team realized it was due to a technical error and a weak call-to-action (CTA). They fixed the bug and reworded the CTA, which led to a 50 percent increase in the number of users who purchased additional coverage.

Why Behavioral Analytics is Different?

What sets behavioral analytics apart from other types of business analytics is that it combines two technologies: user segmentation and event tracking. While some analytics vendors only offer one or the other—user data or event data—behavioral analytics unites the two for a complete customer view. It ties users to the events they trigger to produce a map of their actions, also known as a user flow, or customer journey.

Viewed either alone or in aggregate, user journeys tell stories that teams can use to tweak and improve their product development, marketing, and launch strategies.

Steps to Successful Behavioral Analysis

Customer behavioral analysis requires careful planning and each team's success is a function of how carefully they implement the analytics tool and how seriously they take their tracking plan.

Behavioral analysis is not a race. The first half of the implementation process should be spent planning and all teams who will eventually benefit from user intelligence need to have a hand in selecting and deploying the tool.

Teams can prepare themselves to conduct user behavior analysis in five steps:

Select Goals, KPIs and Metrics

To determine whether users are reaching the right goals, such as purchases or conversions, teams must select the KPIs and metrics that indicate progress toward those goals. A fitness app that makes money through monthly subscriptions, for instance, can track paid subscriber growth. An enterprise resource planning (ERP) software that relies on annual contracts, on the other hand, can track users that complete the onboarding sequence.

Define the Most Desirable user Journeys

Based on the service or app's design, what are the most common paths for users to reach their goals? If the product has already been launched, teams can use actual user data to answer this question. If the product is pre-launch, the team can use the design team's wireframes of the suspected or intended flow.

All user journeys should end in some type of a desirable outcome for the customer or the business. An e-commerce website, for instance, can track a user from their first page visit to adding an item to their shopping cart to checkout because that flow leads to purchases. Alternatively, a streaming music app can track users as they move from its homepage to playing a song and, hopefully, purchasing that song.

Create a Tracking Plan

Based on the user flow, teams can decide which events they'll need to track within the product. It can seem appealing to track everything but this is a mistake—too much data can clutter the analytics and make useful information more difficult to find. Track events and users based on whether the data is actually useful. Some events contain, within them, multiple properties. The event for playing a song within a music app, for instance, could contain properties for the song title, genre, and artist.

To keep events and properties organized, companies typically create a tracking plan in a spreadsheet. This acts as a directory of all events and serves as a map for implementing the analytics tool. A tracking plan is a mutable document that should be revised and updated as the product, team, and goals change. To reduce the burden of trying to share and control access to the spreadsheet, Mixpanel offers a feature called Lexicon which stores the event name taxonomy for all to see.

Involve all teams—analytics, product, marketing, and engineering—in drafting the tracking plan. Members of each will need to understand how the users and events are named and organized if they're going to run reports and understand the results.

Set a Unique Identifier for Users

Most digital products today exist across multiple platforms and this makes it difficult to track unique users. One user can appear to be multiple people unless assigned a unique identifier—either an email or string of characters—that persists across platforms and devices and connects the touch points along their journey. Teams should ensure their behavioral analytics platform vendor provides a unique identifier that won't change over time.

Implement Analytics and Begin Event Tracking

Once the tracking plan is complete, companies can deploy behavioral data analytics software and use its SDK or API to integrate it with their products. That's when they assign a unique identifier for users and set up user and event properties as outlined in the tracking plan. It's not uncommon for teams to discover additional events they want to track during implementation. This isn't an issue as long as they update both the tracking plan and the analytics service.

Before the tracking system goes live, teams should use test devices to verify the event and user tracking is firing properly. Once working, teams are ready to begin analyzing their users.

Apply the Results of Behavioral Analytics

Most teams study their users with segmentation, which allows them to separate users based on characteristics and behaviors. An e-commerce app, for example, can create a segment for recent users who added items to a shopping cart but then abandoned. Or, they could filter for power shop pers who access the app multiple times a day.

Segmentation allows teams to learn about their users to build more complete customer profiles. They can save user segmentations, known as cohorts, and make adjustments to their product and marketing to make it more profitable with each segment.

Media and entertainment company STARZ PLAY, for instance, segmented users that signed up through its free trial offer and found that some users were gaming the system for multiple trials. By creating alerts for the negative behavior, the product team closed the loophole and saved 8x on its marketing spend.

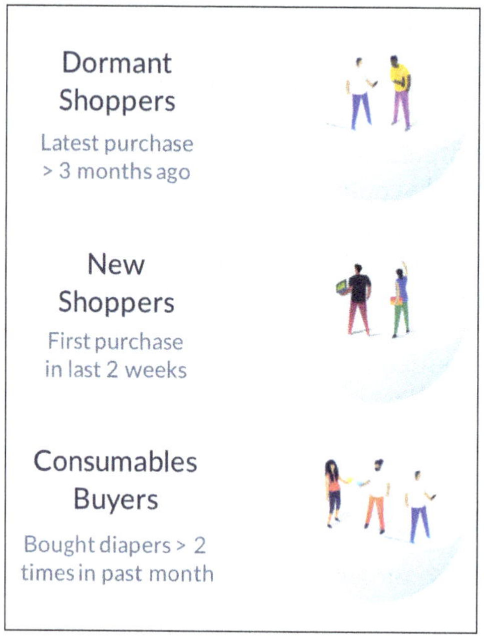

Here are other industry applications for user behavior analytics:

- E-commerce sites can predict future trends and increase conversion rates.
- Consumer messaging apps can increase usage.
- Insurance companies can sell additional products.
- Travel sites can increase bookings.
- Online gaming platforms can attract more users.

Teams can track users' progress toward outcomes such as purchases or signups with funnel reports. Funnels display a series of stages in a user journey, as well as how many users are progressing from one stage to the next. A fitness app could use funnels to see how many users progress from download to signup and purchase. If one stage has a low conversion rate, it's a signal that that stage needs attention.

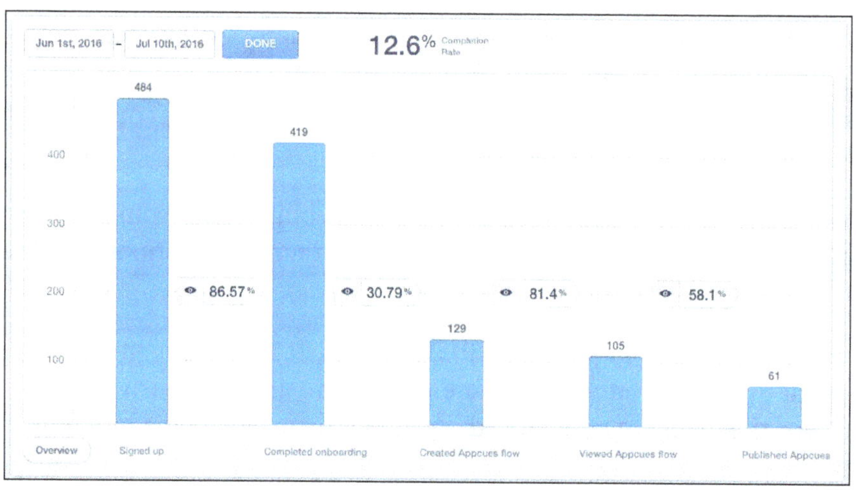

Funnel data allows teams to A/B test different buttons, messages, and images, to see if small changes improve conversions. The peer-to-peer shopping app Grabr, for instance, noticed conversions for referred users was low. The team tested new variants of the landing page and increased referral conversions 2x. The data can also be used to personalize parts of an app or website, say, to greet returning users, or present prospects with content relevant to their industry.

Teams can also use funnel data to deduce which behaviors are correlated with high retention. A media site, for instance, could look at the cohort of users that continue to return to the site eight weeks after signup to see if they share certain behaviors, such as a propensity to leave comments.

With a view of what's happening within the product, teams can run experiments and make alterations to improve the product and help users find more value.

Knowledge Discovery and Data Mining for Predictive Analytics

Business Drivers

Business drivers behind BI solutions are:

- The ability of a BI solution to help produce better business decisions via timely, accurate and more comprehensive analysis of available corporate information assets.
- The ability of BI to identify growth opportunities.
- The ability of BI to reduce costs and wastage by identifying areas of high expenditure, operational inefficiencies and analyzing transactional records.

Other drivers included the ability of BI to help:

- Underpin strategic adjustments in real-time (or near real-time).
- Identify risks and threats.
- Increase customer profitability.
- Improve and measure workplace productivity by employee, department or function.
- Improve operational and supply chain efficiencies.

Factors to Ensure a Successful Business Intelligence Program

The three most critical factors to support a successful BI project, on an ongoing basis, we found to be the ability to:

- Customize dashboards and reports to suite the needs of specific departments and roles.
- Integrate data types across departments to eliminate knowledge silos.
- Cultivate a culture of fact-based decision-making via data analysis.

Other factors identified as important for ensuring a successful BI project included the ability to:

- Establish a repeatable process to allow the constant monitoring and improvement of the quality of organizational data assets.
- Adopt standardized approaches and measures.
- Effectively utilize regular and automated report scheduling and exception reporting.
- Provide users with appropriate training to enable self-service analytics.

Challenges Faced when Implementing a Business Intelligence Program

The three most common barriers to a successful BI rollout were identified as:

- Breaking down departmental knowledge silos.
- Integrating the BI tool with other operational, performance management and transactional systems.
- Establishing and maintaining an appropriate level of data quality to feed into the BI system.

Other major challenges encountered included:

- Securing high rates of user adoption.
- Transforming the workplace from a culture of 'gut feel' to one of data-based decision-making.
- Securing executive sponsorship and necessary financial backing by defining tangible ROI.

Measuring the Performance of a Business Intelligence Platform

Measuring the performance of BI solutions can be problematic. The report lists key metrics that organizations should employ to help identify performance and ROI. The top three are:

- The time it takes to answer user queries.
- The comprehensiveness and usability of information gleaned from data analysis via the BI tool.
- The number and quality of decisions made as a result of the insights generated via the BI tool.

Other useful measures regarding the performance of a BI tool were listed as:

- Sustained user adoption rates.
- Frequency of use.
- Positive user feedback.
- Employee productivity.

Two Styles of Data Mining

1. Directed Data Mining:
    - Top-down approach.
    - Used when we know approximately what we are looking for or what we want to predict.
    - Predictive model uses experience to rank possible outcomes in the future by calculating a score for each outcome.
    - Model is seen as a black box because we care only about the predictions and not how it actually works.
    - Goal of building a predictive model is to apply knowledge gained in the past to the future.
    - Example problem: Which customers are likely to buy a specific type of car?
2. Undirected Data Mining:
    - Bottom-up approach.
    - Finds patterns in the data and leaves it up to the user to determine whether or not these patterns are important.
    - We want to know how the model works and how it comes up with the answer.
    - Human interaction is necessary because only people can determine what significance, if any, the patterns have.
    - Often used during the data exploration steps.
    - Example: A person looks at a decision tree and possibly notices an interesting pattern. For directed data mining a decision tree could make predictions.

Virtuous Cycle of Data Mining

Consists of four major business processes (success in data mining requires all four):

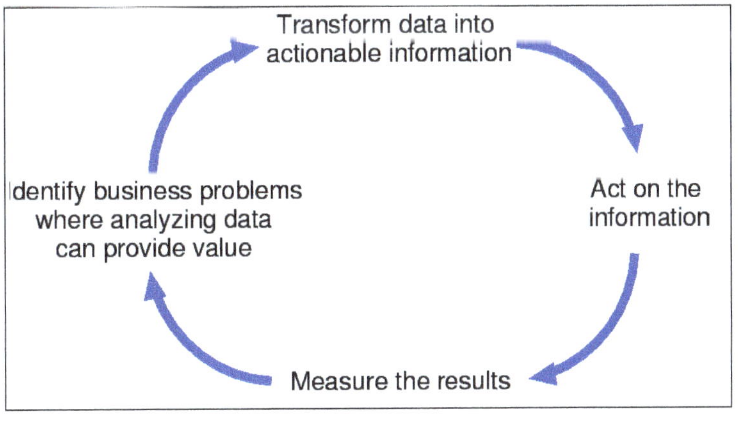

Identify the Business Problem

- Important that technical people understand what the real business needs are.
- Do this by talking to domain experts: the people who understand the business.
- Business people need to be kept informed of the development, so that they may make continuing contributions to the project and the focus remains on the business needs.
- It is important to think outside the confines of domain experts' knowledge to understand the real problem.

Business people's expertise allows you to answer the following questions:

- Is the data mining effort necessary? For example, if the purpose of a marketing campaign is to get every single possible responder, then it would be a waste of money to build a response model, i.e. a model that predicts who will respond to a marketing campaign.
- Should we focus on a particular segment or subgroup? For example, if a marketing campaign wants to focus on people aged 20-30, then modeling this set separately from the set of all people would produce better results.
- What are the relevant business rules? For example, if we are marketing an R-rated movie then we would exclude people under 18 from the model.
- What do they (the business people) know about the data? Domain experts know where data resides and how it is stored. They may know whether some sources are invalid and where certain data should come from.
- What do their intuition and experience say is important? Can be a source of insight.

Checking the opinion of domain experts:

- The data can be used to check that the experience and intuition of domain experts is correct.
- Example: If a domain expert believes that the best customer is aged 24 to 31 with at least one university degree, we can check to see if this is supported by the data.

Transforming Data into Actionable Results

The iterative process of building data mining models:

1. Identify and Obtain Data:
    - The right data is often whatever is available, reasonably clean, and accessible.
    - Data must meet the requirements for solving the business problem, for example - if the business problem is to identify particular customers, then the data must contain information about each individual customer.
    - Data must be as complete as possible.

- When doing predictive modeling the data needs to be complete enough that we can determine the outcome of what we are modelling.

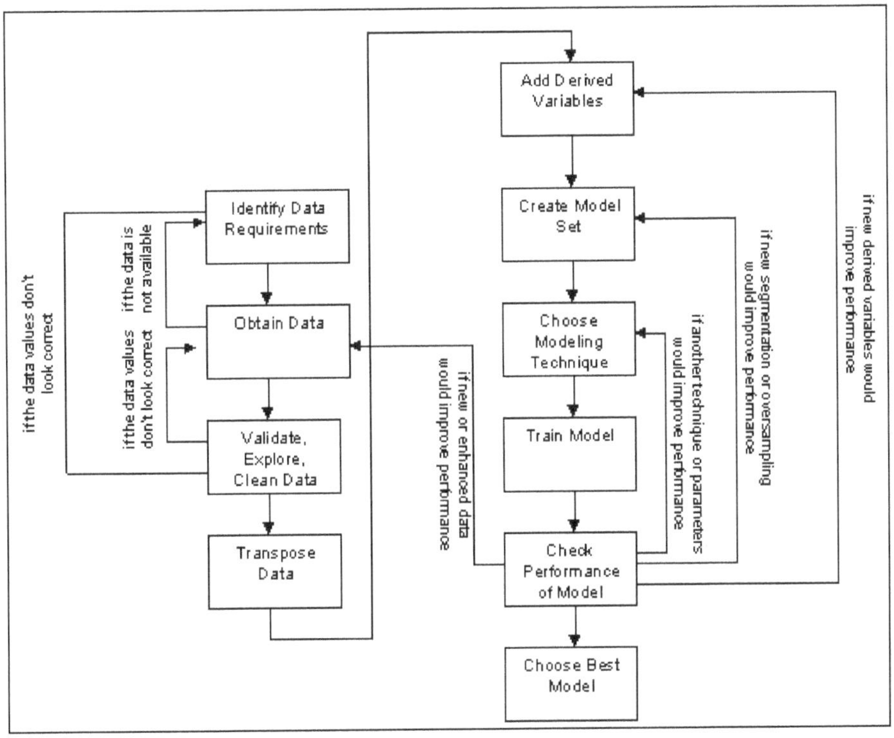

2. Validate, explore and Clean the Data:
   - Is there any missing data and will this be a big problem?
   - Are the field values within legal bounds?
   - Are the field values reasonable?
   - Are the distributions of individual fields explainable?
   - Data fields which are not used are often inaccurate compared to critical data fields.
3. Transpo3se the data to the Right Granularity:
   - Granularity is the level of the data that is being modelled.
   - Some data mining algorithms work on individual rows of data, so all data describing a customer must be in a single row.
4. Add Derived Variables:
   - Derived variables are calculated based on combinations of other values inside the data.
5. Prepare the Model Set:
   - Model set: data used to build the data mining models.

- Need to consider such things as the frequency of the rarer outcomes in the model set. For example, if the frequency of rare outcomes in the model set is too low then the predictions made by the model, although accurate, may never include these rare outcomes.
- The model set can be divided into training, test, and evaluation sets.

6. Choose the modeling technique and train the model:
    - Different data mining tools and algorithms determine the specifics of training a model.
7. Check performance of the models:
    - Evaluation set (part of the model set) is used to see how well the model performs on unseen data.
    - Compare results between different models:
        - A confusion matrix is used to tell us how many of the model's predictions are correct and how many are incorrect.
        - Cumulative gains and lift charts are also used to compare models.

Acting on the Results

- Insights: New facts learned during modeling may lead to insights about the customers and about the business.
- One-time results: Results may be focused on a particular activity and that activity should be carried out.
- Remembered results: Information in the results should be accessible through a data mart or a data warehouse.
- Periodic predictions: Periodically score customers to determine what ongoing marketing efforts should be.
- Real-time scoring: Model may be incorporated into another system.
- Fixing data: May have to fix data problems that have been uncovered.
- Experimental design may be added to the process to add valuable insight. Example: Using an additional random group exposed to a marketing message. This brings in an unbiased sample.

Measuring the Model's Effectiveness

- Compare actual results to predicted results.
- Actual results are usually worse than predicted because models perform less well the farther they get from the model set.

- Over time, actual data will usually be more recent than the model set, so the original patterns become less relevant.

Knowledge Discovery demonstrates intelligent computing at its best, and is the most desirable and interesting end-product of Information Technology. To be able to discover and to extract knowledge from data is a task that many researchers and practitioners are endeavouring to accomplish. There is a lot of hidden knowledge waiting to be discovered – this is the challenge created by today's abundance of data. Knowledge Discovery in Databases (KDD) is the process of identifying valid, novel, useful, and understandable patterns from large datasets.

Data Mining (DM) is the mathematical core of the KDD process, involving the inferring algorithms that explore the data, develop mathematical models and discover significant patterns (implicit or explicit) which are the essence of useful knowledge. Advances in data gathering storage and distribution have created a need for computational tools and techniques to aid in data analysis. Data Mining and Knowledge Discovery in Databases is a rapidly growing area of research and application that builds on techniques and theories from many fields including statistics databases pattern recognition and learning data visualization uncertainty modelling data warehousing and OLAP optimization and high performance computing. KDD is concerned with issues of scalability, the multi-step knowledge discovery process for extracting useful patterns and models from raw data stores (including data cleaning and noise modelling) and issues of making discovered patterns understandable.

Knowledge Discovery includes: Theory and Foundational Issues: Data and knowledge representation; modelling of structured textual and multimedia data; uncertainty management; metrics of interestingness and utility of discovered knowledge; algorithmic complexity efficiency and scalability issues in data mining; statistics over massive data sets. Data Mining Methods: including classification clustering probabilistic modeling prediction and estimation dependency analysis search and optimization. Algorithms for data mining including spatial textual and multimedia data (e.g. the Web) scalability to large databases parallel and distributed data mining techniques and automated discovery agents.

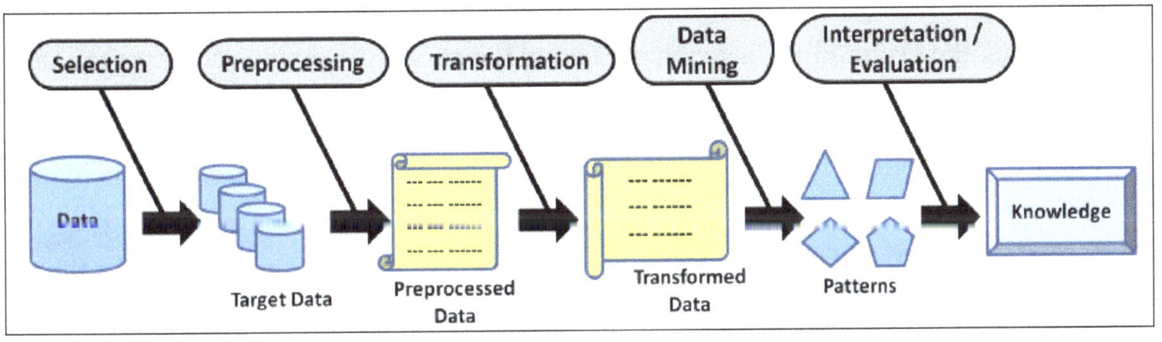

The knowledge discovery process is iterative and interactive, consisting of several steps. The process starts with determining the KDD goals, and "ends" with the implementation of the discovered knowledge. As a result, changes would have to be made in the application domain (such as offering different features to mobile phone users in order to reduce churning). This closes the loop, and the effects are then measured on the new data repositories, and the KDD process is launched again. The following are the steps that are used:

- Developing an understanding of the application domain: This is the initial preparatory step. It prepares the scene for understanding what should be done with the many decisions (about transformation, algorithms, representation, etc.).
- Selecting and creating a data set on which discovery will be performed. Having defined the goals, the data that will be used for the knowledge discovery should be determined. This includes finding out what data is available, obtaining additional necessary data, and then integrating all the data for the knowledge discovery into one data set, including the attributes that will be considered for the process. This process is very important because the Data Mining learns and discovers from the available data. This is the evidence base for constructing the models. If some important attributes are missing, then the entire study may fail.
- Pre-processing and cleansing: In this stage, data reliability is enhanced. It includes data clearing, such as handling missing values and removal of noise or outliers. Several methods are explained in the handbook, from doing nothing to becoming the major part (in terms of time consumed) of a KDD process in certain projects. It may involve complex statistical methods, or using specific Data Mining algorithm in this context.
- Data transformation: In this stage, the generation of better data for the data mining is prepared and developed. Methods here include dimension reduction (such as feature selection and extraction, and record sampling), and attribute transformation (such as Discretization of numerical attributes and functional transformation). This step is often crucial for the success of the entire KDD project, but it is usually very project-specific.
- Choosing the appropriate Data Mining task: We are now ready to decide on which type of Data Mining to use, for example, classification, regression, or clustering. This mostly depends on the KDD goals, and also on the previous steps. There are two major goals in Data Mining: prediction and description. Prediction is often referred to as supervised Data Mining, while descriptive Data Mining includes the unsupervised and visualization aspects of Data Mining.
- Choosing the Data Mining algorithm: Having the strategy, we now decide on the tactics. This stage includes selecting the specific method to be used for searching patterns (including multiple inducers). For example, in considering precision versus understand ability, the former is better with neural networks, while the latter is better with decision trees. For each strategy of meta-learning there are several possibilities of how it can be accomplished.
- Employing the Data Mining algorithm: Finally the implementation of the Data Mining algorithm is reached. In this step we might need to employ the algorithm several times until a satisfied result is obtained, for instance by tuning the algorithm's control parameters, such as the minimum number of instances in a single leaf of a decision tree.
- Evaluation: In this stage we evaluate and interpret the mined patterns (rules, reliability etc.), with respect to the goals defined in the first step.

The following figure presents a summary corresponding to the relative effort spent on each of the DMKD steps.

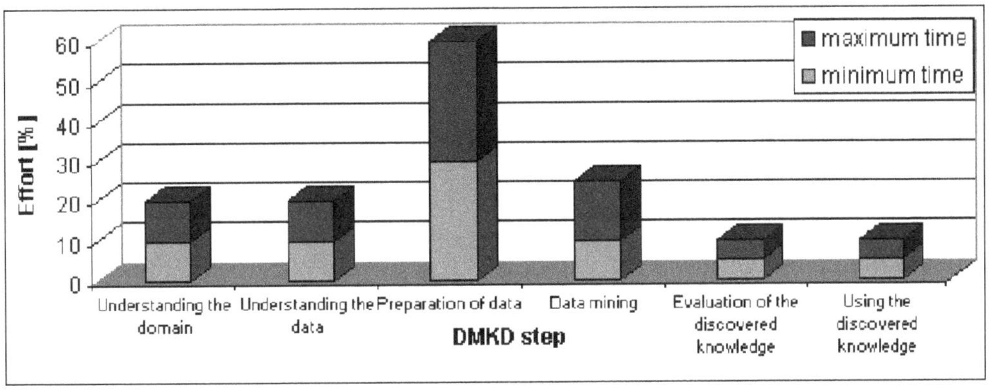

Data Mining Methodology

It should be clear from the above that data mining is not a single technique; any method that will help to get more information out of data is useful. Different methods serve different purposes, each method offering its own advantages and disadvantages. However, most methods commonly used for data mining can be classified into the following groups:

- Statistical Methods: Historically, statistical work has focused mainly on testing of preconceived hypotheses and on fitting models to data. Statistical approaches usually rely on an explicit underlying probability model. In addition, it is generally assumed that these methods will be used by statisticians, and hence human intervention is required for the generation of candidate hypotheses and models.

- Case-Based Reasoning: Case-based reasoning (CBR) is a technology that tries to solve a given problem by making direct use of past experiences and solutions. A case is usually a specific problem that has been previously encountered and solved. Given a particular new problem, case-based reasoning examines the set of stored cases and finds similar ones. If similar cases exist, their solution is applied to the new problem, and the problem is added to the case base for future reference.

- Neural Networks: Neural networks (NN) are a class of systems modeled after the human brain. As the human brain consists of millions of neurons that are interconnected by synapses, neural networks are formed from large numbers of simulated neurons, connected to each other in a manner similar to brain neurons. Like in the human brain, the strength of neuron interconnections may change (or be changed by the learning algorithm) in response to a presented stimulus or an obtained output, which enables the network to "learn".

- Decision Trees: A decision tree is a tree where each non-terminal node represents a test or decision on the considered data item. Depending on the outcome of the test, one chooses a certain branch. To classify a particular data item, we start at the root node and follow the assertions down until we reach a terminal node (or leaf). When a terminal node is reached, a decision is made. Decision trees can also be interpreted as a special form of a rule set, characterized by their hierarchical organization of rules.

- Rule Induction*:* Rules state a statistical correlation between the occurrences of certain attributes in a data item, or between certain data items in a data set. The general form of an association rule is $Xl \wedge ... \wedge Xn => Y [C, S]$, meaning that the attributes $Xl,...,Xn$ predict Y with a confidence C and a significance S.

- Bayesian Belief Networks: Bayesian belief networks (BBN) are graphical representations of probability distributions, derived from co-occurrence counts in the set of data items. Specifically, a BBN is a directed, acyclic graph, where the nodes represent attribute variables and the edges represent probabilistic dependencies between the attribute variables. Associated with each node are conditional probability distributions that describe the relationships between the node and its parents.
- Genetic algorithms/Evolutionary Programming: Genetic algorithms and evolutionary programming are algorithmic optimization strategies that are inspired by the principles observed in natural evolution. Of a collection of potential problem solutions that compete with each other, the best solutions are selected and combined with each other.
- Fuzzy Sets: Fuzzy sets form a key methodology for representing and processing uncertainty. Uncertainty arises in many forms in today's databases: imprecision, non-specificity, inconsistency, vagueness, etc. Fuzzy sets exploit uncertainty in an attempt to make system complexity manageable.
- Rough Sets: A rough set is defined by a lower and upper bound of a set. Every member of the lower bound is a certain member of the set. Every non-member of the upper bound is a certain nonmember of the set. The upper bound of a rough set is the union between the lower bound and the so-called boundary region. A member of the boundary region is possibly (but not certainly) amember of the set.

Knowledge discovery can be broadly defined as the automated discovery of novel and useful information from commercial databases. Data mining is one step at the core of the knowledge discovery process, dealing with the extraction of patterns and relationships from large amounts of data. Today, most enterprises are actively collecting and storing large databases. Many of them have recognized the potential value of these data as an information source for making business decisions.

Data Reuse

Unleashing Big Data Value

The possibility of big data reuse has triggered a number of cutting-edge business models. After all, the world's most successful and innovative companies—Amazon, Google, Walmart, and, last but not least, Facebook— have built their business model on the collection and exploitation of big data.

Based on value creation, Mayer-Schönberger and Cukier differentiate three types of big data business models. The first group are the organizations that own the data but turn to independent firms to license it to others to use. An example is Twitter, which enjoys a massive stream of data flowing through its servers, but is not willing or not able to reuse it in new ways. The second group are the organizations that extract big data value by engaging their employees' analytical skills. Agencies that offer strategic digital consultancy have been flourishing. It is a presumption that big clients from traditional industries lack the skills that would enable them to perform valuable analyses. Data analytics help clients tailor the data to draw useful actions and improve key performance indicators. Finally, there is a group of firms that not only own data and sufficient analytics skills but also the mind-set with ideas about original ways to tap data to unlock new forms of value. For instance, by analysing billions of users' failed search attempts and their typos, Google managed to develop the world's most complete spell checker in basically every living language. The novelty in Google's approach was in showing that 'bad', 'incorrect', or 'defective' data can still be very useful.

Those three groups do not operate in an isolated way but do interact with each other as well as with the rest of business players. The need to liaise with numerous actors on the big data market has triggered the growth of intermediaries—platforms that enable access to data to those that lack the assets and that sell the collected data to those that appreciate it more. Big data benefits are now spreading across the global economy.

Legal Trade-off between Benefits and Risks

The emergence of big data and its proven benefits have demonstrated the complexity of the legal discussion, since current regulation may not sufficiently respond to the challenges related to big data sets, in particular in cases of its reuse. On the one hand, there have been claims that our society should expect a substantial loss of benefits of big data, if it attempts to confine it within an obsolete legal framework. On the other hand, we cannot turn a blind eye to the grey side of the big data revolution and its numerous risks. Big data reuse could be an increasing source of consumer detriment in terms of privacy, security, and consumers' rights.

The European Commission first addressed the questions of data reuse by introducing the Directive 2003/98/ EC of the European Parliament and of the Council on the reuse of public sector information. Due to many positive side effects, various open data initiatives have been also been increasingly interesting for the for-profit businesses, but never really attracted their attention until fairly recently. What the EU has succeeded in, however, has been a more active cooperation between public and private sectors in the form of private–public partnerships. Today, the European legislator has shifted its regula- tory focus to unleashing big data opportunities. Most recently, the Commission has taken important steps towards a more data reuse friendly legal landscape by releasing its Communication on a data-driven economy and proposing changes to the existing legal framework of EU Directive 95/46/EC on the Protection of Personal Data under the umbrella of the Agenda 2020 programme. While the EU has proclaimed the digital improvement its main goal for the future, it has also stressed the import- ance of strong and genuine protection of consumer rights in the information society. A tough trade-off between data protection and business incentives has been well noticed in the lengthy and complex process of adopting the new data protection regulation.

The value of big data is not in the mere data collection but in the insights deduced from it. As the focus of the data industry is shifting towards its value-adding reuse, a number of organizations and business associations have called for legal protections to focus more on how data might be used rather than limit what data can be collected. In the era of big data, the motives let alone the identity of the data reuser may be hidden and in- dividual expectations may be confused. Abstract language of the Data Protection Directive (95/46/EC) adopted 20 years ago does not adequately answer the opaqueness and vagueness of many big data practices, let alone its reuse. The taxonomy of data reuse explained in the following section may be useful to determine the extent to which data reuse is allowed under current data protection laws and to find the right balance between economic incentives and ethical and transparency issues of data reuse.

Data Reuse: Different Categories

A prerequisite for developing a taxonomy for data reuse is addressing the question what exactly is data reuse. The term data reuse in its broadest sense suggests that there is initial (primary) use of data and subsequent (secondary) use of data, ie, the reuse of data. The distinction between use and reuse may imply different aspects, however. In this section, we distinguish different types of data reuse and provide a taxonomy for data reuse. We start with discussing what exactly is data use, since data reuse can only happen after data use. The section 'Data Reuse from the Data Controller's Perspective' will focus on data reuse aspects for data controllers (particularly data recycling, data repurposing, and data recontextuali- zation), and the section 'Data Reuse from the Data Sub- ject's Perspective' will focus on data reuse aspects for data subjects (particularly data sharing, data portability, and the right to be forgotten).

Data use

Before we discuss data reuse, it is necessary to explain data use. This is important since data reuse (secondary use) can only happen after data use (primary use). This may seem an irrelevant question, since everyone will have a basic understanding of data use. Data use is some- thing like using available data for a specific purpose. However, the EU regulation on personal data protection complicates this perception. EU Directive 95/46/EC on the protection of personal data does not deal with the concepts of data use and data reuse, but uses the concept of processing of personal data ('processing'), which is defined in Article 2 as: any operation or set of operations which is performed upon personal data, whether or not by automatic means, such as collection, recording, organization, storage, adaption or alteration, retrieval, consultation, use, disclosure by transmission, dissemination or otherwise making available, alignment or com- bination, blocking, erasure or destruction.

Whereas data use and data reuse may be conceived as an action that takes place after collection and storage of personal data and before erasure or destruction of the personal data, the legal framework considers collection, storage, erasure, and destruction also as forms of data processing. As a result, it may be suggested that data processing always starts with data collection (the first form of processing) and that subsequent actions like data storage, preparation, and analyses are all next steps in data processing and, as such, may be considered as reprocessing or reuse. Since data are always collected (and often stored) before it can be used for any purpose, we do not think data collection and storage, though the first steps in most data processing, should already count as data use. Similarly, we do not think erasure or destruction, if these actions take place at the end of a lifecycle of personal data, should be considered as data reuse. In line with the common under- standing of data use and data reuse, we do not include the collection, storage, erasure, and destruction of personal data as forms of data use or data reuse. To avoid misunderstandings in terminology, we will not use the term data processing, but stick to data use and data reuse.

Data Reuse from the Data Controller's Perspective

There are several ways in which data controllers may like to reuse personal data they have collected. Here, we distinguish data recycling, data repurposing, and data recontextualization.

Data Recycling

The most simplified form of data reuse is using the same data in the same way for more than once. A typical example may be a health insurance company that collects patient data in order to have a proper client database used for billing the insurance premiums that are due and to reimburse medicines, treatments, and therapies. When they use a client's address for sending them a bill, they will do this monthly, quarterly, or annually. In that sense, they periodically reuse the address more than once for the same purpose. This is a form of data reuse that we will call *data recycling*. It is rather straightforward, since the data are used over and over again in the same way. There are no significant legal issues here as long as a data subject does not revoke his or her informed consent. For instance, when a data subject chooses for another health insurance company, the previous insurance company is no longer allowed to use the data for sending bills.

Data Repurposing

In case the same insurance company starts using the data to assess risks of patients in order to deter- mine risk-based insurance premiums (eg, higher premiums for people at risk or showing unhealthy behaviour like smoking, not exercising, etc. and lower premiums for people at low risks showing healthy behaviour), they are reusing the data for a different purpose. This is a form of data reuse that we classify as data repurposing. Data repurposing happens a lot, since data are used for many purposes. Addresses may not only be used for billing purposes but also for advertisements. Data may be combined to find new groups of potential customers, for assessing credit scores, or for assessing medical risks. Using Big Data, all kinds of new insights and predictions can be made about people. Sometimes, such data analysis may even reveal information about people they did not know themselves, such as the risks they run to attract specific forms of cancer or their life expectancy.

It is important to note that data repurposing in a general sense has another meaning than when used in legal terms. In a general sense, data repurposing can be understood as using the same data for several different purposes. From a legal perspective, EU data protection directive 95/46/ EC focuses on data repurposing in Article 6.1(b): personal data must be 'collected for specified, explicit and legitimate purposes and not further processed in a way incompatible with those purposes'. The principle that the purposes for which personal data are collected should be specified in advance and that the data may only be used for these purposes is called the *purpose specification principle*. The principle that person- al data should not be disclosed, made available, or other- wise used for purposes other than those specified, except with the consent of the data subject or by the authority of law is called the *use limitation principle*.

In other words, for data repurposing typically (additional) informed consent of the data subjects has to be obtained or another legal basis (for instance, specific legislation such as criminal investigation laws that allow the use of personal data to help to solve crime) has to be available.

Data Re-contextualization

When the health insurance company in the examples above starts selling the data, other companies may also make use of the data, for instance, for marketing their products to particular target groups. The data are then reused in a (sometimes completely) different context. This may cause issues of contextual integrity, since data may have a different meaning or may be interpreted differently in another context. For instance, health data may be interpreted differently by a physician than by a health insurance company. This is a form of data reuse that we classify as *data recontextualization.*

From a legal perspective, there is no real difference between data repurposing and data recontextualization. Both types of data reuse are usually referred to as *function creep* and are not allowed unless there is a legal basis for it. We introduce the distinction, however, because data recontextualization may bring along different legal issues, for instance, regarding the expectations that data subjects may have regarding the ways in which their data are used (they may know and trust the health insurance company but may not know or trust the marketing company buying their data) and the ways in which they are able to exercise their rights (they may know which data they disclosed to the health insurance company, but may not be aware who has bought their data). In short, when data are used in a new context, the 'distance' between the data subject and the data controller increases and the awareness of the available personal data and for which purposes the personal data is used may decrease among data subjects. As a result, it may become more difficult for data subjects to exercise their rights. Furthermore, the likeliness of interpretation errors may also increase.

When personal data are transferred to a third party and reused, data subject rights like the right to information and transparency do not cease to apply. On the contrary, at this point, it becomes even more important that data subjects are fully informed about the activities in which they are indirectly involved through their own personal data. There are two options how to ensure data subject's awareness. First, data reuse activities that might happen in the future are described and communicated to the data subject before his personal data are collected. Secondly, the data subject renews his consent every time before the data are reused for a new purpose. Both tactics often prove to be difficult to apply. In the first case, it is hard to predict all the purposes for data reuse that may appear in the future. In the second case, it is almost impossible to get in touch with all data subjects and to secure their valid consent. Research has shown that privacy policies nowadays contain information overload and lack a meaningful choice for the users, which leads to the situation where data subjects no longer make informed decisions but simply consent whenever they are asked to do so. Not only are data subjects unaware how their information is processed, and under which conditions, they also lack basic under- standing of whether their data can be and will be reused.

In practice, neither of the two options is frequently used. Describing future uses of personal data may be difficult since it is often unknown for which other purposes collected data may prove to be useful a few years later. Sometimes, new tools for data analyses may also yield new insights like novel patterns and relations in datasets. Not collecting data that can easily be collected is increasingly regarded as a waste of economic resources. For these reasons, many corporations collecting personal data formulate the purposes of their data collection very broadly, so that concrete purposes do not necessarily have to be known at the time of collection. As a result, there are differences in the legal interpretation of repurposing or function creep and the more common understanding of it by data subjects. As mentioned above, from a legal perspective data repurposing or function creep only exists in case the second- ary use of personal data goes beyond the purposes specified in advance. Since these are in general formulated very broadly, this may rarely be the case from a legal perspective. From a more common understand- ing, however, people may consider function creep to be the case when personal data are used for purposes they did not expect their data to be used for.

Literature on expectations of data subjects on how their data are used and what they consider acceptable shows that there is a considerable gap between the practices of data controllers and the expectations of data subjects. For instance, US-based research has shown that race and ethnicity play an influential role in how people use social media and share personal information. Users show concern for privacy, although there seems to be an incongruity between public opinion and public behaviour: people tend to express concern about privacy, but when asked about it, they routinely disclose personal in- formation because of convenience, discounts, and other incentives, or a lack of understanding of the consequences. These tensions between attitudes and practices were also found by Acquisti and Gross. A possible explanation for this tension may be that users do not connect the disclosure of their data at a particular time with the use of their data later, for different purposes, by different organizations and in a different context. Such connections may not be transparent when there are long periods of time between the data collection and actions based upon the processing or sharing of such information and when data are sold to other companies or between the (primary) data use and the (secondary) data reuse. Also, the ways in which data are processed may not be transparent. For instance, when the information collected is used for profiling, such pro- filing techniques, by their nature, tend not to be visible processes for data subjects.

Challenges

Data that is repurposed , as opposed to reused, must be managed with multiple different fitness for use requirements in mind, which complicates any data quality enhancements . While other work has considered context in relation to data quality requirements, including the need to meet multiple fitness for use requirements, in the current fast-paced environment of data repurposing for analytics and business intelligence, there are new challenges for dealing with multiple fitness for use requirements in the context of:

1. Ephemeral data use.
2. Self-service data collection.

Ephemeral data use is when the use of the data is either short-lived or, after collection and transformation, does not prove to be useful at all. The former situation occurs when data analytics results are only used, for example, once or twice (rather than regularly for day-to-day operational decisions). The latter situation occurs when users are performing data analytics with the aim of revealing business insights, which may never materialise because of the exploratory nature of the task. The problem is that discovering that the data is not useful occurs after effort has been expended extracting and transforming the data to get it to the point where it can be analysed. In this case, it is necessary to minimise the time and effort in transforming the data to satisfy the new fitness for use requirements. Otherwise, important results may be missed because of analysts/developers not being willing to invest the time it takes to transform the data to be fit for the new use. If one knows that in many cases the results will be discarded, then there is little incentive to invest large amounts of time and resources to transform the data each time. A specific example of this is investigating whether online public data, such as social media posts and news events, can be used with internal procurement data to provide advanced warning of parts supply shortages to a manufacturing organisation. Even in the exploratory case, effort is required to wrangle the data into a usable form, filter events that do not relate to the manufacturer's suppliers, link events to the relevant part deliveries etc. before any analysis can be done to determine its predictive capability. This effort is wasted for the organisation if it turns out that the data cannot provide useful predictions.

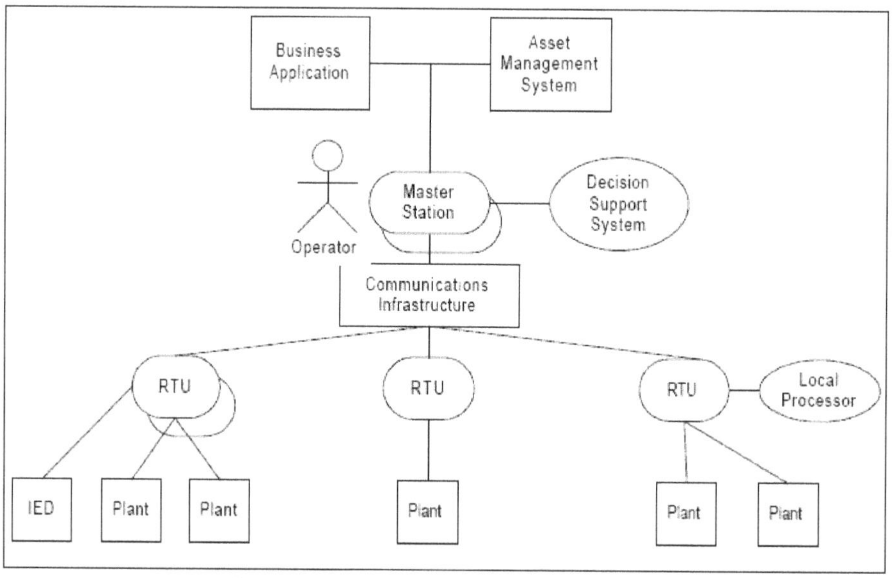

The two key pressures on data repurposing.

Self-service data collection is when users, rather than IT departments, extract, transform and produce their own reports from data. It emerged from both the increased pressure to perform data analytics for business intelligence and the fact that the IT department cannot always meet the increased data demands of the users. The problem is that if users are left to collect and transform the data themselves, how can an organisation be sure that they have the expertise to judge whether it has been done correctly and hence does actually meet the fitness for use requirements? Furthermore, in order to reliably use the data, the analysts must have good visibility of the assumptions and key facts of the data collection and prior transformations, otherwise there is a danger that they may be overlooked leading to the drawing of inaccurate conclusions. This was the case in the example given by Veaux and Hand where a data analyst expected that the data they were using was from a direct measurement when, in fact, it was from the output of a simulation/model. Another example relates to a data analyst at a manufacturer who used expected delivery date and the goods storage date to identify poorly performing suppliers . Comparing these values made many suppliers appear to deliver late because the storage personnel would often wait until the following day before either storing the goods and/or recording them as being stored. These data fields were perfectly accurate for their primary purpose of inventory recording, but were not suitable for their repurposed use in calculations to identify poor supplier performance.

These two pressures are illustrated in figure, which shows how the data is collected, is transformed (T1), is being managed by the Information Technology (IT) personnel (in BD1) for its primary use (Use1), and according to data quality requirements (Req1). Analytics users may also take a copy of this data and collect new data from external sources, integrate and transform it (using T2, or T3 by themselves), hold a copy (in DB2 or their own files, such as spreadsheets), before running it through analytics tools for Use2 and Use3 (the results of which may be discarded immediately or within a short time-scale).

To address these challenges, developing new and enhancing existing data quality tools/methods which focus on further reducing both the time and effort to bring data to the analysis stage is needed. That is, methods in the prior stages of the data analysis pipeline: data acquisition, extraction, cleaning, integration, aggregation, and representation. These could include, (semi) automated methods to discover and evaluate which data sources—including user generated content contain data that is, or can be made, fit for purpose. For the stages after extraction, data quality aware transformation platforms could be designed to support self-service users to make rapid and potentially automated changes to data to enable it to quickly meet different fitness for use requirements. Predictions (e.g. using machine learning) of how data will need to be used/analysed in the future could enable "pre-transforming" or "pre-selection" of data so that it is ready for analysis when (or even before) the analyst needs it. These approaches must also capture key metadata, such as provenance and the context of the data before if it is cleaned, integrated, or aggregated into different forms. Using this metadata, fitness for use validation alerts could warn users when data is being used that does not meet the new quality requirements.

References

- Customer-behavior-modeling target Text-Customer, learning-center: optimove.com, Retrieved 19 May, 2019
- Customer-service: yonyx.com, Retrieved 28 April, 2019
- Modeling-Customer-Lifetime-Value: researchgate.net, Retrieved 21 July, 2019
- Demographic-characteristics-customer-profile-76467: chron.com, Retrieved 10 May, 2019
- Consumer-psychographic: chron.com, Retrieved 15 January, 2019
- Yfcommunitynews-business-intelligence-drivers-challenges-benefits-and-roi: yellowfinbi.com, Retrieved 1 June , 2019
- The-Knowledge-Discovery-in-Databases-KDD-process, figure: researchgate.net, Retrieved 1 August , 2019
- The-Data-Repurposing-Challenge-New-Pressures-from-Data-Analytics: researchgate.net, Retrieved 7 May, 2019

5

Ethics in Business Intelligence

The ethical principles related to the code of conduct which govern the decisions related to the data of consumers, businesses or employees such as data accuracy and involuntary release of personal information are known as professional ethics. This chapter has been carefully written to provide an easy understanding of the varied facets of ethics in business intelligence as well as the diverse principles which fall under it.

The question of whether or not the conduct of activities relating to business intelligence is ethical is really composed of two parts. First, there is the broad question of whether or not the collection and use of business intelligence is an ethical practice. If we come to the conclusion that this "end" is acceptable, then we have to deal with the question of the means. This second question examines which of the specific methods of collection and use of business intelligence are allowable and which methods are not.

Contrary to the opinion that business is an amoral activity (i.e., that it is devoid of any ethical or moral dimension), we believe that business ethics is a viable and necessary field of study. Business, just as any field of human endeavour, is a human activity and, therefore, has a moral dimension. However, unlike other human activities that are founded on the central motive of love or charity toward one's fellow human, the primary motive behind business is profit.

Ethicists and moralists have pronounced this motivation as being acceptable in the eyes of God and man. Some apologists for capitalism have even called the concepts of profit and individual success divinely inspired by an invisible hand that governs the actions of every rational economic man; to the benefit of society as a whole. To profit from one's business dealings is not, in itself, unethical. While one might judge this motivation to be base, it cannot be said that it is immoral or amoral. Profit as an end is perfectly acceptable to most; however, the means to attain that goal can be a problem.

The judgement as to whether or not an action is ethical should be made within the moral frame work of the business environment. The purpose of business intelligence is to help managers assess their competition, their vendors, their customers, and the business and technological environment. This allows the managers to avoid surprises, forecast changes in business relationships, identify opportunities, predict a competitor's strategy and develop a successful business plan. M1 of these motives are aimed at making a business more effective and efficient, hence more profitable. That added efficiency benefits not only the owner but society as a whole.

The type of ethics in business intelligence (BI) is the ethical principles of conduct that govern an individual in the workplace or a company in general.

It is also known as professional ethics and not to be confused with other forms of philosophical ethics including religious conviction, or popular conviction. Professional ethics according to

Griffin is that profit is not the only important strategy of a business anymore. There is also more of a concern and motivator of companies to do what is right.

Companies must acknowledge that they have a common good to protects there local community, improve employee relations and promote informational press to the public. While back in 1986, Griffin was directing his argument towards ethics in accounting but it is also true today in Business Intelligence. Government regulations are not changing fast enough to cover all the changes in technology that bombards users on day to day bases. It is up to corporations to create a code of ethics, and to persistently be receptive to the needs of the public being served.

Everyday in BI management professionals may be at risk of making unethical practices in there decisions that regards the consumer, business and/or other employees data. Ethics is a touchy subject, there is always going to be controversy on how companies choose to handle business decisions. There is no definite decision to make when it comes to ethical decisions. While sometimes it may involve illegal practices, other times it is just a decision that needs to be made in a company to promote a better way of life for all.

An example of an Ethical Decision: A manager of a BI system that chooses to use cheaper data in his/her data mining activities to save money. The data he/she chooses to implement involves personal credit score reports. The cheaper data sets have a 20% possibility of being incorrect. The manager did not see it as being an unethical decision when it was made, just a way to continue to generate close-to-accurate reports and save money.

The impacting decision on 20% of the company's customers may have different results as more people are turned down for credit because inaccurate reports. It is not a crime to have implemented the inaccurate data sets but it may seem as an unethical practice to others. While it is important for managers to be able to make their own decisions, this example decision being made should have involved more managers since it affected the whole business.

The manager's choice could bankrupt the company as user start to leave their business for more accurate competitive companies. As the example points out, sometimes there is no really clear answer to wither an issue involves an ethical or legal choice and each situation can be different. Trying to make decisions based on individuals' beliefs when dealing with a company can amount to intellectual stalls and trying to come to a decision can be expensive and time consuming.

Business Globalization

Today's society has come to the point where there are more solutions to problems than ever before. What once was impossible can now be accomplished through the use of BI and other technology similar to BI. It is not going to stop; technology is going to keep advancing. What seems improbable now may be common in the near future.

Because of business globalization, there is also a larger separation between companies and customers, companies and competitors than there was when everything was done locally in the past. Larger separation between companies and the consumer has resulted in unethical and sometimes illegal business decisions like data theft. Because of all the technology used in big businesses, and resulting exposure to unethical practices by some of the larger corporations like Enron, there is growing anxiety of large companies to be free of unethical practices.

Additionally the general trust level of users has eroded to the point were trust really has to be earned. Users are very aware of cases of identity information being lost to theft as well as other case examples in the media. Users have taken up with the attitude of show me or prove to me that they are safe, that there information is safe or they will not do business.

IT Personnel in Ethics

It is so easy for BI managers to sit behind their desk and manage the data on a day to day business thinking that ethical practices do not concern them. That is not the correct attitude to have. Everyone employed in the information technology field has an obligation to be part of company ethical policies and practices. It is not just about creating schemas and data models, as IT managers they have more of an ethical decision to make than their employers.

The BI manager knows more about the emerging technology, and has the best knowledge of a company's technologies capabilities of what is possible. With all the work that is done in an informational system and what is involved in information delivery and business ethical dilemmas.

Code of Ethics

Every technologically backed association deals with ethical issues in their own way. The Association for Computing Machinery (ACM) has set some great code of ethics including:

"Computing professionals have a responsibility to share technical knowledge with the public by encouraging understanding of computing, including the impacts of computer systems and their limitations. This imperative implies an obligation to counter any false views related to computing."

While most of the code of ethics covers general ethical issues, it also covers leadership and other professional responsibility in information technology and is worth looking up.

PAPA Framework

PAPA is an acronym for privacy, accuracy, property, and accessibility. A framework proposed by Richard Mason as the four ethical issues of the information age. He proposed this framework 25 years ago in 1986. To date it is still acknowledge as the four subjects of ethics in information technology and covers ethics in BI as more and more data is extracted, transformed and loaded into data warehouse silos.

A lot of are private information is handle with BI in Customer Relationship Management (CRM) systems like Amazons customer web portal. While Amazon is making web application business services for users better and geared towards individual use, it also demands that some of your private information is given in return for the CRM to accurately predict what you may need and want.

Elements of privacy should contain a notice of what data is being collected, how it is being used, a option to participate of not, security measures to protect from data misuse, the ability to access your person information to review and correct and steps are assigned to enforce set policies. On opposing side of privacy is the need to create security, any inadequate security measures can be viewed as carelessness also while the option to participate in the data collection is an option, choosing to not participate usually means that the company will also not provide their services to you.

Accurate Data

Accuracy Data Mining (DM) and BI systems is very costly and the percentage of accurate data is a business decision. Some companies can ethically choose less accurate data and still maintain a competitive edge, and supply the users with their services while other systems like a Hospital Information System (HIS) cannot afford to reduce accuracy when a person life in hanging on the line. When it comes down to who is responsible for the accuracy of the data, executives may set business processes for guidelines but the main responsibility stills falls to the BI manager to be able to understand their BI database and also for when new data must be integrated. Executives do not care how the analytics works, just that they are presented with accurate reports and/or dashboards.

The whole reliability and integrity of a BI system eventually is placed on the personnel who can transfers the sea of technology used, not the end users. When there is an ethical situation within the company who will be helped liable, the executive who did not know the technology or the BI manager in charge of data accuracy? Accessibility of data in the past was only privileged to a significantly smaller group of user than now. With the technology explosion of BI and web interfaces, anyone with a smart phone, computer, laptop or PDA can gain access DM information. The technology gap, also known as the digital divide, is growing smaller.

Information is power, users have a right to be on a level playing field, we have a moral obligation to provide skills to understand and manage, understand, and access information throughout the world so that users are on a level playing field when it comes down to access of data that provides basic survival information, so a larger technology gap is not created based on poverty, sex, age, or race.

While sharing data freely is a goal to help individuals, there is a limit to what can be shared among business partners, customers and competitors yet they should also have the right to come to the same results using technology.

Ethical Issues in BI

While many ethical issue are obscure and hard to notice at the surface there is one a number one concern brought up by most users and according to Hackathorn, the ethical issue in BI that is known by most is the involuntary release of personal information that has leads to identity theft.

The theft of personal information like social security numbers, birth-dates, and credit card numbers has allowed for technology skilled criminals to possibly walk away with billions of dollars in innocent victims' money nationally.

Organization Accountability

Organization need to be accountable for financial data. The U.S. has required financial accountability through regulations like the Sarbanes-Oxley (SOX) of 2002. Yet according to Wallice, the main focus of SOX is to measure internal effectiveness of business controls and does not explicitly address IT.

Because of the lack of security for IT in SOX, ISO 17700, the International Standard for the Code and Practice for Informational Security Management is being executed by companies as a framework for maintaining informational security to protect information systems from unauthorized admission, usage, modification, and destruction.

Government use

The pressing issue of homeland security and the U.S. patriot Act after the attack on the World Trade Center in New York, left the Government with a strong ability to analyze anyone in the United States as a threat by collecting almost any type of data that they wish including financial activities and how they may be related to terrorism.

Technology is being implemented at airports in order to fight terrorism. The Transport Security Administration (TSA), according to Worthen is continuously conducting test with different data mining techniques in order to find the most effective way of weeding out terrorist so that they never gain access to be airlines again. The lack of an almost never ending budget and a lack of a well define scope allow the TSA to try newer technologies in the name of security, compared to other sectors of business. After 9/11 the Computer Automated Passenger Pre-screening (CAPPS) system that used consumers', names, credit card information, and address to screen for criminals was change to CAPPS II. CAPPS II combined previous technology of its predecessor with information purchased from data stores run by Choice Point and Lexis-Nexis. CAPPS was eventually replaced with a newer system called Secure Flight that shares the same process of combining passenger data with information purchased from commercial data providers. Over $125 million has been spent in the name of homeland security just in the first 5 years after 9/11.

Framework for Solving Ethical Dilemmas

- The ability to solve any ethical problem is to first be aware that there is an ethical situation.
- Try to be open and honest about the situation while at the same time you need to avoid discussions that could magnify the problem.
- Try to make the subject of ethics in the work place an acceptable activity.
- The next step is to thoroughly research the ethical problem and at the same time stay focused on the problem at hand and not try to solve the greater issues, if it is necessary for a person to solve the greater ethical issues that do not impact the company then it should be done on their own personal time. Once all research has been done on the subject and you are able to gain a better understanding to the root of the problem you need to come to a decision on what should be done to fix the ethical problem.
- Once you have made the proper decision make sure that it is properly documented for you and future employees can learn from it. Solving ethical solutions is the same as solving any

decision making process effectively and can be broken down into 6 simple steps: Identify the decision, get the facts, develop alternatives, rate each alternative, make the decision and implement the decision. Make sure to be clear about your actions, if you cannot come to a valuable solution on your own consider hiring someone who can.

Benefits of Ethics in IT

Employers may see that: "Although data are mixed, numerous studies in the field of computer ethics support the hypothesis that a written and clearly transmitted code of ethics is a strong influence on employee behavior when an ethical decision is involved."

Companies that can change there thinking to become more ethical will also beat government regulations while implementing ethical solutions at the companies' own affordable base without having to hurry up and match such regulations and will save themselves from the costs of future fines and fees for data misuses in their BI system.

If a company is well known for being able to protect the companies BI systems not only from security hacks but also from unethical practices, that company will most likely have the competitive advantage over their rivals and companies can align the business processes of their BI better to cover the broader strategy.

Ethics of Competitive Intelligence

Competitive Intelligence Business intelligence intends to support improved business decision-making, though the term business intelligence is sometimes used as a synonym for competitive intelligence, because they both maintain decision making, BI uses technologies, processes, and applications to analyze mostly internal, structured data and business processes while competitive intelligence gathers, analyzes and disseminates information with a topical focus on company competitors. Business intelligence understood generally can include the division of competitive intelligence. Competitive intelligence is really using all legal means at organizations disposal, i.e. information found on the internet or using specialist software and any other information which is publicly accessible or via a subscription source, organizing the information, analyzing it and using it to help make important decisions for the future of your company.

The ethics of competitive intelligence has been the topic of much discussion over the years the trouble is where to draw the line between competitive intelligence and industrial espionage. The five principles of ethical intelligence are: Do No Harm, Make Things Better, Respect Others, Be Fair, and Be Loving. It's not always easy to do the right thing, or even to know what the right thing is. The principles of ethical intelligence present the base for making the accurate choices in every area of life. The Ethics of Competitive Intelligence can really be subdivided into three main categories:

1. Clarification of what constitutes ethical and legal competitive intelligence activities.

2. Developing and implementing a competitive intelligence ethics policy. Honest competitive intelligence practitioners do however follow a strict code of conduct, which have been formulated by the SCIP, Society of Competitive Intelligence Professionals.
3. To abide by all applicable laws – this includes domestic and international laws, covering things like bribery, bugging and other illegal codes of conduct to accurately disclose the correct information including identity and organization, prior to any interviews. You can't expect to gain ground on your competitors by filling them with lies – it's just not on.
    - Provide honest, complete and realistic conclusions to the organization they are working for.

In general and in competitive intelligence in particular, what is legal can be ethically questionable. There are many gray areas. The Society of Competitive Intelligence Professionals (SCIP) has published the following ethical guidelines for CI professionals. When joining, its members voluntarily agree to abide by the SCIP Code of Ethics: To continually strive to increase the recognition and respect of the profession, to comply with all applicable laws, domestic and international, to accurately disclose all relevant information, including one's identity and organization, prior to all interviews, to evade conflicts of interest in fulfilling one's duties, to provide honest and sensible recommendations and conclusions in the execution of one's duties. To endorse this code of ethics within one's company, with third-party contractors and within the entire profession, to faithfully stick to and abide by one's company policies, objectives, and guidelines.

Ethical Challenges in Competitive Intelligence

Misrepresentation is falsely identifying oneself in order to receive or access information that would not have been provided if one's identity was used. There are three common cases of misrepresentation where there is some ambiguity: excluding some details about one's identity, not revealing one's identity in a public venue after overhearing classified information, not disclosing true intent on how information will be used usually clients often seek CI consultants to gather information about their competitors. The ethical issue is at what cost or length does the clients expect the CI consultants to get the information. One of the reasons the clients hire a CI consultant is to try to distance themselves from facing those ethical situations.

Principles of Ethics

Data science professionals and practitioners should strive to perpetuate these principles:

1. The highest priority is to respect the persons behind the data: When insights derived from data could impact the human condition, the potential harm to individuals and communities should be the paramount consideration. Big data can produce compelling insights about populations, but those same insights can be used to unfairly limit an individual's possibilities.

2. Attend to the downstream uses of datasets: Data professionals should strive to use data in ways that are consistent with the intentions and understanding of the disclosing party.

Many regulations govern datasets on the basis of the status of the data, such as "public," "private" or "proprietary." However, what is *done with* datasets is ultimately more consequential to subjects/users than the type of data or the context in which it is collected. Correlative uses of repurposed data in research and industry represent both the greatest promise and the greatest risk posed by data analytics.

3. Provenance of the data and analytical tools shapes the consequences of their use: There is no such thing as raw data—all datasets and accompanying analytic tools carry a history of human decision-making. As much as possible, that history should be auditable, including mechanisms for tracking the context of collection, methods of consent, the chain of responsibility, and assessments of quality and accuracy of the data.

4. Strive to match privacy and security safeguards with privacy and security expectations: Data subjects hold a range of expectations about the privacy and security of their data and those expectations are often context-dependent. Designers and data professionals should give due consideration to those expectations and align safeguards and expectations as much as possible.

5. Always follow the law, but understand that the law is often a minimum bar: As digital transformations have become a standard evolutionary path for businesses, governments and laws have largely failed to keep up with the pace of digital innovation and existing regulations are often mis-calibrated to present risks. In this context, compliance means complacency. To excel in data ethics, leaders must define their own compliance frameworks that outperform legislated requirements.

6. Be wary of collecting data just for the sake of more data: The power and peril of data analytics is that data collected today will be useful for unpredictable purposes in the future. Give due consideration to the possibility that less data may result in both better analysis and less risk.

7. Data can be a tool of inclusion and exclusion: While everyone deserves the social and economic benefits of data, not everyone is equally impacted by the processes of data collection, correlation, and prediction. Data professionals should strive to mitigate the disparate impacts of their products and listen to the concerns of affected communities.

8. As much as possible, explain methods for analysis and marketing to data disclosers: Maximizing transparency at the point of data collection can minimize more significant risks as data travels through the data supply chain.

9. Data scientists and practitioners should accurately represent their qualifications, limits to their expertise, adhere to professional standards, and strive for peer accountability. The long-term success of the field depends on public and client trust. Data professionals should develop practices for holding themselves and peers accountable to shared standards.

10. Aspire to design practices that incorporate transparency, configurability, accountability, and auditability. Not all ethical dilemmas have design solutions, but being aware of design practices can break down many of the practical barriers that stand in the way of shared, robust ethical standards. Data ethics is an engineering challenge worthy of the best minds in the field.

11. Products and research practices should be subject to internal and potentially external ethical review. Organizations should prioritize establishing consistent, efficient, and actionable ethics review practices for new products, services, and research programs. Internal peer-review practices can mitigate risk, and an external review board can contribute significantly to public trust.

12. Governance practices should be robust, known to all team members and reviewed regularly. Data ethics poses organizational challenges that cannot be resolved by familiar compliance regimes alone. Because the regulatory, social, and engineering terrains are so unsettled, organizations engaged in data analytics require collaborative, routine and transparent practices for ethical governance.

Permissions

All chapters in this book are published with permission under the Creative Commons Attribution Share Alike License or equivalent. Every chapter published in this book has been scrutinized by our experts. Their significance has been extensively debated. The topics covered herein carry significant information for a comprehensive understanding. They may even be implemented as practical applications or may be referred to as a beginning point for further studies.

We would like to thank the editorial team for lending their expertise to make the book truly unique. They have played a crucial role in the development of this book. Without their invaluable contributions this book wouldn't have been possible. They have made vital efforts to compile up to date information on the varied aspects of this subject to make this book a valuable addition to the collection of many professionals and students.

This book was conceptualized with the vision of imparting up-to-date and integrated information in this field. To ensure the same, a matchless editorial board was set up. Every individual on the board went through rigorous rounds of assessment to prove their worth. After which they invested a large part of their time researching and compiling the most relevant data for our readers.

The editorial board has been involved in producing this book since its inception. They have spent rigorous hours researching and exploring the diverse topics which have resulted in the successful publishing of this book. They have passed on their knowledge of decades through this book. To expedite this challenging task, the publisher supported the team at every step. A small team of assistant editors was also appointed to further simplify the editing procedure and attain best results for the readers.

Apart from the editorial board, the designing team has also invested a significant amount of their time in understanding the subject and creating the most relevant covers. They scrutinized every image to scout for the most suitable representation of the subject and create an appropriate cover for the book.

The publishing team has been an ardent support to the editorial, designing and production team. Their endless efforts to recruit the best for this project, has resulted in the accomplishment of this book. They are a veteran in the field of academics and their pool of knowledge is as vast as their experience in printing. Their expertise and guidance has proved useful at every step. Their uncompromising quality standards have made this book an exceptional effort. Their encouragement from time to time has been an inspiration for everyone.

The publisher and the editorial board hope that this book will prove to be a valuable piece of knowledge for students, practitioners and scholars across the globe.

Index

www.ingramcontent.com/pod-product-compliance
Lightning Source LLC
LaVergne TN
LVHW080646210926
848485LV00003B/335